THE MISSING BOOKS OF THE BIBLE

VOLUME II

HALO PRESS

CONTENTS

VOLUME II

THE WISDOM OF JESUS THE SON OF SIRACH

A Prologue Made by an Uncertain Author: This Jesus was the son of Sirach, and grandchild to Jesus of the same name with him: this man therefore lived in the latter times, after the people had been led away captive, and called home again, and almost after all the prophets. Now his grandfather Jesus, as he himself witnesseth, was a man of great diligence and wisdom among the Hebrews, who did not only gather the grave and short sentences of wise men, that had been before him, but himself also uttered some of his own, full of much understanding and wisdom. When as therefore the first Jesus died, leaving this book almost perfected, Sirach his son receiving it after him left it to his own son Jesus, who, having gotten it into his hands, compiled it all orderly into one volume, and called it Wisdom, entitling it both by his own name, his father's name, and his grandfather's; alluring the hearer by the very name of Wisdom to have a greater love to the study of this book. It containeth therefore wise sayings, dark sentences, and parables, and certain particular ancient godly stories of men that pleased God; also his prayer and song; moreover, what benefits God had vouchsafed his people, and what plagues he had heaped upon their enemies. This Jesus did imitate Solomon, and was no less famous for wisdom and learning, both being indeed a man of great learning, and so reputed also.

The Prologue of the Wisdom of Jesus the Son of Sirach: Whereas many and great things have been delivered unto us by the law and the prophets, and by others that have followed their steps, for the which things Israel ought to be commended for learning and wisdom; and whereof not only the readers must needs become skilful themselves, but also they that desire to learn be able to profit them which are without, both by speaking and writing: my grandfather Jesus, when he had much given himself to the reading of the law, and the prophets, and other books of our fathers, and had gotten therein good judgment, was drawn on also himself to write something pertaining to learning and wisdom; to the intent that those which are desirous to learn, and are addicted to these things, might profit much more in living according to the law. Wherefore let me intreat you to read it with favour and attention, and to pardon us, wherein we may seem to come short of some words, which we have laboured to interpret. For the same things uttered in Hebrew, and translated into another tongue, have not the same force in them: and not only these things, but the law itself, and the prophets, and the rest of the books, have no small difference, when they are spoken in their own language. For in the eight and thirtieth year coming into Egypt, when Euergetes was king, and continuing there some time, I found a book of no small learning: therefore I thought it most necessary for me to bestow some diligence and travail to interpret it; using great watchfulness and skill in that space to bring the book to an end, and set it forth for them also, which in a strange country are willing to learn, being prepared before in manners to live after the law.

1 ¹ All wisdom cometh from the Lord, and is with him for ever. ² Who can number the sand of the sea, and the drops of rain, and the days of eternity? ³ Who can find out the height of heaven, and the breadth of the earth, and the deep, and wisdom? ⁴ Wisdom hath been created before all things, and the understanding of prudence from everlasting. ⁵ The word of God most high is the fountain of wisdom; and her ways are everlasting commandments. ⁶ To whom hath the root of wisdom been revealed? or who hath known her wise counsels? ⁷ [Unto whom hath the knowledge of wisdom been made manifest? and who hath understood her great experience?] ⁸ There is one wise and greatly to be feared, the Lord sitting upon his throne. ⁹ He created her, and saw her, and numbered her, and poured her out upon all his works. ¹⁰ She is with all flesh according to his gift, and he hath given her to them that love him. ¹¹ The fear of the Lord is honour, and glory, and gladness, and a crown of rejoicing. ¹² The fear of the Lord maketh a merry heart, and giveth joy, and gladness, and a long life. ¹³ Whoso feareth the Lord, it shall go well with him at the last, and he shall find favour in the day of his death. ¹⁴ To fear the Lord is the beginning of wisdom: and it was created with the faithful in the womb. ¹⁵ She hath built an everlasting foundation with men, and she shall continue with their seed. ¹⁶ To fear the

Lord is fulness of wisdom, and filleth men with her fruits. [17] She filleth all their house with things desirable, and the garners with her increase. [18] The fear of the Lord is a crown of wisdom, making peace and perfect health to flourish; both which are the gifts of God: and it enlargeth their rejoicing that love him. [19] Wisdom raineth down skill and knowledge of understanding, and exalteth them to honour that hold her fast. [20] The root of wisdom is to fear the Lord, and the branches thereof are long life. [21] The fear of the Lord driveth away sins: and where it is present, it turneth away wrath. [22] A furious man cannot be justified; for the sway of his fury shall be his destruction. [23] A patient man will bear for a time, and afterward joy shall spring up unto him. [24] He will hide his words for a time, and the lips of many shall declare his wisdom. [25] The parables of knowledge are in the treasures of wisdom: but godliness is an abomination to a sinner. [26] If thou desire wisdom, keep the commandments, and the Lord shall give her unto thee. [27] For the fear of the Lord is wisdom and instruction: and faith and meekness are his delight. [28] Distrust not the fear of the Lord when thou art poor: and come not unto him with a double heart. [29] Be not an hypocrite in the sight of men, and take good heed what thou speakest. [30] Exalt not thyself, lest thou fall, and bring dishonour upon thy soul, and so God discover thy secrets, and cast thee down in the midst of the congregation, because thou camest not in truth to the fear of the Lord, but thy heart is full of deceit.

2 [1] My son, if thou come to serve the Lord, prepare thy soul for temptation. [2] Set thy heart aright, and constantly endure, and make not haste in time of trouble.

³ Cleave unto him, and depart not away, that thou mayest be increased at thy last end. ⁴ Whatsoever is brought upon thee take cheerfully, and be patient when thou art changed to a low estate. ⁵ For gold is tried in the fire, and acceptable men in the furnace of adversity. ⁶ Believe in him, and he will help thee; order thy way aright, and trust in him. ⁷ Ye that fear the Lord, wait for his mercy; and go not aside, lest ye fall. ⁸ Ye that fear the Lord, believe him; and your reward shall not fail. ⁹ Ye that fear the Lord, hope for good, and for everlasting joy and mercy. ¹⁰ Look at the generations of old, and see; did ever any trust in the Lord, and was confounded? or did any abide in his fear, and was forsaken? or whom did he ever despise, that called upon him? ¹¹ For the Lord is full of compassion and mercy, long suffering, and very pitiful, and forgiveth sins, and saveth in time of affliction. ¹² Woe be to fearful hearts, and faint hands, and the sinner that goeth two ways! ¹³ Woe unto him that is fainthearted! for he believeth not; therefore shall he not be defended. ¹⁴ Woe unto you that have lost patience! and what will ye do when the Lord shall visit you? ¹⁵ They that fear the Lord will not disobey his Word; and they that love him will keep his ways. ¹⁶ They that fear the Lord will seek that which is well-pleasing unto him; and they that love him shall be filled with the law. ¹⁷ They that fear the Lord will prepare their hearts, and humble their souls in his sight, ¹⁸ saying, We will fall into the hands of the Lord, and not into the hands of men: for as his majesty is, so is his mercy.

3 ¹ Hear me your father, O children, and do thereafter, that ye may be safe. ² For the Lord hath given the father honour over the children, and hath confirmed

the authority of the mother over the sons. ³ Whoso honoureth his father maketh an atonement for his sins: ⁴ And he that honoureth his mother is as one that layeth up treasure. ⁵ Whoso honoureth his father shall have joy of his own children; and when he maketh his prayer, he shall be heard. ⁶ He that honoureth his father shall have a long life; and he that is obedient unto the Lord shall be a comfort to his mother. ⁷ He that feareth the Lord will honour his father, and will do service unto his parents, as to his masters. ⁸ Honour thy father and mother, both in word and deed, that a blessing may come upon thee from them. ⁹ For the blessing of the father establisheth the houses of children; but the curse of the mother rooteth out foundations. ¹⁰ Glory not in the dishonour of thy father; for thy father's dishonour is no glory unto thee. ¹¹ For the glory of a man is from the honour of his father; and a mother in dishonour is a reproach to the children. ¹² My son, help thy father in his age, and grieve him not as long as he liveth. ¹³ And if his understanding fail, have patience with him; and despise him not when thou art in thy full strength. ¹⁴ For the relieving of thy father shall not be forgotten: and instead of sins it shall be added to build thee up. ¹⁵ In the day of thine affliction it shall be remembered; thy sins also shall melt away, as the ice in the fair warm weather. ¹⁶ He that forsaketh his father is as a blasphemer; and he that angereth his mother is cursed of God. ¹⁷ My son, go on with thy business in meekness; so shalt thou be beloved of him that is approved. ¹⁸ The greater thou art, the more humble thyself, and thou shalt find favour before the Lord. ¹⁹ Many are in high place, and of renown: but mysteries are revealed unto the meek. ²⁰ For the power of the Lord is great, and he is honoured of the lowly.

²¹ Seek not out things that are too hard for thee, neither search the things that are above thy strength. ²² But what is commanded thee, think thereupon with reverence, for it is not needful for thee to see with thine eyes the things that are in secret. ²³ Be not curious in unnecessary matters: for more things are shewed unto thee than men understand. ²⁴ For many are deceived by their own vain opinion; and an evil suspicion hath overthrown their judgment. ²⁵ Without eyes thou shalt want light: profess not the knowledge therefore that thou hast not. ²⁶ A stubborn heart shall fare evil at the last; and he that loveth danger shall perish therein. ²⁷ An obstinate heart shall be laden with sorrows; and the wicked man shall heap sin upon sin. ²⁸ In the punishment of the proud there is no remedy; for the plant of wickedness hath taken root in him. ²⁹ The heart of the prudent will understand a parable; and an attentive ear is the desire of a wise man. ³⁰ Water will quench a flaming fire; and alms maketh an atonement for sins. ³¹ And he that requiteth good turns is mindful of that which may come hereafter; and when he falleth, he shall find a stay.

4 ¹ My son, defraud not the poor of his living, and make not the needy eyes to wait long. ² Make not an hungry soul sorrowful; neither provoke a man in his distress. ³ Add not more trouble to an heart that is vexed; and defer not to give to him that is in need. ⁴ Reject not the supplication of the afflicted; neither turn away thy face from a poor man. ⁵ Turn not away thine eye from the needy, and give him none occasion to curse thee: ⁶ For if he curse thee in the bitterness of his soul, his prayer shall be heard of him that made him. ⁷ Get thyself the love of the congregation, and bow thy head to a great

man. [8] Let it not grieve thee to bow down thine ear to the poor, and give him a friendly answer with meekness. [9] Deliver him that suffereth wrong from the hand of the oppressor; and be not fainthearted when thou sittest in judgment. [10] Be as a father unto the fatherless, and instead of an husband unto their mother: so shalt thou be as the son of the most High, and he shall love thee more than thy mother doth. [11] Wisdom exalteth her children, and layeth hold of them that seek her. [12] He that loveth her loveth life; and they that seek to her early shall be filled with joy. [13] He that holdeth her fast shall inherit glory; and wheresoever she entereth, the Lord will bless. [14] They that serve her shall minister to the Holy One: and them that love her the Lord doth love. [15] Whoso giveth ear unto her shall judge the nations: and he that attendeth unto her shall dwell securely. [16] If a man commit himself unto her, he shall inherit her; and his generation shall hold her in possession. [17] For at the first she will walk with him by crooked ways, and bring fear and dread upon him, and torment him with her discipline, until she may trust his soul, and try him by her laws. [18] Then will she return the straight way unto him, and comfort him, and shew him her secrets. [19] But if he go wrong, she will forsake him, and give him over to his own ruin. [20] Observe the opportunity, and beware of evil; and be not ashamed when it concerneth thy soul. [21] For there is a shame that bringeth sin; and there is a shame which is glory and grace. [22] Accept no person against thy soul, and let not the reverence of any man cause thee to fall. [23] And refrain not to speak, when there is occasion to do good, and hide not thy wisdom in her beauty. [24] For by speech wisdom shall be known: and learning by the word of the tongue. [25] In no wise speak against the truth; but be

abashed of the error of thine ignorance. ²⁶ Be not
ashamed to confess thy sins; and force not the course of
the river. ²⁷ Make not thyself an underling to a foolish
man; neither accept the person of the mighty. ²⁸ Strive
for the truth unto death, and the Lord shall fight for
thee. ²⁹ Be not hasty in thy tongue, and in thy deeds
slack and remiss. ³⁰ Be not as a lion in thy house, nor
frantic among thy servants. ³¹ Let not thine hand be
stretched out to receive, and shut when thou shouldest
repay.

5 ¹ Set not thy heart upon thy goods; and say not, I have
enough for my life. ² Follow not thine own mind and
thy strength, to walk in the ways of thy heart: ³ And say
not, Who shall control me for my works? for the Lord
will surely revenge thy pride. ⁴ Say not, I have sinned,
and what harm hath happened unto me? for the Lord is
long-suffering, he will in no wise let thee go.
⁵ Concerning propitiation, be not without fear to add
sin unto sin: ⁶ And say not, His mercy is great; he will
be pacified for the multitude of my sins: for mercy and
wrath come from him, and his indignation resteth upon
sinners. ⁷ Make no tarrying to turn to the Lord, and put
not off from day to day: for suddenly shall the wrath of
the Lord come forth, and in thy security thou shalt be
destroyed, and perish in the day of vengeance. ⁸ Set not
thine heart upon goods unjustly gotten, for they shall
not profit thee in the day of calamity. ⁹ Winnow not
with every wind, and go not into every way: for so doth
the sinner that hath a double tongue. ¹⁰ Be stedfast in
thine understanding; and let thy word be the same.
¹¹ Be swift to hear; and let thy life be sincere; and with
patience give answer. ¹² If thou hast understanding,
answer thy neighbour; if not, lay thy hand upon thy

mouth. [13] Honour and shame is in talk: and the tongue of man is his fall. [14] Be not called a whisperer, and lie not in wait with thy tongue: for a foul shame is upon the thief, and an evil condemnation upon the double tongue. [15] Be not ignorant of any thing in a great matter or a small.

6 [1] Instead of a friend become not an enemy; for [thereby] thou shalt inherit an ill name, shame, and reproach: even so shall a sinner that hath a double tongue. [2] Extol not thyself in the counsel of thine own heart; that thy soul be not torn in pieces as a bull [straying alone]. [3] Thou shalt eat up thy leaves, and lose thy fruit, and leave thyself as a dry tree. [4] A wicked soul shall destroy him that hath it, and shall make him to be laughed to scorn of his enemies. [5] Sweet language will multiply friends: and a fairspeaking tongue will increase kind greetings. [6] Be in peace with many: nevertheless have but one counsellor of a thousand. [7] If thou wouldest get a friend, prove him first and be not hasty to credit him. [8] For some man is a friend for his own occasion, and will not abide in the day of thy trouble. [9] And there is a friend, who being turned to enmity and strife, will discover thy reproach. [10] Again, some friend is a companion at the table, and will not continue in the day of thine affliction. [11] But in thy prosperity he will be as thyself, and will be bold over thy servants. [12] If thou be brought low, he will be against thee, and will hide himself from thy face. [13] Separate thyself from thine enemies, and take heed of thy friends. [14] A faithful friend is a strong defence: and he that hath found such an one hath found a treasure. [15] Nothing doth countervail a faithful friend, and his excellency is invaluable. [16] A faithful friend is the medicine of life;

and they that fear the Lord shall find him. ¹⁷ Whoso feareth the Lord shall direct his friendship aright: for as he is, so shall his neighbour be also. ¹⁸ My son, gather instruction from thy youth up: so shalt thou find wisdom till thine old age. ¹⁹ Come unto her as one that ploweth and soweth, and wait for her good fruits: for thou shalt not toil much in labouring about her, but thou shalt eat of her fruits right soon. ²⁰ She is very unpleasant to the unlearned: he that is without understanding will not remain with her. ²¹ She will lie upon him as a mighty stone of trial; and he will cast her from him ere it be long. ²² For wisdom is according to her name, and she is not manifest unto many. ²³ Give ear, my son, receive my advice, and refuse not my counsel, ²⁴ and put thy feet into her fetters, and thy neck into her chain. ²⁵ Bow down thy shoulder, and bear her, and be not grieved with her bonds. ²⁶ Come unto her with thy whole heart, and keep her ways with all thy power. ²⁷ Search, and seek, and she shall be made known unto thee: and when thou hast got hold of her, let her not go. ²⁸ For at the last thou shalt find her rest, and that shall be turned to thy joy. ²⁹ Then shall her fetters be a strong defence for thee, and her chains a robe of glory. ³⁰ For there is a golden ornament upon her, and her bands are purple lace. ³¹ Thou shalt put her on as a robe of honour, and shalt put her about thee as a crown of joy. ³² My son, if thou wilt, thou shalt be taught: and if thou wilt apply thy mind, thou shalt be prudent. ³³ If thou love to hear, thou shalt receive understanding: and if thou bow thine ear, thou shalt be wise. ³⁴ Stand in the multitude of the elders; and cleave unto him that is wise. ³⁵ Be willing to hear every godly discourse; and let not the parables of understanding escape thee. ³⁶ And if thou seest a man of understanding, get thee betimes unto him, and let thy foot wear the steps of his door. [37] Let thy mind be upon the ordinances of the Lord and meditate continually in his commandments: he shall establish thine heart, and give thee wisdom at thine own desire.

7 [1] Do no evil, so shall no harm come unto thee. [2] Depart from the unjust, and iniquity shall turn away from thee. [3] My son, sow not upon the furrows of unrighteousness, and thou shalt not reap them sevenfold. [4] Seek not of the Lord preeminence, neither of the king the seat of honour. [5] Justify not thyself before the Lord; and boast not of thy wisdom before the king. [6] Seek not to be judge, being not able to take away iniquity; lest at any time thou fear the person of the mighty, and lay a stumbling-block in the way of thy uprightness. [7] Offend not against the multitude of a city, and then thou shalt not cast thyself down among the people. [8] Bind not one sin upon another; for in one thou shalt not be unpunished. [9] Say not, God will look upon the multitude of my oblations, and when I offer to the most high God, he will accept it. [10] Be not fainthearted when thou makest thy prayer, and neglect not to give alms. [11] Laugh no man to scorn in the bitterness of his soul: for there is one which humbleth and exalteth. [12] Devise not a lie against thy brother; neither do the like to thy friend. [13] Use not to make any manner of lie: for the custom thereof is not good. [14] Use not many words in a multitude of elders, and make not much babbling when thou prayest. [15] Hate not laborious work, neither husbandry, which the most High hath ordained. [16] Number not thyself among the multitude of sinners, but remember that wrath will not tarry long. [17] Humble thyself greatly: for the vengeance of the ungodly is fire and worms.

[18] Change not a friend for any good, by no means; neither a faithful brother for the gold of Ophir. [19] Forego not a wise and good woman: for her grace is above gold. [20] Whereas thy servant worketh truly, entreat him not evil, nor the hireling that bestoweth himself wholly for thee. [21] Let thy soul love a good servant, and defraud him not of liberty. [22] Hast thou cattle? have an eye to them: and if they be for thy profit, keep them with thee. [23] Hast thou children? instruct them, and bow down their neck from their youth. [24] Hast thou daughters? have a care of their body, and shew not thyself cheerful toward them. [25] Marry thy daughter, and so shalt thou have performed a weighty matter: but give her to a man of understanding. [26] Hast thou a wife after thy mind? forsake her not: but give not thyself over to a light woman. [27] Honour thy father with thy whole heart, and forget not the sorrows of thy mother. [28] Remember that thou wast begotten of them; and how canst thou recompense them the things that they have done for thee? [29] Fear the Lord with all thy soul, and reverence his priests. [30] Love him that made thee with all thy strength, and forsake not his ministers. [31] Fear the Lord, and honour the priest; and give him his portion, as it is commanded thee; the firstfruits, and the trespass offering, and the gift of the shoulders, and the sacrifice of sanctification, and the firstfruits of the holy things. [32] And stretch thine hand unto the poor, that thy blessing may be perfected. [33] A gift hath grace in the sight of every man living; and for the dead detain it not. [34] Fail not to be with them that weep, and mourn with them that mourn. [35] Be not slow to visit the sick: for that shall make thee to be beloved. [36] Whatsoever thou takest in hand, remember the end, and thou shalt never do amiss.

8 [1] Strive not with a mighty man, lest thou fall into his hands. [2] Be not at variance with a rich man, lest he overweigh thee: for gold hath destroyed many, and perverted the hearts of kings. [3] Strive not with a man that is full of tongue, and heap not wood upon his fire. [4] Jest not with a rude man, lest thine ancestors be disgraced. [5] Reproach not a man that turneth from sin, but remember that we are all worthy of punishment. [6] Dishonour not a man in his old age: for even some of us wax old. [7] Rejoice not over thy greatest enemy being dead, but remember that we die all. [8] Despise not the discourse of the wise, but acquaint thyself with their proverbs: for of them thou shalt learn instruction, and how to serve great men with ease. [9] Miss not the discourse of the elders: for they also learned of their fathers, and of them thou shalt learn understanding, and to give answer as need requireth. [10] Kindle not the coals of a sinner, lest thou be burnt with the flame of his fire. [11] Rise not up [in anger] at the presence of an injurious person, lest he lie in wait to entrap thee in thy words. [12] Lend not unto him that is mightier than thyself; for if thou lendest him, count it but lost. [13] Be not surety above thy power: for if thou be surety, take care to pay it. [14] Go not to law with a judge; for they will judge for him according to his honour. [15] Travel not by the way with a bold fellow, lest he become grievous unto thee: for he will do according to his own will, and thou shalt perish with him through his folly. [16] Strive not with an angry man, and go not with him into a solitary place: for blood is as nothing in his sight, and where there is no help, he will overthrow thee. [17] Consult not with a fool; for he cannot keep counsel. [18] Do no secret thing before a stranger; for thou knowest not what he will bring forth. [19] Open not thine

heart to every man, lest he requite thee with a shrewd turn.

9 [1] Be not jealous over the wife of thy bosom, and teach her not an evil lesson against thyself. [2] Give not thy soul unto a woman to set her foot upon thy substance. [3] Meet not with an harlot, lest thou fall into her snares. [4] Use not much the company of a woman that is a singer, lest thou be taken with her attempts. [5] Gaze not on a maid, that thou fall not by those things that are precious in her. [6] Give not thy soul unto harlots, that thou lose not thine inheritance. [7] Look not around about thee in the streets of the city, neither wander thou in the solitary places thereof. [8] Turn away thine eye from a beautiful woman, and look not upon another's beauty; for many have been deceived by the beauty of a woman; for herewith love is kindled as a fire. [9] Sit not at all with another man's wife, nor sit down with her in thine arms, and spend not thy money with her at the wine; lest thine heart incline unto her, and so through thy desire thou fall into destruction. [10] Forsake not an old friend; for the new is not comparable to him: a new friend is as new wine; when it is old, thou shalt drink it with pleasure. [11] Envy not the glory of a sinner: for thou knowest not what shall be his end. [12] Delight not in the thing that the ungodly have pleasure in; but remember they shall not go unpunished unto their grave. [13] Keep thee far from the man that hath power to kill; so shalt thou not doubt the fear of death: and if thou come unto him, make no fault, lest he take away thy life presently: remember that thou goest in the midst of snares, and that thou walkest upon the battlements of the city. [14] As near as thou canst, guess at thy neighbour, and consult with the wise. [15] Let thy talk be

253

with the wise, and all thy communication in the law of the most High. [16] And let just men eat and drink with thee; and let thy glorying be in the fear of the Lord. [17] For the hand of the artificer the work shall be commended: and the wise ruler of the people for his speech. [18] A man of an ill tongue is dangerous in his city; and he that is rash in his talk shall be hated.

10 [1] A wise judge will instruct his people; and the government of a prudent man is well ordered. [2] As the judge of the people is himself, so are his officers; and what manner of man the ruler of the city is, such are all they that dwell therein. [3] An unwise king destroyeth his people; but through the prudence of them which are in authority, the city shall be inhabited. [4] The power of the earth is in the hand of the Lord, and in due time he will set over it one that is profitable. [5] In the hand of God is the prosperity of man: and upon the person of the scribe shall he lay his honour. [6] Bear not hatred to thy neighbour for every wrong; and do nothing at all by injurious practices. [7] Pride is hateful before God and man: and by both doth one commit iniquity. [8] Because of unrighteous dealings, injuries, and riches got by deceit, the kingdom is translated from one people to another. [9] Why is earth and ashes proud? There is not a more wicked thing than a covetous man: for such an one setteth his own soul to sale; because while he liveth he casteth away his bowels. [10] The physician cutteth off a long disease; and he that is to-day a king to-morrow shall die. [11] For when a man is dead, he shall inherit creeping things, beasts, and worms. [12] The beginning of pride is when one departeth from God, and his heart is turned away from his Maker. [13] For pride is the beginning of sin, and he that hath it shall pour out abomination: and therefore the Lord brought upon them strange calamities, and overthrew them utterly. [14] The Lord hath cast down the thrones of proud princes, and set up the meek in their stead. [15] The Lord hath plucked up the roots of the proud nations, and planted the lowly in their place. [16] The Lord overthrew countries of the heathen, and destroyed them to the foundations of the earth. [17] He took some of them away, and destroyed them, and hath made their memorial to cease from the earth. [18] Pride was not made for men, nor furious anger for them that are born of a woman. [19] They that fear the Lord are a sure seed, and they that love him an honourable plant: they that regard not the law are a dishonourable seed; they that transgress the commandments are a deceivable seed. [20] Among brethren he that is chief is honourable; so are they that fear the Lord in his eyes. [21] The fear of the Lord goeth before the obtaining of authority; but roughness and pride is the losing thereof. [22] Whether he be rich, noble, or poor, their glory is the fear of the Lord. [23] It is not meet to despise the poor man that hath understanding; neither is it convenient to magnify a sinful man. [24] Great men, and judges, and potentates, shall be honoured; yet is there none of them greater than he that feareth the Lord. [25] Unto the servant that is wise shall they that are free do service: and he that hath knowledge will not grudge when he is reformed. [26] Be not overwise in doing thy business; and boast not thyself in the time of thy distress. [27] Better is he that laboureth, and aboundeth in all things, than he that boasteth himself, and wanteth bread. [28] My son, glorify thy soul in meekness, and give it honour according to the dignity thereof. [29] Who will justify him that sinneth against his own soul? and who will honour him that dishonoureth his own life? [30] The poor man is honoured for his skill, and the rich man is honoured for his riches. [31] He that is honoured in poverty, how much more in riches? and he that is dishonourable in riches, how much more in poverty?

11 [1] Wisdom lifteth up the head of him that is of low degree, and maketh him to sit among great men. [2] Commend not a man for his beauty; neither abhor a man for his outward appearance. [3] The bee is little among such as fly; but her fruit is the chief of sweet things. [4] Boast not of thy clothing and raiment, and exalt not thyself in the day of honour: for the works of the Lord are wonderful, and his works among men are hidden. [5] Many kings have sat down upon the ground; and one that was never thought of hath worn the crown. [6] Many mighty men have been greatly disgraced; and the honourable delivered into other men's hands. [7] Blame not before thou hast examined the truth: understand first, and then rebuke. [8] Answer not before thou hast heard the cause: neither interrupt men in the midst of their talk. [9] Strive not in a matter that concerneth thee not; and sit not in judgment with sinners. [10] My son, meddle not with many matters: for if thou meddle much, thou shalt not be innocent; and if thou follow after, thou shalt not obtain, neither shalt thou escape by fleeing. [11] There is one that laboureth, and taketh pains, and maketh haste, and is so much the more behind. [12] Again, there is another that is slow, and hath need of help, wanting ability, and full of poverty; yet the eye of the Lord looked upon him for good, and set him up from his low estate, [13] and lifted up his head from misery; so that many that saw it marvelled at him. [14] Prosperity and adversity, life and death, poverty and riches, come of the Lord. ¹⁵ Wisdom, knowledge, and understanding of the law, are of the Lord: love, and the way of good works, are from him. ¹⁶ Error and darkness had their beginning together with sinners: and evil shall wax old with them that glory therein. ¹⁷ The gift of the Lord remaineth with the godly, and his favour bringeth prosperity for ever. ¹⁸ There is that waxeth rich by his wariness and pinching, and this is the portion of his reward: ¹⁹ Whereas he saith, I have found rest, and now will eat continually of my goods; and yet he knoweth not what time shall come upon him, and that he must leave those things to others, and die. ²⁰ Be stedfast in thy covenant, and be conversant therein, and wax old in thy work. ²¹ Marvel not at the works of sinners; but trust in the Lord, and abide in thy labour: for it is an easy thing in the sight of the Lord on the sudden to make a poor man rich. ²² The blessing of the Lord is in the reward of the godly, and suddenly he maketh his blessing flourish. ²³ Say not, What profit is there of my service? and what good things shall I have hereafter? ²⁴ Again, say not, I have enough, and possess many things, and what evil shall I have hereafter? ²⁵ In the day of prosperity there is a forgetfulness of affliction: and in the day of affliction there is no more remembrance of prosperity. ²⁶ For it is an easy thing unto the Lord in the day of death to reward a man according to his ways. ²⁷ The affliction of an hour maketh a man forget pleasure: and in his end his deeds shall be discovered. ²⁸ Judge none blessed before his death: for a man shall be known in his children. ²⁹ Bring not every man into thine house: for the deceitful man hath many trains. ³⁰ Like as a partridge taken [and kept] in a cage, so is the heart of the proud; and like as a spy, watcheth he for thy fall: [31] For he lieth in wait, and turneth good into evil, and in things worthy praise will lay blame upon thee. [32] Of a spark of fire a heap of coals is kindled: and a sinful man layeth wait for blood. [33] Take heed of a mischievous man, for he worketh wickedness; lest he bring upon thee a perpetual blot. [34] Receive a stranger into thine house, and he will disturb thee, and turn thee out of thine own.

12

[1] When thou wilt do good, know to whom thou doest it; so shalt thou be thanked for thy benefits. [2] Do good to the godly man, and thou shalt find a recompence; and if not from him, yet from the most High. [3] There can no good come to him that is always occupied in evil, nor to him that giveth no alms. [4] Give to the godly man, and help not a sinner. [5] Do well unto him that is lowly, but give not to the ungodly: hold back thy bread, and give it not unto him, lest he overmaster thee thereby: for [else] thou shalt receive twice as much evil for all the good thou shalt have done unto him. [6] For the most High hateth sinners, and will repay vengeance unto the ungodly, and keepeth them against the mighty day of their punishment. [7] Give unto the good, and help not the sinner. [8] A friend cannot be known in prosperity: and an enemy cannot be hidden in adversity. [9] In the prosperity of a man, enemies will be grieved: but in his adversity, even a friend will depart. [10] Never trust thine enemy: for like as iron rusteth, so is his wickedness. [11] Though he humble himself, and go crouching, yet take good heed and beware of him, and thou shalt be unto him as if thou hadst wiped a looking-glass, and thou shalt know that his rust hath not been altogether wiped away. [12] Set him not by thee, lest, when he hath overthrown thee,

he stand up in thy place; neither let him sit at thy right hand, lest he seek to take thy seat, and thou at the last remember my words, and be pricked therewith. [13] Who will pity a charmer that is bitten with a serpent, or any such as come nigh wild beasts? [14] So one that goeth to a sinner, and is defiled with him in his sins, who will pity? [15] For a while he will abide with thee, but if thou begin to fall, he will not tarry. [16] An enemy speaketh sweetly with his lips, but in his heart he imagineth how to throw thee into a pit: he will weep with his eyes, but if he find opportunity, he will not be satisfied with blood. [17] If adversity come upon thee, thou shalt find him there first; and though he pretend to help thee, yet shall he undermine thee. [18] He will shake his head, and clap his hands, and whisper much, and change his countenance.

13 [1] He that toucheth pitch shall be defiled therewith; and he that hath fellowship with a proud man shall be like unto him. [2] Burden not thyself above thy power while thou livest; and have no fellowship with one that is mightier and richer than thyself: for how agree the kettle and the earthen pot together? for if the one be smitten against the other, it shall be broken. [3] The rich man hath done wrong, and yet he threateneth withal: the poor is wronged, and he must intreat also. [4] If thou be for his profit, he will use thee: but if thou have nothing, he will forsake thee. [5] If thou have any thing, he will live with thee: yea, he will make thee bare, and will not be sorry for it. [6] If he have need of thee, he will deceive thee, and smile upon thee, and put thee in hope; he will speak thee fair, and say, What wantest thou? [7] And he will shame thee by his meats, until he have drawn thee dry twice or thrice, and at the last he will laugh thee to scorn: afterward, when he seeth thee, he will forsake thee, and shake his head at thee. [8] Beware that thou be not deceived, and brought down in thy jollity. [9] If thou be invited of a mighty man, withdraw thyself, and so much the more will he invite thee. [10] Press thou not upon him, lest thou be put back; stand not far off, lest thou be forgotten. [11] Affect not to be made equal unto him in talk, and believe not his many words: for with much communication will he tempt thee, and smiling upon thee will get out thy secrets: [12] But cruelly he will lay up thy words, and will not spare to do thee hurt, and to put thee in prison. [13] Observe, and take good heed, for thou walkest in peril of thy overthrowing: when thou hearest these things, awake in thy sleep. [14] Love the Lord all thy life, and call upon him for thy salvation. [15] Every beast loveth his like, and every man loveth his neighbour. [16] All flesh consorteth according to kind, and a man will cleave to his like. [17] What fellowship hath the wolf with the lamb? so the sinner with the godly. [18] What agreement is there between the hyena and a dog? and what peace between the rich and the poor? [19] As the wild ass is the lion's prey in the wilderness: so the rich eat up the poor. [20] As the proud hate humility: so doth the rich abhor the poor. [21] A rich man beginning to fall is held up of his friends: but a poor man being down is thrust away by his friends. [22] When a rich man is fallen, he hath many helpers: he speaketh things not to be spoken, and yet men justify him: the poor man slipped, and yet they rebuked him too; he spake wisely, and could have no place. [23] When a rich man speaketh, every man holdeth his tongue, and, look, what he saith, they extol it to the clouds: but if the poor man speak, they say, What fellow is this? and if he stumble, they will help to overthrow him. ²⁴ Riches are good unto him that hath no sin, and poverty is evil in the mouth of the ungodly. ²⁵ The heart of a man changeth his countenance, whether it be for good or evil: and a merry heart maketh a cheerful countenance. ²⁶ A cheerful countenance is a token of a heart that is in prosperity; and the finding out of parables is a wearisome labour of the mind.

14

¹ Blessed is the man that hath not slipped with his mouth, and is not pricked with the multitude of sins. ² Blessed is he whose conscience hath not condemned him, and who is not fallen from his hope in the Lord. ³ Riches are not comely for a niggard: and what should an envious man do with money? ⁴ He that gathereth by defrauding his own soul gathereth for others, that shall spend his goods riotously. ⁵ He that is evil to himself, to whom will he be good? he shall not take pleasure in his goods. ⁶ There is none worse than he that envieth himself; and this is a recompence of his wickedness. ⁷ And if he doeth good, he doeth it unwillingly; and at the last he will declare his wickedness. ⁸ The envious man hath a wicked eye; he turneth away his face, and despiseth men. ⁹ A covetous man's eye is not satisfied with his portion; and the iniquity of the wicked drieth up his soul. ¹⁰ A wicked eye envieth [his] bread, and he is a niggard at his table. ¹¹ My son, according to thy ability do good to thyself, and give the Lord his due offering. ¹² Remember that death will not be long in coming, and that the covenant of the grave is not shewed unto thee. ¹³ Do good unto thy friend before thou die, and according to thy ability stretch out thy hand and give to him. ¹⁴ Defraud not thyself of the good day, and let not the part of a good desire overpass thee. ¹⁵ Shalt

thou not leave thy travails unto another? and thy labours to be divided by lot? [16] Give, and take, and sanctify thy soul; for there is no seeking of dainties in the grave. [17] All flesh waxeth old as a garment: for the covenant from the beginning is, Thou shalt die the death. [18] As of the green leaves on a thick tree, some fall, and some grow; so is the generation of flesh and blood, one cometh to an end, and another is born. [19] Every work rotteth and consumeth away, and the worker thereof shall go withal. [20] Blessed is the man that doth meditate good things in wisdom, and that reasoneth of holy things by his understanding. [21] He that considereth her ways in his heart shall also have understanding in her secrets. [22] Go after her as one that traceth, and lie in wait in her ways. [23] He that prieth in at her windows shall also hearken at her doors. [24] He that doth lodge near her house shall also fasten a pin in her walls. [25] He shall pitch his tent nigh unto her, and shall lodge in a lodging where good things are. [26] He shall set his children under her shelter, and shall lodge under her branches. [27] By her he shall be covered from heat, and in her glory shall he dwell.

15 [1] He that feareth the Lord will do good, and he that hath the knowledge of the law shall obtain her. [2] And as a mother shall she meet him, and receive him as a wife married of a virgin. [3] With the bread of understanding shall she feed him, and give him the water of wisdom to drink. [4] He shall be stayed upon her, and shall not be moved; and shall rely upon her, and shall not be confounded. [5] She shall exalt him above his neighbours, and in the midst of the congregation shall she open his mouth. [6] He shall find joy and a crown of gladness, and she shall cause him to inherit an ever-

lasting name. ⁷ But foolish men shall not attain unto her, and sinners shall not see her. ⁸ For she is far from pride, and men that are liars cannot remember her. ⁹ Praise is not seemly in the mouth of a sinner, for it was not sent him of the Lord. ¹⁰ For praise shall be uttered in wisdom, and the Lord will prosper it. ¹¹ Say not thou, It is through the Lord that I fell away: for thou oughtest not to do the things that he hateth. ¹² Say not thou, He hath caused me to err: for he hath no need of the sinful man. ¹³ The Lord hateth all abomination; and they that fear God love it not. ¹⁴ He himself made man from the beginning, and left him in the hand of his counsel; ¹⁵ if thou wilt, to keep the commandments, and to perform acceptable faithfulness. ¹⁶ He hath set fire and water before thee: stretch forth thy hand unto whether thou wilt. ¹⁷ Before man is life and death; and whether him liketh shall be given him. ¹⁸ For the wisdom of the Lord is great, and he is mighty in power, and beholdeth all things: ¹⁹ And his eyes are upon them that fear him, and he knoweth every work of man. ²⁰ He hath commanded no man to do wickedly, neither hath he given any man licence to sin.

16

¹ Desire not a multitude of unprofitable children, neither delight in ungodly sons. ² Though they multiply, rejoice not in them, except the fear of the Lord be with them. ³ Trust not thou in their life, neither respect their multitude: for one that is just is better than a thousand; and better it is to die without children, than to have them that are ungodly. ⁴ For by one that hath understanding shall the city be replenished: but the kindred of the wicked shall speedily become desolate. ⁵ Many such things have I seen with mine eyes, and mine ear hath heard greater things than these. ⁶ In the

congregation of the ungodly shall a fire be kindled; and in a rebellious nation wrath is set on fire. [7] He was not pacified toward the old giants, who fell away in the strength of their foolishness. [8] Neither spared he the place where Lot sojourned, but abhorred them for their pride. [9] He pitied not the people of perdition, who were taken away in their sins: [10] nor the six hundred thousand footmen, who were gathered together in the hardness of their hearts. [11] And if there be one stiffnecked among the people, it is marvel if he escape unpunished: for mercy and wrath are with him; he is mighty to forgive, and to pour out displeasure. [12] As his mercy is great, so is his correction also: he judgeth a man according to his works. [13] The sinner shall not escape with his spoils: and the patience of the godly shall not be frustrate. [14] Make way for every work of mercy: for every man shall find according to his works. [15] The Lord hardened Pharaoh, that he should not know him, that his powerful works might be known to the world. [16] His mercy is manifest to every creature; and he hath separated his light from the darkness with an adamant. [17] Say not thou, I will hide myself from the Lord: shall any remember me from above? I shall not be remembered among so many people: for what is my soul among such an infinite number of creatures? [18] Behold, the heaven, and the heaven of heavens, the deep, and the earth, and all that therein is, shall be moved when he shall visit. [19] The mountains also and foundations of the earth be shaken with trembling, when the Lord looketh upon them. [20] No heart can think upon these things worthily: and who is able to conceive his ways? [21] It is a tempest which no man can see: for the most part of his works are hid. [22] Who can declare the works of his justice? or who can endure them? for his covenant is afar off, and the trial of all things is in the end. ²³ He that wanteth understanding will think upon vain things: and a foolish man erring imagineth follies. ²⁴ My son, hearken unto me, and learn knowledge, and mark my words with thy heart. ²⁵ I will shew forth doctrine in weight, and declare his knowledge exactly. ²⁶ The works of the Lord are done in judgment from the beginning: and from the time he made them he disposed the parts thereof. ²⁷ He garnished his works for ever, and in his hand are the chief of them unto all generations: they neither labour, nor are weary, nor cease from their works. ²⁸ None of them hindereth another, and they shall never disobey his word. ²⁹ After this the Lord looked upon the earth, and filled it with his blessings. ³⁰ With all manner of living things hath he covered the face thereof; and they shall return into it again.

17 ¹ The Lord created man of the earth, and turned him into it again. ² He gave them few days, and a short time, and power also over the things therein. ³ He endued them with strength by themselves, and made them according to his image, ⁴ and put the fear of man upon all flesh, and gave him dominion over beasts and fowls. ⁵ [They received the use of the five operations of the Lord, and in the sixth place he imparted them understanding, and in the seventh speech, an interpreter of the cogitations thereof.] ⁶ Counsel, and a tongue, and eyes, ears, and a heart, gave he them to understand. ⁷ Withal he filled them with the knowledge of understanding, and shewed them good and evil. ⁸ He set his eye upon their hearts, that he might shew them the greatness of his works. ⁹ He gave them to glory in his marvellous acts for ever, that they might declare his works with understanding. ¹⁰ And the elect shall praise his holy name. [11] Besides this he gave them knowledge, and the law of life for an heritage. [12] He made an everlasting covenant with them, and shewed them his judgments. [13] Their eyes saw the majesty of his glory, and their ears heard his glorious voice. [14] And he said unto them, Beware of all unrighteousness; and he gave every man commandment concerning his neighbour. [15] Their ways are ever before him, and shall not be hid from his eyes. [16] Every man from his youth is given to evil; neither could they make to themselves fleshey hearts for stony. [17] For in the division of the nations of the whole earth he set a ruler over every people, but Israel is the Lord's portion: [18] whom, being his firstborn, he nourisheth with discipline, and giving him the light of his love doth not forsake him. [19] Therefore all their works are as the sun before him, and his eyes are continually upon their ways. [20] None of their unrighteous deeds are hid from him, but all their sins are before the Lord. [21] But the Lord being gracious and knowing his workmanship, neither left nor forsook them, but spared them. [22] The alms of a man is as a signet with him, and he will keep the good deeds of man as the apple of his eye, and give repentance to his sons and daughters. [23] Afterwards he will rise up and reward them, and render their recompence upon their heads. [24] But unto them that repent, he granted them return, and comforted those that failed in patience. [25] Return unto the Lord, and forsake thy sins, make thy prayer before his face, and offend less. [26] Turn again to the most High, and turn away from iniquity: for he will lead thee out of darkness into the light of health, and hate thou abomination vehemently. [27] Who shall praise the most High in the grave, instead of them which live and give thanks? [28] Thanksgiving perisheth from the dead, as from one that is not: the living and sound in heart shall praise the Lord. ²⁹ How great is the lovingkindness of the Lord our God, and his compassion unto such as turn unto him in holiness! ³⁰ For all things cannot be in men, because the son of man is not immortal. ³¹ What is brighter than the sun? yet the light thereof faileth; and flesh and blood will imagine evil. ³² He vieweth the power of the height of heaven; and all men are but earth and ashes.

18

¹ He that liveth for ever hath created all things in general. ² The Lord only is righteous, and there is none other but he, ³ who governeth the world with the palm of his hand, and all things obey his will: for he is the King of all, by his power dividing holy things among them from profane. ⁴ To whom hath he given power to declare his works? and who shall find out his noble acts? ⁵ Who shall number the strength of his majesty? and who shall also tell out his mercies? ⁶ As for the wondrous works of the Lord, there may nothing be taken from them, neither may any thing be put unto them, neither can the ground of them be found out. ⁷ When a man hath done, then he beginneth; and when he leaveth off, then he shall be doubtful. ⁸ What is man, and whereto serveth he? what is his good, and what is his evil? ⁹ The number of a man's days at the most are an hundred years. ¹⁰ As a drop of water unto the sea, and a gravelstone in comparison of the sand; so are a thousand years to the days of eternity. ¹¹ Therefore is God patient with them, and poureth forth his mercy upon them. ¹² He saw and perceived their end to be evil; therefore he multiplied his compassion. ¹³ The mercy of man is toward his neighbour; but the mercy of the Lord is upon all flesh: he reproveth, and nurtureth,

and teacheth and bringeth again, as a shepherd his flock. [14] He hath mercy on them that receive discipline, and that diligently seek after his judgments. [15] My son, blemish not thy good deeds, neither use uncomfortable words when thou givest any thing. [16] Shall not the dew assuage the heat? so is a word better than a gift. [17] Lo, is not a word better than a gift? but both are with a gracious man. [18] A fool will upbraid churlishly, and a gift of the envious consumeth the eyes. [19] Learn before thou speak, and use physic or ever thou be sick. [20] Before judgment examine thyself, and in the day of visitation thou shalt find mercy. [21] Humble thyself before thou be sick, and in the time of sins shew repentance. [22] Let nothing hinder thee to pay thy vow in due time, and defer not until death to be justified. [23] Before thou prayest, prepare thyself; and be not as one that tempteth the Lord. [24] Think upon the wrath that shall be at the end, and the time of vengeance, when he shall turn away his face. [25] When thou hast enough, remember the time of hunger: and when thou art rich, think upon poverty and need. [26] From the morning until the evening the time is changed, and all things are soon done before the Lord. [27] A wise man will fear in every thing, and in the day of sinning he will beware of offence: but a fool will not observe time. [28] Every man of understanding knoweth wisdom, and will give praise unto him that found her. [29] They that were of understanding in sayings became also wise themselves, and poured forth exquisite parables. [30] Go not after thy lusts, but refrain thyself from thine appetites. [31] If thou givest thy soul the desires that please her, she will make thee a laughingstock to thine enemies that malign thee. [32] Take not pleasure in much good cheer, neither be tied to the expence thereof. ³³ Be not made a beggar by banqueting upon borrowing, when thou hast nothing in thy purse: for thou shalt lie in wait for thine own life, and be talked on.

19

¹ A labouring man that is given to drunkenness shall not be rich: and he that contemneth small things shall fall by little and little. ² Wine and women will make men of understanding to fall away: and he that cleaveth to harlots will become impudent. ³ Moths and worms shall have him to heritage, and a bold man shall be taken away. ⁴ He that is hasty to give credit is lightminded; and he that sinneth shall offend against his own soul. ⁵ Whoso taketh pleasure in wickedness shall be condemned: but he that resisteth pleasures crowneth his life. ⁶ He that can rule his tongue shall live without strife; and he that hateth babbling shall have less evil. ⁷ Rehearse not unto another that which is told unto thee, and thou shalt fare never the worse. ⁸ Whether it be to friend or foe, talk not of other men's lives; and if thou canst without offence, reveal them not. ⁹ For he heard and observed thee, and when time cometh he will hate thee. ¹⁰ If thou hast heard a word, let it die with thee; and be bold, it will not burst thee. ¹¹ A fool travaileth with a word, as a woman in labour of a child. ¹² As an arrow that sticketh in a man's thigh, so is a word within a fool's belly. ¹³ Admonish a friend, it may be he hath not done it: and if he have done it, that he do it no more. ¹⁴ Admonish thy friend, it may be he hath not said it: and if he have, that he speak it not again. ¹⁵ Admonish a friend: for many times it is a slander, and believe not every tale. ¹⁶ There is one that slippeth in his speech, but not from his heart; and who is he that hath not offended with his tongue? ¹⁷ Admonish thy neighbour before thou threaten him;

and not being angry, give place to the law of the most High. ¹⁸ The fear of the Lord is the first step to be accepted [of him,] and wisdom obtaineth his love. ¹⁹ The knowledge of the commandments of the Lord is the doctrine of life: and they that do things that please him shall receive the fruit of the tree of immortality. ²⁰ The fear of the Lord is all wisdom; and in all wisdom is the performance of the law, and the knowledge of his omnipotency. ²¹ If a servant say to his master, I will not do as it pleaseth thee; though afterward he do it, he angereth him that nourisheth him. ²² The knowledge of wickedness is not wisdom, neither at any time the counsel of sinners prudence. ²³ There is a wickedness, and the same an abomination; and there is a fool wanting in wisdom. ²⁴ He that hath small understanding, and feareth God, is better than one that hath much wisdom, and transgresseth the law of the most High. ²⁵ There is an exquisite subtilty, and the same is unjust; and there is one that turneth aside to make judgment appear; and there is a wise man that justifieth in judgment. ²⁶ There is a wicked man that hangeth down his head sadly; but inwardly he is full of deceit, ²⁷ casting down his countenance, and making as if he heard not: where he is not known, he will do thee a mischief before thou be aware. ²⁸ And if for want of power he be hindered from sinning, yet when he findeth opportunity he will do evil. ²⁹ A man may be known by his look, and one that hath understanding by his countenance, when thou meetest him. ³⁰ A man's attire, and excessive laughter, and gait, shew what he is.

20 ¹ There is a reproof that is not comely: again, some man holdeth his tongue, and he is wise. ² It is much better to reprove, than to be angry secretly: and he that confesseth his fault shall be preserved from hurt. ³ How good is it, when thou art reproved, to shew repentance! for so shalt thou escape wilful sin. ⁴ As is the lust of an eunuch to deflower a virgin; so is he that executeth judgment with violence. ⁵ There is one that keepeth silence, and is found wise: and another by much babbling becometh hateful. ⁶ Some man holdeth his tongue, because he hath not to answer: and some keepeth silence, knowing his time. ⁷ A wise man will hold his tongue till he see opportunity: but a babbler and a fool will regard no time. ⁸ He that useth many words shall be abhorred; and he that taketh to himself authority therein shall be hated. ⁹ There is a sinner that hath good success in evil things; and there is a gain that turneth to loss. ¹⁰ There is a gift that shall not profit thee; and there is a gift whose recompence is double. ¹¹ There is an abasement because of glory; and there is that lifteth up his head from a low estate. ¹² There is that buyeth much for a little, and repayeth it sevenfold. ¹³ A wise man by his words maketh himself beloved: but the graces of fools shall be poured out. ¹⁴ The gift of a fool shall do thee no good when thou hast it; neither yet of the envious for his necessity: for he looketh to receive many things for one. ¹⁵ He giveth little, and upbraideth much; he openeth his mouth like a crier; to day he lendeth, and to morrow will he ask it again: such an one is to be hated of God and man. ¹⁶ The fool saith, I have no friends, I have no thanks for all my good deeds, and they that eat my bread speak evil of me. ¹⁷ How oft, and of how many shall he be laughed to scorn! for he knoweth not aright what it is to have; and it is all one unto him as if he had it not. ¹⁸ To slip upon a pavement is better than to slip with the tongue: so the fall of the wicked shall come speedily. ¹⁹ An unseasonable tale will always be in the mouth of the unwise. [20] A wise sentence shall be rejected when it cometh out of a fool's mouth; for he will not speak it in due season. [21] There is that is hindered from sinning through want: and when he taketh rest, he shall not be troubled. [22] There is that destroyeth his own soul through bashfulness, and by accepting of persons overthroweth himself. [23] There is that for bashfulness promiseth to his friend, and maketh him his enemy for nothing. [24] A lie is a foul blot in a man, yet it is continually in the mouth of the untaught. [25] A thief is better than a man that is accustomed to lie: but they both shall have destruction to heritage. [26] The disposition of a liar is dishonourable, and his shame is ever with him. [27] A wise man shall promote himself to honour with his words: and he that hath understanding will please great men. [28] He that tilleth his land shall increase his heap: and he that pleaseth great men shall get pardon for iniquity. [29] Presents and gifts blind the eyes of the wise, and stop up his mouth that he cannot reprove. [30] Wisdom that is hid, and treasure that is hoarded up, what profit is in them both? [31] Better is he that hideth his folly than a man that hideth his wisdom. [32] Necessary patience in seeking the Lord is better than he that leadeth his life without a guide.

21 [1] My son, hast thou sinned? do so no more, but ask pardon for thy former sins. [2] Flee from sin as from the face of a serpent: for if thou comest too near it, it will bite thee: the teeth thereof are as the teeth of a lion, slaying the souls of men. [3] All iniquity is as a two-edged sword, the wounds whereof cannot be healed. [4] To terrify and do wrong will waste riches: thus the house of proud men shall be made desolate. [5] A prayer out of a poor man's mouth reacheth to the ears of God, and his judgment cometh speedily. ⁶ He that hateth to be reproved is in the way of sinners: but he that feareth the Lord will repent from his heart. ⁷ An eloquent man is known far and near; but a man of understanding knoweth when he slippeth. ⁸ He that buildeth his house with other men's money is like one that gathereth himself stones for the tomb of his burial. ⁹ The congregation of the wicked is like tow wrapped together: and the end of them is a flame of fire to destroy them. ¹⁰ The way of sinners is made plain with stones, but at the end thereof is the pit of hell. ¹¹ He that keepeth the law of the Lord getteth the understanding thereof: and the perfection of the fear of the Lord is wisdom. ¹² He that is not wise will not be taught: but there is a wisdom which multiplieth bitterness. ¹³ The knowledge of a wise man shall abound like a flood: and his counsel is like a pure fountain of life. ¹⁴ The inner parts of a fool are like a broken vessel, and he will hold no knowledge as long as he liveth. ¹⁵ If a skilful man hear a wise word, he will commend it, and add unto it: but as soon as one of no understanding heareth it, it displeaseth him, and he casteth it behind his back. ¹⁶ The talking of a fool is like a burden in the way: but grace shall be found in the lips of the wise. ¹⁷ They enquire at the mouth of the wise man in the congregation, and they shall ponder his words in their heart. ¹⁸ As is a house that is destroyed, so is wisdom to a fool: and the knowledge of the unwise is as talk without sense. ¹⁹ Doctrine unto fools is as fetters on the feet, and like manacles on the right hand. ²⁰ A fool lifteth up his voice with laughter; but a wise man doth scarce smile a little. ²¹ Learning is unto a wise man as an ornament of gold, and like a bracelet upon his right arm.

²² A foolish man's foot is soon in his [neighbour's] house: but a man of experience is ashamed of him. ²³ A fool will peep in at the door into the house: but he that is well nurtured will stand without. ²⁴ It is the rudeness of a man to hearken at the door: but a wise man will be grieved with the disgrace. ²⁵ The lips of talkers will be telling such things as pertain not unto them: but the words of such as have understanding are weighed in the balance. ²⁶ The heart of fools is in their mouth: but the mouth of the wise is in their heart. ²⁷ When the ungodly curseth Satan, he curseth his own soul. ²⁸ A whisperer defileth his own soul, and is hated wheresoever he dwelleth.

22 ¹ A slothful man is compared to a filthy stone, and every one will hiss him out to his disgrace. ² A slothful man is compared to the filth of a dunghill: every man that takes it up will shake his hand. ³ An evil-nurtured son is the dishonour of his father that begat him: and a [foolish] daughter is born to his loss. ⁴ A wise daughter shall bring an inheritance to her husband: but she that liveth dishonestly is her father's heaviness. ⁵ She that is bold dishonoureth both her father and her husband, but they both shall despise her. ⁶ A tale out of season [is as] music in mourning: but stripes and correction of wisdom are never out of time. ⁷ Whoso teacheth a fool is as one that glueth a potsherd together, and as he that waketh one from a sound sleep. ⁸ He that telleth a tale to a fool speaketh to one in a slumber: when he hath told his tale, he will say, What is the matter? ⁹ If children live honestly, and have wherewithal, they shall cover the baseness of their parents. ¹⁰ But children, being haughty, through disdain and want of nurture do stain the nobility of their kindred. ¹¹ Weep for the

dead, for he hath lost the light: and weep for the fool, for he wanteth understanding: make little weeping for the dead, for he is at rest: but the life of the fool is worse than death. ¹² Seven days do men mourn for him that is dead; but for a fool and an ungodly man all the days of his life. ¹³ Talk not much with a fool, and go not to him that hath no understanding: beware of him, lest thou have trouble, and thou shalt never be defiled with his fooleries: depart from him, and thou shalt find rest, and never be disquieted with madness. ¹⁴ What is heavier than lead? and what is the name thereof, but a fool? ¹⁵ Sand, and salt, and a mass of iron, is easier to bear, than a man without understanding. ¹⁶ As timber girt and bound together in a building cannot be loosed with shaking: so the heart that is established by advised counsel shall fear at no time. ¹⁷ A heart settled upon a thought of understanding is as a fair plaistering on the wall of a gallery. ¹⁸ Pales set on an high place will never stand against the wind: so a fearful heart in the imagination of a fool cannot stand against any fear. ¹⁹ He that pricketh the eye will make tears to fall: and he that pricketh the heart maketh it to shew her knowledge. ²⁰ Whoso casteth a stone at the birds frayeth them away: and he that upbraideth his friend breaketh friendship. ²¹ Though thou drewest a sword at thy friend, yet despair not: for there may be a returning [to favour.] ²² If thou hast opened thy mouth against thy friend, fear not; for there may be a reconciliation: except for upbraiding, or pride, or disclosing of secrets, or a treacherous wound: for, for these things every friend will depart. ²³ Be faithful to thy neighbour in his poverty, that thou mayest rejoice in his prosperity: abide stedfast unto him in the time of his trouble, that thou mayest be heir with him in his heritage: for a mean estate is not always to be contemned: nor the rich that is foolish to be had in admiration. 24 As the vapour and smoke of a furnace goeth before the fire; so reviling before blood. 25 I will not be ashamed to defend a friend; neither will I hide myself from him. 26 And if any evil happen unto me by him, every one that heareth it will beware of him. 27 Who shall set a watch before my mouth, and a seal of wisdom upon my lips, that I fall not suddenly by them, and that my tongue destroy me not?

23 1 O Lord, Father and Governor of all my whole life, leave me not to their counsels, and let me not fall by them. 2 Who will set scourges over my thoughts, and the discipline of wisdom over mine heart? that they spare me not for mine ignorances, and it pass not by my sins: 3 lest mine ignorances increase, and my sins abound to my destruction, and I fall before mine adversaries, and mine enemy rejoice over me, whose hope is far from thy mercy. 4 O Lord, Father and God of my life, give me not a proud look, but turn away from thy servants always a haughty mind. 5 Turn away from me vain hopes and concupiscence, and thou shalt hold him up that is desirous always to serve thee. 6 Let not the greediness of the belly nor lust of the flesh take hold of me; and give not over me thy servant into an impudent mind. 7 Hear, O ye children, the discipline of the mouth: he that keepeth it shall never be taken in his lips. 8 The sinner shall be left in his foolishness: both the evil speaker and the proud shall fall thereby. 9 Accustom not thy mouth to swearing; neither use thyself to the naming of the Holy One. 10 For as a servant that is continually beaten shall not be without a blue mark: so he that sweareth and nameth God con-

tinually shall not be faultless. ¹¹ A man that useth much swearing shall be filled with iniquity, and the plague shall never depart from his house: if he shall offend, his sin shall be upon him: and if he acknowledge not his sin, he maketh a double offence: and if he swear in vain, he shall not be innocent, but his house shall be full of calamities. ¹² There is a word that is clothed about with death: God grant that it be not found in the heritage of Jacob; for all such things shall be far from the godly, and they shall not wallow in their sins. ¹³ Use not thy mouth to intemperate swearing, for therein is the word of sin. ¹⁴ Remember thy father and thy mother, when thou sittest among great men. Be not forgetful before them, and so thou by thy custom become a fool, and wish that thou hadst not been born, and curse the day of thy nativity. ¹⁵ The man that is accustomed to opprobrious words will never be reformed all the days of his life. ¹⁶ Two sorts of men multiply sin, and the third will bring wrath: a hot mind is as a burning fire, it will never be quenched till it be consumed: a fornicator in the body of his flesh will never cease till he hath kindled a fire. ¹⁷ All bread is sweet to a whoremonger, he will not leave off till he die. ¹⁸ A man that breaketh wedlock, saying thus in his heart, Who seeth me? I am compassed about with darkness, the walls cover me, and no body seeth me; what need I to fear? the most High will not remember my sins: ¹⁹ Such a man only feareth the eyes of men, and knoweth not that the eyes of the Lord are ten thousand times brighter than the sun, beholding all the ways of men, and considering the most secret parts. ²⁰ He knew all things ere ever they were created; so also after they were perfected he looked upon them all. ²¹ This man shall be punished in the streets of the city, and where he suspecteth not he shall be taken. [22] Thus shall it go also with the wife that leaveth her husband, and bringeth in an heir by another. [23] For first, she hath disobeyed the law of the most High; and secondly, she hath trespassed against her own husband; and thirdly, she hath played the whore in adultery, and brought children by another man. [24] She shall be brought out into the congregation, and inquisition shall be made of her children. [25] Her children shall not take root, and her branches shall bring forth no fruit. [26] She shall leave her memory to be cursed, and her reproach shall not be blotted out. [27] And they that remain shall know that there is nothing better than the fear of the Lord, and that there is nothing sweeter than to take heed unto the commandments of the Lord. [28] It is great glory to follow the Lord, and to be received of him is long life.

24 [1] Wisdom shall praise herself, and shall glory in the midst of her people. [2] In the congregation of the most High shall she open her mouth, and triumph before his power. [3] I came out of the mouth of the most High, and covered the earth as a cloud. [4] I dwelt in high places, and my throne is in a cloudy pillar. [5] I alone compassed the circuit of heaven, and walked in the bottom of the deep. [6] In the waves of the sea and in all the earth, and in every people and nation, I got a possession. [7] With all these I sought rest: and in whose inheritance shall I abide? [8] So the Creator of all things gave me a commandment, and he that made me caused my tabernacle to rest, and said, Let thy dwelling be in Jacob, and thine inheritance in Israel. [9] He created me from the beginning before the world, and I shall never fail. [10] In the holy tabernacle I served before him; and so was I

established in Sion. ¹¹ Likewise in the beloved city he gave me rest, and in Jerusalem was my power. ¹² And I took root in an honourable people, even in the portion of the Lord's inheritance. ¹³ I was exalted like a cedar in Libanus, and as a cypress tree upon the mountains of Hermon. ¹⁴ I was exalted like a palm tree in Engaddi, and as a rose plant in Jericho, as a fair olive tree in a pleasant field, and grew up as a plane tree by the water. ¹⁵ I gave a sweet smell like cinnamon and aspalathus, and I yielded a pleasant odour like the best myrrh, as galbanum, and onyx, and sweet storax, and as the fume of frankincense in the tabernacle. ¹⁶ As the turpentine tree I stretched out my branches, and my branches are the branches of honour and grace. ¹⁷ As the vine brought I forth pleasant savour, and my flowers are the fruit of honour and riches. ¹⁸ I am the mother of fair love, and fear, and knowledge, and holy hope: I therefore, being eternal, am given to all my children which are named of him. ¹⁹ Come unto me, all ye that be desirous of me, and fill yourselves with my fruits. ²⁰ For my memorial is sweeter than honey, and mine inheritance than the honeycomb. ²¹ They that eat me shall yet be hungry, and they that drink me shall yet be thirsty. ²² He that obeyeth me shall never be confounded, and they that work by me shall not do amiss. ²³ All these things are the book of the covenant of the most high God, even the law which Moses commanded for an heritage unto the congregations of Jacob. ²⁴ Faint not to be strong in the Lord; that he may confirm you, cleave unto him: for the Lord Almighty is God alone, and besides him there is no other Saviour. ²⁵ He filleth all things with his wisdom, as Phison and as Tigris in the time of the new fruits. ²⁶ He maketh the understanding to abound like Euphrates, and as Jordan in the time of the harvest. [27] He maketh the doctrine of knowledge appear as the light, and as Geon in the time of vintage. [28] The first man knew her not perfectly: no more shall the last find her out. [29] For her thoughts are more than the sea, and her counsels profounder than the great deep. [30] I also came out as a brook from a river, and as a conduit into a garden. [31] I said, I will water my best garden, and will water abundantly my garden bed: and, lo, my brook became a river, and my river became a sea. [32] I will yet make doctrine to shine as the morning, and will send forth her light afar off. [33] I will yet pour out doctrine as prophecy, and leave it to all ages for ever. [34] Behold that I have not laboured for myself only, but for all them that seek wisdom.

25 [1] In three things I was beautified, and stood up beautiful both before God and men: the unity of brethren, the love of neighbours, a man and a wife that agree together. [2] Three sorts of men my soul hateth, and I am greatly offended at their life: a poor man that is proud, a rich man that is a liar, and an old adulterer that doteth. [3] If thou hast gathered nothing in thy youth, how canst thou find any thing in thine age? [4] O how comely a thing is judgment for gray hairs, and for ancient men to know counsel! [5] O how comely is the wisdom of old men, and understanding and counsel to men of honour. [6] Much experience is the crown of old men, and the fear of God is their glory. [7] There be nine things which I have judged in mine heart to be happy, and the tenth I will utter with my tongue: A man that hath joy of his children; and he that liveth to see the fall of his enemy: [8] Well is him that dwelleth with a wife of understanding, and that hath not slipped with

his tongue, and that hath not served a man more unworthy than himself: ⁹ Well is him that hath found prudence, and he that speaketh in the ears of them that will hear: ¹⁰ O how great is he that findeth wisdom! yet is there none above him that feareth the Lord. ¹¹ But the love of the Lord passeth all things for illumination: he that holdeth it, whereto shall he be likened? ¹² The fear of the Lord is the beginning of his love: and faith is the beginning of cleaving unto him. ¹³ [Give me] any plague, but the plague of the heart: and any wickedness, but the wickedness of a woman: ¹⁴ And any affliction, but the affliction from them that hate me: and any revenge, but the revenge of enemies. ¹⁵ There is no head above the head of a serpent; and there is no wrath above the wrath of an enemy. ¹⁶ I had rather dwell with a lion and a dragon, than to keep house with a wicked woman. ¹⁷ The wickedness of a woman changeth her face, and darkeneth her countenance like sackcloth. ¹⁸ Her husband shall sit among his neighbours; and when he heareth it shall sigh bitterly. ¹⁹ All wickedness is but little to the wickedness of a woman: let the portion of a sinner fall upon her. ²⁰ As the climbing of a sandy way is to the feet of the aged, so is a wife full of words to a quiet man. ²¹ Stumble not at the beauty of a woman, and desire her not for pleasure. ²² A woman, if she maintain her husband, is full of anger, impudence, and much reproach. ²³ A wicked woman abateth the courage, maketh an heavy countenance and a wounded heart: a woman that will not comfort her husband in distress maketh weak hands and feeble knees. ²⁴ Of the woman came the beginning of sin, and through her we all die. ²⁵ Give the water no passage; neither a wicked woman liberty to gad abroad. ²⁶ If she go not as thou wouldest have her, cut her off from thy flesh, and give her a bill of divorce, and let her go.

26 ¹ Blessed is the man that hath a virtuous wife, for the number of his days shall be double. ² A virtuous woman rejoiceth her husband, and he shall fulfil the years of his life in peace ³ A good wife is a good portion, which shall be given in the portion of them that fear the Lord. ⁴ Whether a man be rich or poor, if he have a good heart toward the Lord, he shall at all times rejoice with a cheerful countenance. ⁵ There be three things that mine heart feareth; and for the fourth I was sore afraid: the slander of a city, the gathering together of an unruly multitude, and a false accusation: all these are worse than death. ⁶ But a grief of heart and sorrow is a woman that is jealous over another woman, and a scourge of the tongue which communicateth with all. ⁷ An evil wife is a yoke shaken to and fro: he that hath hold of her is as though he held a scorpion. ⁸ A drunken woman and a gadder abroad causeth great anger, and she will not cover her own shame. ⁹ The whoredom of a woman may be known in her haughty looks and eyelids. ¹⁰ If thy daughter be shameless, keep her in straitly, lest she abuse herself through overmuch liberty. ¹¹ Watch over an impudent eye: and marvel not if she trespass against thee. ¹² She will open her mouth, as a thirsty traveller when he hath found a fountain, and drink of every water near her: by every hedge will she sit down, and open her quiver against every arrow. ¹³ The grace of a wife delighteth her husband, and her discretion will fatten his bones. ¹⁴ A silent and loving woman is a gift of the Lord; and there is nothing so much worth as a mind well instructed. ¹⁵ A shamefaced and faithful woman is a double grace, and her continent mind cannot be valued. ¹⁶ As the sun when it ariseth in the high heaven; so is the beauty of a good wife in the ordering of her house. ¹⁷ As the clear light is upon the holy candlestick; so is the beauty of the face in ripe age. ¹⁸ As the golden pillars are upon the sockets of silver; so are the fair feet with a constant heart. ¹⁹ My son, keep the flower of thine age sound; and give not thy strength to strangers. ²⁰ When thou hast gotten a fruitful possession through all the field, sow it with thine own seed, trusting in the goodness of thy stock. ²¹ So thy race which thou leavest shall be magnified, having the confidence of their good descent. ²² An harlot shall be accounted as spittle; but a married woman is a tower against death to her husband. ²³ A wicked woman is given as a portion to a wicked man: but a godly woman is given to him that feareth the Lord. ²⁴ A dishonest woman contemneth shame: but an honest woman will reverence her husband. ²⁵ A shameless woman shall be counted as a dog; but she that is shamefaced will fear the Lord. ²⁶ A woman that honoureth her husband shall be judged wise of all; but she that dishonoureth him in her pride shall be counted ungodly of all. ²⁷ A loud crying woman and a scold shall be sought out to drive away the enemies. ²⁸ There be two things that grieve my heart; and the third maketh me angry: a man of war that suffereth poverty; and men of understanding that are not set by; and one that returneth from righteousness to sin; the Lord prepareth such an one for the sword. ²⁹ A merchant shall hardly keep himself from doing wrong; and an huckster shall not be freed from sin.

27 ¹ Many have sinned for a small matter; and he that seeketh for abundance will turn his eyes away. ² As a

nail sticketh fast between the joinings of the stones; so doth sin stick close between buying and selling. [3] Unless a man hold himself diligently in the fear of the Lord, his house shall soon be overthrown. [4] As when one sifteth with a sieve, the refuse remaineth; so the filth of man in his talk. [5] The furnace proveth the potter's vessels; so the trial of man is in his reasoning. [6] The fruit declareth if the tree have been dressed; so is the utterance of a conceit in the heart of man. [7] Praise no man before thou hearest him speak; for this is the trial of men. [8] If thou followest righteousness, thou shalt obtain her, and put her on, as a glorious long robe. [9] The birds will resort unto their like; so will truth return unto them that practise in her. [10] As the lion lieth in wait for the prey; so sin for them that work iniquity. [11] The discourse of a godly man is always with wisdom; but a fool changeth as the moon. [12] If thou be among the indiscreet, observe the time; but be continually among men of understanding. [13] The discourse of fools is irksome, and their sport is the wantonness of sin. [14] The talk of him that sweareth much maketh the hair stand upright; and their brawls make one stop his ears. [15] The strife of the proud is bloodshedding, and their revilings are grievous to the ear. [16] Whoso discovereth secrets loseth his credit; and shall never find a friend to his mind. [17] Love thy friend, and be faithful unto him: but if thou betrayest his secrets, follow no more after him. [18] For as a man hath destroyed his enemy; so hast thou lost the love of thy neighbour. [19] As one that letteth a bird go out of his hand, so hast thou let thy neighbour go, and shalt not get him again. [20] Follow after him no more, for he is too far off; he is as a roe escaped out of the snare. [21] As for a wound, it may be bound up; and after reviling there may be reconcilement: but he that betrayeth secrets is without hope. ²² He that winketh with the eyes worketh evil: and he that knoweth him will depart from him. ²³ When thou art present, he will speak sweetly, and will admire thy words: but at the last he will writhe his mouth, and slander thy sayings. ²⁴ I have hated many things, but nothing like him; for the Lord will hate him. ²⁵ Whoso casteth a stone on high casteth it on his own head; and a deceitful stroke shall make wounds. ²⁶ Whoso diggeth a pit shall fall therein: and he that setteth a trap shall be taken therein. ²⁷ He that worketh mischief, it shall fall upon him, and he shall not know whence it cometh. ²⁸ Mockery and reproach are from the proud; but vengeance, as a lion, shall lie in wait for them. ²⁹ They that rejoice at the fall of the righteous shall be taken in the snare; and anguish shall consume them before they die. ³⁰ Malice and wrath, even these are abominations; and the sinful man shall have them both.

28

¹ He that revengeth shall find vengeance from the Lord, and he will surely keep his sins [in remembrance]. ² Forgive thy neighbour the hurt that he hath done unto thee, so shall thy sins also be forgiven when thou prayest. ³ One man beareth hatred against another, and doth he seek pardon from the Lord? ⁴ He sheweth no mercy to a man, which is like himself: and doth he ask forgiveness of his own sins? ⁵ If he that is but flesh nourish hatred, who will intreat for pardon of his sins? ⁶ Remember thy end, and let enmity cease; [remember] corruption and death, and abide in the commandments. ⁷ Remember the commandments, and bear no malice to thy neighbour: [remember] the covenant of the Highest, and wink at ignorance. ⁸ Abstain from

strife, and thou shalt diminish thy sins: for a furious man will kindle strife. [9] A sinful man disquieteth friends, and maketh debate among them that be at peace. [10] As the matter of the fire is, so it burneth: and as a man's strength is, so is his wrath; and according to his riches his anger riseth; and the stronger they are which contend, the more they will be inflamed. [11] An hasty contention kindleth a fire: and an hasty fighting sheddeth blood. [12] If thou blow the spark, it shall burn: if thou spit upon it, it shall be quenched: and both these come out of thy mouth. [13] Curse the whisperer and doubletongued: for such have destroyed many that were at peace. [14] A backbiting tongue hath disquieted many, and driven them from nation to nation: strong cities hath it pulled down, and overthrown the houses of great men. [15] A backbiting tongue hath cast out virtuous women, and deprived them of their labours. [16] Whoso hearkeneth unto it shall never find rest, and never dwell quietly. [17] The stroke of the whip maketh marks in the flesh: but the stroke of the tongue breaketh the bones. [18] Many have fallen by the edge of the sword: but not so many as have fallen by the tongue. [19] Well is he that is defended from it, and hath not passed through the venom thereof; who hath not drawn the yoke thereof, nor hath been bound in her bands. [20] For the yoke thereof is a yoke of iron, and the bands thereof are bands of brass. [21] The death thereof is an evil death, the grave were better than it. [22] It shall not have rule over them that fear God, neither shall they be burned with the flame thereof. [23] Such as forsake the Lord shall fall into it; and it shall burn in them, and not be quenched; it shall be sent upon them as a lion, and devour them as a leopard. [24] Look that thou hedge thy possession about with thorns, and bind up thy silver and gold, ²⁵ and weigh thy words in a balance, and make a door and bar for thy mouth. ²⁶ Beware thou slide not by it, lest thou fall before him that lieth in wait.

29

¹ He that is merciful will lend unto his neighbour; and he that strengtheneth his hand keepeth the commandments. ² Lend to thy neighbour in time of his need, and pay thou thy neighbour again in due season. ³ Keep thy word, and deal faithfully with him, and thou shalt always find the thing that is necessary for thee. ⁴ Many, when a thing was lent them, reckoned it to be found, and put them to trouble that helped them. ⁵ Till he hath received, he will kiss a man's hand; and for his neighbour's money he will speak submissively: but when he should repay, he will prolong the time, and return words of grief, and complain of the time. ⁶ If he prevail, he shall hardly receive the half, and he will count as if he had found it: if not, he hath deprived him of his money, and he hath gotten him an enemy without cause: he payeth him with cursings and railings; and for honour he will pay him disgrace. ⁷ Many therefore have refused to lend for other men's ill dealing, fearing to be defrauded. ⁸ Yet have thou patience with a man in poor estate, and delay not to shew him mercy. ⁹ Help the poor for the commandment's sake, and turn him not away because of his poverty. ¹⁰ Lose thy money for thy brother and thy friend, and let it not rust under a stone to be lost. ¹¹ Lay up thy treasure according to the commandments of the most High, and it shall bring thee more profit than gold. ¹² Shut up alms in thy storehouses: and it shall deliver thee from all affliction. ¹³ It shall fight for thee against thine enemies better than a mighty shield and strong spear. ¹⁴ An honest man is surety for his neighbour: but he that is impudent will

forsake him. [15] Forget not the friendship of thy surety, for he hath given his life for thee. [16] A sinner will overthrow the good estate of his surety: [17] And he that is of an unthankful mind will leave him [in danger] that delivered him. [18] Suretiship hath undone many of good estate, and shaken them as a wave of the sea: mighty men hath it driven from their houses, so that they wandered among strange nations. [19] A wicked man transgressing the commandments of the Lord shall fall into suretiship: and he that undertaketh and followeth other men's business for gain shall fall into suits. [20] Help thy neighbour according to thy power, and beware that thou thyself fall not into the same. [21] The chief thing for life is water, and bread, and clothing, and an house to cover shame. [22] Better is the life of a poor man in a mean cottage, than delicate fare in another man's house. [23] Be it little or much, hold thee contented, that thou hear not the reproach of thy house. [24] For it is a miserable life to go from house to house: for where thou art a stranger, thou darest not open thy mouth. [25] Thou shalt entertain, and feast, and have no thanks: moreover thou shalt hear bitter words: [26] Come, thou stranger, and furnish a table, and feed me of that thou hast ready. [27] Give place, thou stranger, to an honourable man; my brother cometh to be lodged, and I have need of mine house. [28] These things are grievous to a man of understanding; the upbraiding of houseroom, and reproaching of the lender.

30

[1] He that loveth his son causeth him oft to feel the rod, that he may have joy of him in the end. [2] He that chastiseth his son shall have joy in him, and shall rejoice of him among his acquaintance. [3] He that teacheth his son grieveth the enemy: and before his friends he shall

rejoice of him. ⁴ Though his father die, yet he is as though he were not dead: for he hath left one behind him that is like himself. ⁵ While he lived, he saw and rejoiced in him: and when he died, he was not sorrowful. ⁶ He left behind him an avenger against his enemies, and one that shall requite kindness to his friends. ⁷ He that maketh too much of his son shall bind up his wounds; and his bowels will be troubled at every cry. ⁸ An horse not broken becometh headstrong: and a child left to himself will be wilful. ⁹ Cocker thy child, and he shall make thee afraid: play with him, and he will bring thee to heaviness. ¹⁰ Laugh not with him, lest thou have sorrow with him, and lest thou gnash thy teeth in the end. ¹¹ Give him no liberty in his youth, and wink not at his follies. ¹² Bow down his neck while he is young, and beat him on the sides while he is a child, lest he wax stubborn, and be disobedient unto thee, and so bring sorrow to thine heart. ¹³ Chastise thy son, and hold him to labour, lest his lewd behaviour be an offence unto thee. ¹⁴ Better is the poor, being sound and strong of constitution, than a rich man that is afflicted in his body. ¹⁵ Health and good estate of body are above all gold, and a strong body above infinite wealth. ¹⁶ There is no riches above a sound body, and no joy above the joy of the heart. ¹⁷ Death is better than a bitter life or continual sickness. ¹⁸ Delicacies poured upon a mouth shut up are as messes of meat set upon a grave. ¹⁹ What good doeth the offering unto an idol? for neither can it eat nor smell: so is he that is persecuted of the Lord. ²⁰ He seeth with his eyes and groaneth, as an eunuch that embraceth a virgin and sigheth. ²¹ Give not over thy mind to heaviness, and afflict not thyself in thine own counsel. ²² The gladness of the heart is the life of man, and the joyfulness of a man prolongeth his days. ²³ Love thine own soul, and comfort thy heart, remove sorrow far from thee: for sorrow hath killed many, and there is no profit therein. ²⁴ Envy and wrath shorten the life, and carefulness bringeth age before the time. ²⁵ A cheerful and good heart will have a care of his meat and diet.

31

¹ Watching for riches consumeth the flesh, and the care thereof driveth away sleep. ² Watching care will not let a man slumber, as a sore disease breaketh sleep. ³ The rich hath great labour in gathering riches together; and when he resteth, he is filled with his delicacies. ⁴ The poor laboureth in his poor estate; and when he leaveth off, he is still needy. ⁵ He that loveth gold shall not be justified, and he that followeth corruption shall have enough thereof. ⁶ Gold hath been the ruin of many, and their destruction was present. ⁷ It is a stumbling-block unto them that sacrifice unto it, and every fool shall be taken therewith. ⁸ Blessed is the rich that is found without blemish, and hath not gone after gold. ⁹ Who is he? and we will call him blessed: for wonderful things hath he done among his people. ¹⁰ Who hath been tried thereby, and found perfect? then let him glory. Who might offend, and hath not offended? or done evil, and hath not done it? ¹¹ His goods shall be established, and the congregation shall declare his alms. ¹² If thou sit at a bountiful table, be not greedy upon it, and say not, There is much meat on it. ¹³ Remember that a wicked eye is an evil thing: and what is created more wicked than an eye? therefore it weepeth upon every occasion. ¹⁴ Stretch not thine hand whithersoever it looketh, and thrust it not with him into the dish. ¹⁵ Judge not thy neighbour by thyself: and be discreet in every point. ¹⁶ Eat as it becometh a man, those things

which are set before thee; and devour not, lest thou be hated. ¹⁷ Leave off first for manners' sake; and be not unsatiable, lest thou offend. ¹⁸ When thou sittest among many, reach not thine hand out first of all. ¹⁹ A very little is sufficient for a man well nurtured, and he fetcheth not his wind short upon his bed. ²⁰ Sound sleep cometh of moderate eating: he riseth early, and his wits are with him: but the pain of watching, and choler, and pangs of the belly, are with an unsatiable man. ²¹ And if thou hast been forced to eat, arise, go forth, vomit, and thou shalt have rest. ²² My son, hear me, and despise me not, and at the last thou shalt find as I told thee: in all thy works be quick, so shall there no sickness come unto thee. ²³ Whoso is liberal of his meat, men shall speak well of him; and the report of his good housekeeping will be believed. ²⁴ But against him that is a niggard of his meat the whole city shall murmur; and the testimonies of his niggardness shall not be doubted of. ²⁵ Shew not thy valiantness in wine; for wine hath destroyed many. ²⁶ The furnace proveth the edge by dipping: so doth wine the hearts of the proud by drunkeness. ²⁷ Wine is as good as life to a man, if it be drunk moderately: what is life then to a man that is without wine? for it was made to make men glad. ²⁸ Wine measurably drunk and in season bringeth gladness of the heart, and cheerfulness of the mind: ²⁹ but wine drunken with excess maketh bitterness of the mind, with brawling and quarrelling. ³⁰ Drunkenness increaseth the rage of a fool till he offend: it diminisheth strength, and maketh wounds. ³¹ Rebuke not thy neighbour at the wine, and despise him not in his mirth: give him no despiteful words, and press not upon him with urging him [to drink.]

32 [1] If thou be made the master [of a feast,] lift not thyself up, but be among them as one of the rest; take diligent care for them, and so sit down. [2] And when thou hast done all thy office, take thy place, that thou mayest be merry with them, and receive a crown for thy well ordering of the feast. [3] Speak, thou that art the elder, for it becometh thee, but with sound judgment; and hinder not music. [4] Pour not out words where there is a musician, and shew not forth wisdom out of time. [5] A concert of music in a banquet of wine is as a signet of carbuncle set in gold. [6] As a signet of an emerald set in a work of gold, so is the melody of music with pleasant wine. [7] Speak, young man, if there be need of thee: and yet scarcely when thou art twice asked. [8] Let thy speech be short, comprehending much in few words; be as one that knoweth and yet holdeth his tongue. [9] If thou be among great men, make not thyself equal with them; and when ancient men are in place, use not many words. [10] Before the thunder goeth lightning; and before a shamefaced man shall go favour. [11] Rise up betimes, and be not the last; but get thee home without delay. [12] There take thy pastime, and do what thou wilt: but sin not by proud speech. [13] And for these things bless him that made thee, and hath replenished thee with his good things. [14] Whoso feareth the Lord will receive his discipline; and they that seek him early shall find favour. [15] He that seeketh the law shall be filled therewith: but the hypocrite will be offended thereat. [16] They that fear the Lord shall find judgment, and shall kindle justice as a light. [17] A sinful man will not be reproved, but findeth an excuse according to his will. [18] A man of counsel will be considerate; but a strange and proud man is not daunted with fear, even when of himself he hath done without counsel. [19] Do

nothing without advice; and when thou hast once done, repent not. ²⁰ Go not in a way wherein thou mayest fall, and stumble not among the stones. ²¹ Be not confident in a plain way. ²² And beware of thine own children. ²³ In every good work trust thy own soul; for this is the keeping of the commandments. ²⁴ He that believeth in the Lord taketh heed to the commandment; and he that trusteth in him shall fare never the worse.

33

¹ There shall no evil happen unto him that feareth the Lord; but in temptation even again he will deliver him. ² A wise man hateth not the law; but he that is an hypocrite therein is as a ship in a storm. ³ A man of understanding trusteth in the law; and the law is faithful unto him, as an oracle. ⁴ Prepare what to say, and so thou shalt be heard: and bind up instruction, and then make answer. ⁵ The heart of the foolish is like a cartwheel; and his thoughts are like a rolling axletree. ⁶ A stallion horse is as a mocking friend, he neigheth under every one that sitteth upon him. ⁷ Why doth one day excel another, when as all the light of every day in the year is of the sun? ⁸ By the knowledge of the Lord they were distinguished: and he altered seasons and feasts. ⁹ Some of them hath he made high days, and hallowed them, and some of them hath he made ordinary days. ¹⁰ And all men are from the ground, and Adam was created of earth. ¹¹ In much knowledge the Lord hath divided them, and made their ways diverse. ¹² Some of them hath he blessed and exalted and some of them he sanctified, and set near himself: but some of them hath he cursed and brought low, and turned out of their places. ¹³ As the clay is in the potter's hand, to fashion it at his pleasure: so man is in the hand of him that

made him, to render to them as liketh him best.
14 Good is set against evil, and life against death: so is
the godly against the sinner, and the sinner against the
godly. 15 So look upon all the works of the most High;
and there are two and two, one against another. 16 I
awaked up last of all, as one that gathereth after the
grapegatherers: by the blessing of the Lord I profited,
and tred my winepress like a gatherer of grapes.
17 Consider that I laboured not for myself only, but for
all them that seek learning. 18 Hear me, O ye great men
of the people, and hearken with your ears, ye rulers of
the congregation. 19 Give not thy son and wife, thy
brother and friend, power over thee while thou livest,
and give not thy goods to another: lest it repent thee,
and thou intreat for the same again. 20 As long as thou
livest and hast breath in thee, give not thyself over to
any. 21 For better it is that thy children should seek to
thee, than that thou shouldest stand to their courtesy.
22 In all thy works keep to thyself the preeminence;
leave not a stain in thine honour. 23 At the time when
thou shalt end thy days, and finish thy life, distribute
thine inheritance. 24 Fodder, a wand, and burdens, are
for the ass; and bread, correction, and work, for a servant. 25 If thou set thy servant to labour, thou shalt find
rest: but if thou let him go idle, he shall seek liberty.
26 A yoke and a collar do bow the neck: so are tortures
and torments for an evil servant. 27 Send him to labour,
that he be not idle; for idleness teacheth much evil.
28 Set him to work, as is fit for him: if he be not obedient, put on more heavy fetters. 29 But be not excessive
toward any; and without discretion do nothing. 30 If
thou have a servant, let him be unto thee as thyself,
because thou hast bought him with a price. 31 If thou
have a servant, entreat him as a brother: for thou hast

need of him, as of thine own soul: if thou entreat him evil, and he run from thee, which way wilt thou go to seek him?

34

[1] The hopes of a man void of understanding are vain and false: and dreams lift up fools. [2] Whoso regardeth dreams is like him that catcheth at a shadow, and followeth after the wind. [3] The vision of dreams is the resemblance of one thing to another, even as the likeness of a face to a face. [4] Of an unclean thing what can be cleansed? and from that thing which is false what truth can come? [5] Divinations, and soothsayings, and dreams, are vain: and the heart fancieth, as a woman's heart in travail. [6] If they be not sent from the most High in thy visitation, set not thy heart upon them. [7] For dreams have deceived many, and they have failed that put their trust in them. [8] The law shall be found perfect without lies: and wisdom is perfection to a faithful mouth. [9] A man that hath travelled knoweth many things; and he that hath much experience will declare wisdom. [10] He that hath no experience knoweth little: but he that hath travelled is full of prudence. [11] When I travelled, I saw many things; and I understand more than I can express. [12] I was oft-times in danger of death: yet I was delivered because of these things. [13] The spirit of those that fear the Lord shall live; for their hope is in him that saveth them. [14] Whoso feareth the Lord shall not fear nor be afraid; for he is his hope. [15] Blessed is the soul of him that feareth the Lord: to whom doth he look? and who is his strength? [16] For the eyes of the Lord are upon them that love him, he is their mighty protection and strong stay, a defence from heat, and a cover from the sun at noon, a preservation from stumbling, and an help from

falling. [17] He raiseth up the soul, and lighteneth the eyes: he giveth health, life, and blessing. [18] He that sacrificeth of a thing wrongfully gotten, his offering is ridiculous; and the gifts of unjust men are not accepted. [19] The most High is not pleased with the offerings of the wicked; neither is he pacified for sin by the multitude of sacrifices. [20] Whoso bringeth an offering of the goods of the poor doeth as one that killeth the son before his father's eyes. [21] The bread of the needy is their life: he that defraudeth him thereof is a man of blood. [22] He that taketh away his neighbour's living slayeth him; and he that defraudeth the labourer of his hire is a bloodshedder. [23] When one buildeth, and another pulleth down, what profit have they then but labour? [24] When one prayeth, and another curseth, whose voice will the Lord hear? [25] He that washeth himself after the touching of a dead body, if he touch it again, what availeth his washing? [26] So is it with a man that fasteth for his sins, and goeth again, and doeth the same: who will hear his prayer? or what doth his humbling profit him?

35

[1] He that keepeth the law bringeth offerings enough: he that taketh heed to the commandment offereth a peace offering. [2] He that requiteth a good turn offereth fine flour; and he that giveth alms sacrificeth praise. [3] To depart from wickedness is a thing pleasing to the Lord; and to forsake unrighteousness is a propitiation. [4] Thou shalt not appear empty before the Lord. [5] For all these things [are to be done] because of the commandment. [6] The offering of the righteous maketh the altar fat, and the sweet savour thereof is before the most High. [7] The sacrifice of a just man is acceptable, and the memorial thereof shall never be forgotten. [8] Give

the Lord his honour with a good eye, and diminish not the firstfruits of thine hands. [9] In all thy gifts shew a cheerful countenance, and dedicate thy tithes with gladness. [10] Give unto the most High according as he hath enriched thee; and as thou hast gotten, give with a cheerful eye. [11] For the Lord recompenseth, and will give thee seven times as much. [12] Do not think to corrupt with gifts; for such he will not receive: and trust not to unrighteous sacrifices; for the Lord is judge, and with him is no respect of persons. [13] He will not accept any person against a poor man, but will hear the prayer of the oppressed. [14] He will not despise the supplication of the fatherless; nor the widow, when she poureth out her complaint. [15] Do not the tears run down the widow's cheeks? and is not her cry against him that causeth them to fall? [16] He that serveth the Lord shall be accepted with favour, and his prayer shall reach unto the clouds. [17] The prayer of the humble pierceth the clouds: and till it come nigh, he will not be comforted; and will not depart, till the most High shall behold to judge righteously, and execute judgment. [18] For the Lord will not be slack, neither will the Mighty be patient toward them, till he have smitten in sunder the loins of the unmerciful, and repaid vengeance to the heathen; till he have taken away the multitude of the proud, and broken the sceptre of the unrighteous; [19] till he have rendered to every man according to his deeds, and to the works of men according to their devices; till he have judged the cause of his people, and made them to rejoice in his mercy. [20] Mercy is seasonable in the time of affliction, as clouds of rain in the time of drought.

36

[1] Have mercy upon us, O Lord God of all, and behold us: [2] And send thy fear upon all the nations that seek not after thee. [3] Lift up thy hand against the strange nations, and let them see thy power. [4] As thou wast sanctified in us before them: so be thou magnified among them before us. [5] And let them know thee, as we have known thee, that there is no God but only thou, O God. [6] Shew new signs, and make other strange wonders: glorify thy hand and thy right arm, that they may set forth thy wondrous works. [7] Raise up indignation, and pour out wrath: take away the adversary, and destroy the enemy. [8] Make the time short, remember the covenant, and let them declare thy wonderful works. [9] Let him that escapeth be consumed by the rage of the fire; and let them perish that oppress the people. [10] Smite in sunder the heads of the rulers of the heathen, that say, There is none other but we. [11] Gather all the tribes of Jacob together, and inherit thou them, as from the beginning. [12] O Lord, have mercy upon the people that is called by thy name, and upon Israel, whom thou hast named thy firstborn. [13] O be merciful unto Jerusalem, thy holy city, the place of thy rest. [14] Fill Sion with thine unspeakable oracles, and thy people with thy glory: [15] Give testimony unto those that thou hast possessed from the beginning, and raise up prophets that have been in thy name. [16] Reward them that wait for thee, and let thy prophets be found faithful. [17] O Lord, hear the prayer of thy servants, according to the blessing of Aaron over thy people, that all they which dwell upon the earth may know that thou art the Lord, the eternal God. [18] The belly devoureth all meats, yet is one meat better than another. [19] As the palate tasteth divers kinds of venison: so doth an heart of understanding false speeches. [20] A

froward heart causeth heaviness: but a man of experience will recompense him. ²¹ A woman will receive every man, yet is one daughter better than another. ²² The beauty of a woman cheereth the countenance, and a man loveth nothing better. ²³ If there be kindness, meekness, and comfort in her tongue, then is not her husband like other men. ²⁴ He that getteth a wife beginneth a possession, a help like unto himself, and a pillar of rest. ²⁵ Where no hedge is, there the possession is spoiled: and he that hath no wife will wander up and down mourning. ²⁶ Who will trust a thief well appointed, that skippeth from city to city? so [who will believe] a man that hath no house, and lodgeth wheresoever the night taketh him?

37 ¹ Every friend saith, I am his friend also: but there is a friend, which is only a friend in name. ² Is it not a grief unto death, when a companion and friend is turned to an enemy? ³ O wicked imagination, whence camest thou in to cover the earth with deceit? ⁴ There is a companion, which rejoiceth in the prosperity of a friend, but in the time of trouble will be against him. ⁵ There is a companion, which helpeth his friend for the belly, and taketh up the buckler against the enemy. ⁶ Forget not thy friend in thy mind, and be not unmindful of him in thy riches. ⁷ Every counsellor extolleth counsel; but there is some that counselleth for himself. ⁸ Beware of a counsellor, and know before what need he hath; for he will counsel for himself; lest he cast the lot upon thee, ⁹ and say unto thee, Thy way is good: and afterward he stand on the other side, to see what shall befall thee. ¹⁰ Consult not with one that suspecteth thee: and hide thy counsel from such as envy thee. ¹¹ Neither consult with a woman touching her of

whom she is jealous; neither with a coward in matters of war; nor with a merchant concerning exchange; nor with a buyer of selling; nor with an envious man of thankfulness; nor with an unmerciful man touching kindness; nor with the slothful for any work; nor with an hireling for a year of finishing work; nor with an idle servant of much business: hearken not unto these in any matter of counsel. [12] But be continually with a godly man, whom thou knowest to keep the commandments of the Lord, whose mind is according to thy mind, and will sorrow with thee, if thou shalt miscarry. [13] And let the counsel of thine own heart stand: for there is no man more faithful unto thee than it. [14] For a man's mind is sometime wont to tell him more than seven watchmen, that sit above in an high tower. [15] And above all this pray to the most High, that he will direct thy way in truth. [16] Let reason go before every enterprise, and counsel before every action. [17] The countenance is a sign of changing of the heart. [18] Four manner of things appear: good and evil, life and death: but the tongue ruleth over them continually. [19] There is one that is wise and teacheth many, and yet is unprofitable to himself. [20] There is one that sheweth wisdom in words, and is hated: he shall be destitute of all food. [21] For grace is not given him from the Lord, because he is deprived of all wisdom. [22] Another is wise to himself; and the fruits of understanding are commendable in his mouth. [23] A wise man instructeth his people; and the fruits of his understanding fail not. [24] A wise man shall be filled with blessing; and all they that see him shall count him happy. [25] The days of the life of man may be numbered: but the days of Israel are innumerable. [26] A wise man shall inherit glory among his people, and his name shall be perpetual. [27] My son, prove thy soul in thy life, and see what is evil for it, and give not that unto it. ²⁸ For all things are not profitable for all men, neither hath every soul pleasure in every thing. ²⁹ Be not unsatiable in any dainty thing, nor too greedy upon meats: ³⁰ for excess of meats bringeth sickness, and surfeiting will turn into choler. ³¹ By surfeiting have many perished; but he that taketh heed prolongeth his life.

38

¹ Honour a physician with the honour due unto him for the uses which ye may have of him: for the Lord hath created him. ² For of the most High cometh healing, and he shall receive honour of the king. ³ The skill of the physician shall lift up his head: and in the sight of great men he shall be in admiration. ⁴ The Lord hath created medicines out of the earth; and he that is wise will not abhor them. ⁵ Was not the water made sweet with wood, that the virtue thereof might be known? ⁶ And he hath given men skill, that he might be honoured in his marvellous works. ⁷ With such doth he heal [men,] and taketh away their pains. ⁸ Of such doth the apothecary make a confection; and of his works there is no end; and from him is peace over all the earth. ⁹ My son, in thy sickness be not negligent: but pray unto the Lord, and he will make thee whole. ¹⁰ Leave off from sin, and order thine hands aright, and cleanse thy heart from all wickedness. ¹¹ Give a sweet savour, and a memorial of fine flour; and make a fat offering, as not being. ¹² Then give place to the physician, for the Lord hath created him: let him not go from thee, for thou hast need of him. ¹³ There is a time when in their hands there is good success. ¹⁴ For they shall also pray unto the Lord, that he would prosper that which they give for ease and remedy to prolong

life. [15] He that sinneth before his Maker, let him fall into the hand of the physician. [16] My son, let tears fall down over the dead, and begin to lament, as if thou hadst suffered great harm thyself; and then cover his body according to the custom, and neglect not his burial. [17] Weep bitterly, and make great moan, and use lamentation, as he is worthy, and that a day or two, lest thou be evil spoken of: and then comfort thyself for thy heaviness. [18] For of heaviness cometh death, and the heaviness of the heart breaketh strength. [19] In affliction also sorrow remaineth: and the life of the poor is the curse of the heart. [20] Take no heaviness to heart: drive it away, and remember the last end. [21] Forget it not, for there is no turning again: thou shalt not do him good, but hurt thyself. [22] Remember my judgment: for thine also shall be so; yesterday for me, and today for thee. [23] When the dead is at rest, let his remembrance rest; and be comforted for him, when his spirit is departed from him. [24] The wisdom of a learned man cometh by opportunity of leisure: and he that hath little business shall become wise. [25] How can he get wisdom that holdeth the plough, and that glorieth in the goad, that driveth oxen, and is occupied in their labours, and whose talk is of bullocks? [26] He giveth his mind to make furrows; and is diligent to give the kine fodder. [27] So every carpenter and workmaster, that laboureth night and day: and they that cut and grave seals, and are diligent to make great variety, and give themselves to counterfeit imagery, and watch to finish a work: [28] The smith also sitting by the anvil, and considering the iron work, the vapour of the fire wasteth his flesh, and he fighteth with the heat of the furnace: the noise of the hammer and the anvil is ever in his ears, and his eyes look still upon the pattern of the thing that he maketh; he setteth his mind to finish his work, and watcheth to polish it perfectly: ²⁹ So doth the potter sitting at his work, and turning the wheel about with his feet, who is always carefully set at his work, and maketh all his work by number; ³⁰ he fashioneth the clay with his arm, and boweth down his strength before his feet; he applieth himself to lead it over; and he is diligent to make clean the furnace: ³¹ All these trust to their hands: and every one is wise in his work. ³² Without these cannot a city be inhabited: and they shall not dwell where they will, nor go up and down: ³³ They shall not be sought for in public counsel, nor sit high in the congregation: they shall not sit on the judges' seat, nor understand the sentence of judgment: they cannot declare justice and judgment; and they shall not be found where parables are spoken. ³⁴ But they will maintain the state of the world, and [all] their desire is in the work of their craft.

39 ¹ But he that giveth his mind to the law of the most High, and is occupied in the meditation thereof, will seek out the wisdom of all the ancient, and be occupied in prophecies. ² He will keep the sayings of the renowned men: and where subtil parables are, he will be there also. ³ He will seek out the secrets of grave sentences, and be conversant in dark parables. ⁴ He shall serve among great men, and appear before princes: he will travel through strange countries; for he hath tried the good and the evil among men. ⁵ He will give his heart to resort early to the Lord that made him, and will pray before the most High, and will open his mouth in prayer, and make supplication for his sins. ⁶ When the great Lord will, he shall be filled with the spirit of understanding: he shall pour out wise sentences, and give thanks unto the Lord in his prayer. [7] He shall direct his counsel and knowledge, and in his secrets shall he meditate. [8] He shall shew forth that which he hath learned, and shall glory in the law of the covenant of the Lord. [9] Many shall commend his understanding; and so long as the world endureth, it shall not be blotted out; his memorial shall not depart away, and his name shall live from generation to generation. [10] Nations shall shew forth his wisdom, and the congregation shall declare his praise. [11] If he die, he shall leave a greater name than a thousand: and if he live, he shall increase it. [12] Yet have I more to say, which I have thought upon; for I am filled as the moon at the full. [13] Hearken unto me, ye holy children, and bud forth as a rose growing by the brook of the field: [14] And give ye a sweet savour as frankincense, and flourish as a lily, send forth a smell, and sing a song of praise, bless the Lord in all his works. [15] Magnify his name, and shew forth his praise with the songs of your lips, and with harps, and in praising him ye shall say after this manner: [16] All the works of the Lord are exceeding good, and whatsoever he commandeth shall be accomplished in due season. [17] And none may say, What is this? wherefore is that? for at time convenient they shall all be sought out: at his commandment the waters stood as an heap, and at the words of his mouth the receptacles of waters. [18] At his commandment is done whatsoever pleaseth him; and none can hinder, when he will save. [19] The works of all flesh are before him, and nothing can be hid from his eyes. [20] He seeth from everlasting to everlasting; and there is nothing wonderful before him. [21] A man need not to say, What is this? wherefore is that? for he hath made all things for their uses. [22] His blessing covered the dry land as a river, and watered it as a flood. ²³ As he hath turned the waters into saltness: so shall the heathen inherit his wrath. ²⁴ As his ways are plain unto the holy; so are they stumbling blocks unto the wicked. ²⁵ For the good are good things created from the beginning: so evil things for sinners. ²⁶ The principal things for the whole use of man's life are water, fire, iron, and salt, flour of wheat, honey, milk, and the blood of the grape, and oil, and clothing. ²⁷ All these things are for good to the godly: so to the sinners they are turned into evil. ²⁸ There be spirits that are created for vengeance, which in their fury lay on sore strokes; in the time of destruction they pour out their force, and appease the wrath of him that made them. ²⁹ Fire, and hail, and famine, and death, all these were created for vengeance; ³⁰ teeth of wild beasts, and scorpions, serpents, and the sword, punishing the wicked to destruction. ³¹ They shall rejoice in his commandment, and they shall be ready upon earth, when need is; and when their time is come, they shall not transgress his word. ³² Therefore from the beginning I was resolved, and thought upon these things, and have left them in writing. ³³ All the works of the Lord are good: and he will give every needful thing in due season. ³⁴ So that a man cannot say, This is worse than that: for in time they shall all be well approved. ³⁵ And therefore praise ye the Lord with the whole heart and mouth, and bless the name of the Lord.

40 ¹ Great travail is created for every man, and an heavy yoke is upon the sons of Adam, from the day that they go out of their mother's womb, till the day that they return to the mother of all things. ² Their imagination of things to come, and the day of death, [trouble] their

thoughts, and [cause] fear of heart; [3] from him that sitteth on a throne of glory, unto him that is humbled in earth and ashes; [4] from him that weareth purple and a crown, unto him that is clothed with a linen frock. [5] Wrath, and envy, trouble, and unquietness, fear of death, and anger, and strife, and in the time of rest upon his bed, his night sleep, do change his knowledge. [6] A little or nothing is his rest, and afterward he is in his sleep, as in a day of keeping watch, troubled in the vision of his heart, as if he were escaped out of a battle. [7] When all is safe, he awaketh, and marvelleth that the fear was nothing. [8] [Such things happen] unto all flesh, both man and beast, and that is sevenfold more upon sinners. [9] Death, and bloodshed, strife, and sword, calamities, famine, tribulation, and the scourge; [10] these things are created for the wicked, and for their sakes came the flood. [11] All things that are of the earth shall turn to the earth again: and that which is of the waters doth return into the sea. [12] All bribery and injustice shall be blotted out: but true dealing shall endure for ever. [13] The goods of the unjust shall be dried up like a river, and shall vanish with noise, like a great thunder in rain. [14] While he openeth his hand he shall rejoice: so shall transgressors come to nought. [15] The children of the ungodly shall not bring forth many branches: but are as unclean roots upon a hard rock. [16] The weed growing upon every water and bank of a river shall be pulled up before all grass. [17] Bountifulness is as a most fruitful garden, and mercifulness endureth for ever. [18] To labour, and to be content with that a man hath, is a sweet life: but he that findeth a treasure is above them both. [19] Children and the building of a city continue a man's name: but a blameless wife is counted above them both. [20] Wine and music rejoice the heart: but the love of wisdom is above them both. ²¹ The pipe and the psaltery make sweet melody: but a pleasant tongue is above them both. ²² Thine eye desireth favour and beauty: but more than both, corn while it is green. ²³ A friend and companion never meet amiss: but above both is a wife with her husband. ²⁴ Brethren and help are against time of trouble: but alms shall deliver more than them both. ²⁵ Gold and silver make the foot stand sure: but counsel is esteemed above them both. ²⁶ Riches and strength lift up the heart: but the fear of the Lord is above them both: there is no want in the fear of the Lord, and it needeth not to seek help. ²⁷ The fear of the Lord is a fruitful garden, and covereth him above all glory. ²⁸ My son, lead not a beggar's life; for better it is to die than to beg. ²⁹ The life of him that dependeth on another man's table is not to be counted for a life; for he polluteth himself with other men's meat: but a wise man well nurtured will beware thereof. ³⁰ Begging is sweet in the mouth of the shameless: but in his belly there shall burn a fire.

41

¹ O death, how bitter is the remembrance of thee to a man that liveth at rest in his possessions, unto the man that hath nothing to vex him, and that hath prosperity in all things: yea, unto him that is yet able to receive meat! ² O death, acceptable is thy sentence unto the needy, and unto him whose strength faileth, that is now in the last age, and is vexed with all things, and to him that despaireth, and hath lost patience! ³ Fear not the sentence of death, remember them that have been before thee, and that come after; for this is the sentence of the Lord over all flesh. ⁴ And why art thou against the pleasure of the most High? there is no inquisition

in the grave, whether thou have lived ten, or an hundred, or a thousand years. [5] The children of sinners are abominable children, and they that are conversant in the dwelling of the ungodly. [6] The inheritance of sinners' children shall perish, and their posterity shall have a perpetual reproach. [7] The children will complain of an ungodly father, because they shall be reproached for his sake. [8] Woe be unto you, ungodly men, which have forsaken the law of the most high God! for if ye increase, it shall be to your destruction: [9] And if ye be born, ye shall be born to a curse: and if ye die, a curse shall be your portion. [10] All that are of the earth shall turn to earth again: so the ungodly shall go from a curse to destruction. [11] The mourning of men is about their bodies: but an ill name of sinners shall be blotted out. [12] Have regard to thy name; for that shall continue with thee above a thousand great treasures of gold. [13] A good life hath but few days: but a good name endureth for ever. [14] My children, keep discipline in peace: for wisdom that is hid, and a treasure that is not seen, what profit is in them both? [15] A man that hideth his foolishness is better than a man that hideth his wisdom. [16] Therefore be shamefaced according to my word: for it is not good to retain all shamefacedness; neither is it altogether approved in every thing. [17] Be ashamed of whoredom before father and mother: and of a lie before a prince and a mighty man; [18] of an offence before a judge and ruler; of iniquity before a congregation and people; of unjust dealing before thy partner and friend; [19] and of theft in regard to the place where thou sojournest, and in regard of the truth of God and his covenant; and to lean with thine elbow upon the meat; and of scorning to give and take; [20] and of silence before them that salute thee; and to look upon an harlot; ²¹ and to turn away thy face from thy kinsman; or to take away a portion or a gift; or to gaze upon another man's wife; ²² or to be overbusy with his maid, and come not near her bed; or of upbraiding speeches before friends; and after thou hast given, upbraid not; ²³ or of iterating and speaking again that which thou hast heard; and of revealing of secrets. ²⁴ So shalt thou be truly shamefaced and find favour before all men.

42

¹ Of these things be not thou ashamed, and accept no person to sin thereby: ² Of the law of the most High, and his covenant; and of judgment to justify the ungodly; ³ of reckoning with thy partners and travellers; or of the gift of the heritage of friends; ⁴ of exactness of balance and weights; or of getting much or little; ⁵ and of merchants' indifferent selling; of much correction of children; and to make the side of an evil servant to bleed. ⁶ Sure keeping is good, where an evil wife is; and shut up, where many hands are. ⁷ Deliver all things in number and weight; and put all in writing that thou givest out, or receivest in. ⁸ Be not ashamed to inform the unwise and foolish, and the extreme aged that contendeth with those that are young: thus shalt thou be truly learned, and approved of all men living. ⁹ The father waketh for the daughter, when no man knoweth; and the care for her taketh away sleep: when she is young, lest she pass away the flower of her age; and being married, lest she should be hated: ¹⁰ in her virginity, lest she should be defiled and gotten with child in her father's house; and having an husband, lest she should misbehave herself; and when she is married, lest she should be barren. ¹¹ Keep a sure watch over a shameless daughter, lest she make thee a laughingstock to thine enemies, and a byword in the city, and a

reproach among the people, and make thee ashamed before the multitude. [12] Behold not every body's beauty, and sit not in the midst of women. [13] For from garments cometh a moth, and from women wickedness. [14] Better is the churlishness of a man than a courteous woman, a woman, I say, which bringeth shame and reproach. [15] I will now remember the works of the Lord, and declare the things that I have seen: In the words of the Lord are his works. [16] The sun that giveth light looketh upon all things, and the work thereof is full of the glory of the Lord. [17] The Lord hath not given power to the saints to declare all his marvellous works, which the Almighty Lord firmly settled, that whatsoever is, might be established for his glory. [18] He seeketh out the deep, and the heart, and considereth their crafty devices: for the Lord knoweth all that may be known, and he beholdeth the signs of the world. [19] He declareth the things that are past, and for to come, and revealeth the steps of hidden things. [20] No thought escapeth him, neither any word is hidden from him. [21] He hath garnished the excellent works of his wisdom, and he is from everlasting to everlasting: unto him may nothing be added, neither can he be diminished, and he hath no need of any counsellor. [22] Oh how desirable are all his works! and that a man may see even to a spark. [23] All these things live and remain for ever for all uses, and they are all obedient. [24] All things are double one against another: and he hath made nothing imperfect. [25] One thing establisheth the good of another: and who shall be filled with beholding his glory?

43

[1] The pride of the height, the clear firmament, the beauty of heaven, with his glorious shew; [2] the sun when it appeareth, declaring at his rising a marvellous

instrument, the work of the most High: ³ At noon it parcheth the country, and who can abide the burning heat thereof? ⁴ A man blowing a furnace is in works of heat, but the sun burneth the mountains three times more; breathing out fiery vapours, and sending forth bright beams, it dimmeth the eyes. ⁵ Great is the Lord that made it; and at his commandment runneth hastily. ⁶ He made the moon also to serve in her season for a declaration of times, and a sign of the world. ⁷ From the moon is the sign of feasts, a light that decreaseth in her perfection. ⁸ The month is called after her name, increasing wonderfully in her changing, being an instrument of the armies above, shining in the firmament of heaven; ⁹ the beauty of heaven, the glory of the stars, an ornament giving light in the highest places of the Lord. ¹⁰ At the commandment of the Holy One they will stand in their order, and never faint in their watches. ¹¹ Look upon the rainbow, and praise him that made it; very beautiful it is in the brightness thereof. ¹² It compasseth the heaven about with a glorious circle, and the hands of the most High have bended it. ¹³ By his commandment he maketh the snow to fall apace, and sendeth swiftly the lightnings of his judgment. ¹⁴ Through this the treasures are opened: and clouds fly forth as fowls. ¹⁵ By his great power he maketh the clouds firm, and the hailstones are broken small. ¹⁶ At his sight the mountains are shaken, and at his will the south wind bloweth. ¹⁷ The noise of the thunder maketh the earth to tremble: so doth the northern storm and the whirlwind: as birds flying he scattereth the snow, and the falling down thereof is as the lighting of grasshoppers: ¹⁸ The eye marvelleth at the beauty of the whiteness thereof, and the heart is astonished at the raining of it. ¹⁹ The hoarfrost also as salt he poureth on the earth, and being congealed, it lieth on the top of sharp stakes. [20] When the cold north wind bloweth, and the water is congealed into ice, it abideth upon every gathering together of water, and clotheth the water as with a breastplate. [21] It devoureth the mountains, and burneth the wilderness, and consumeth the grass as fire. [22] A present remedy of all is a mist coming speedily, a dew coming after heat refresheth. [23] By his counsel he appeaseth the deep, and planteth islands therein. [24] They that sail on the sea tell of the danger thereof; and when we hear it with our ears, we marvel thereat. [25] For therein be strange and wondrous works, variety of all kinds of beasts and whales created. [26] By him the end of them hath prosperous success, and by his word all things consist. [27] We may speak much, and yet come short: wherefore in sum, he is all. [28] How shall we be able to magnify him? for he is great above all his works. [29] The Lord is terrible and very great, and marvellous is his power. [30] When ye glorify the Lord, exalt him as much as ye can; for even yet will he far exceed: and when ye exalt him, put forth all your strength, and be not weary; for ye can never go far enough. [31] Who hath seen him, that he might tell us? and who can magnify him as he is? [32] There are yet hid greater things than these be, for we have seen but a few of his works. [33] For the Lord hath made all things; and to the godly hath he given wisdom.

44

[1] Let us now praise famous men, and our fathers that begat us. [2] The Lord hath wrought great glory by them through his great power from the beginning. [3] Such as did bear rule in their kingdoms, men renowned for their power, giving counsel by their understanding, and declaring prophecies: [4] Leaders of the people by their

counsels, and by their knowledge of learning meet for the people, wise and eloquent are their instructions: ⁵ Such as found out musical tunes, and recited verses in writing: ⁶ Rich men furnished with ability, living peaceably in their habitations: ⁷ All these were honoured in their generations, and were the glory of their times. ⁸ There be of them, that have left a name behind them, that their praises might be reported. ⁹ And some there be, which have no memorial; who are perished, as though they had never been; and are become as though they had never been born; and their children after them. ¹⁰ But these were merciful men, whose righteousness hath not been forgotten. ¹¹ With their seed shall continually remain a good inheritance, and their children are within the covenant. ¹² Their seed standeth fast, and their children for their sakes. ¹³ Their seed shall remain for ever, and their glory shall not be blotted out. ¹⁴ Their bodies are buried in peace; but their name liveth for evermore. ¹⁵ The people will tell of their wisdom, and the congregation will shew forth their praise. ¹⁶ Enoch pleased the Lord, and was translated, being an example of repentance to all generations. ¹⁷ Noah was found perfect and righteous; in the time of wrath he was taken in exchange [for the world]; therefore was he left as a remnant unto the earth, when the flood came. ¹⁸ An everlasting covenant was made with him, that all flesh should perish no more by the flood. ¹⁹ Abraham was a great father of many people: in glory was there none like unto him; ²⁰ who kept the law of the most High, and was in covenant with him: he established the covenant in his flesh; and when he was proved, he was found faithful. ²¹ Therefore he assured him by an oath, that he would bless the nations in his seed, and that he would multiply him as the dust of the earth, and exalt his seed as the stars, and cause them to inherit from sea to sea, and from the river unto the utmost part of the land. ²² With Isaac did he establish likewise [for Abraham his father's sake] the blessing of all men, and the covenant, ²³ and made it rest upon the head of Jacob. He acknowledged him in his blessing, and gave him an heritage, and divided his portions; among the twelve tribes did he part them.

45 ¹ And he brought out of him a merciful man, which found favour in the sight of all flesh, even Moses, beloved of God and men, whose memorial is blessed. ² He made him like to the glorious saints, and magnified him, so that his enemies stood in fear of him. ³ By his words he caused the wonders to cease, and he made him glorious in the sight of kings, and gave him a commandment for his people, and shewed him part of his glory. ⁴ He sanctified him in his faithfulness and meekness, and chose him out of all men. ⁵ He made him to hear his voice, and brought him into the dark cloud, and gave him commandments before his face, even the law of life and knowledge, that he might teach Jacob his covenants, and Israel his judgments. ⁶ He exalted Aaron, an holy man like unto him, even his brother, of the tribe of Levi. ⁷ An everlasting covenant he made with him and gave him the priesthood among the people; he beautified him with comely ornaments, and clothed him with a robe of glory. ⁸ He put upon him perfect glory; and strengthened him with rich garments, with breeches, with a long robe, and the ephod. ⁹ And he compassed him with pomegranates, and with many golden bells round about, that as he went there might be a sound, and a noise made that might be heard in the temple, for a memorial to the children of his people; [10] with an holy garment, with gold, and blue silk, and purple, the work of the embroiderer, with a breastplate of judgment, and with Urim and Thummim; [11] with twisted scarlet, the work of the cunning workman, with precious stones graven like seals, and set in gold, the work of the jeweller, with a writing engraved for a memorial, after the number of the tribes of Israel. [12] He set a crown of gold upon the mitre, wherein was engraved Holiness, an ornament of honour, a costly work, the desires of the eyes, goodly and beautiful. [13] Before him there were none such, neither did ever any stranger put them on, but only his children and his children's children perpetually. [14] Their sacrifices shall be wholly consumed every day twice continually. [15] Moses consecrated him, and anointed him with holy oil: this was appointed unto him by an everlasting covenant, and to his seed, so long as the heavens should remain, that they should minister unto him, and execute the office of the priesthood, and bless the people in his name. [16] He chose him out of all men living to offer sacrifices to the Lord, incense, and a sweet savour, for a memorial, to make reconciliation for his people. [17] He gave unto him his commandments, and authority in the statutes of judgments, that he should teach Jacob the testimonies, and inform Israel in his laws. [18] Strangers conspired together against him, and maligned him in the wilderness, even the men that were of Dathan's and Abiron's side, and the congregation of Core, with fury and wrath. [19] This the Lord saw, and it displeased him, and in his wrathful indignation were they consumed: he did wonders upon them, to consume them with the fiery flame. [20] But he made Aaron more honourable, and gave him an heritage, and divided unto him the firstfruits of the increase; especially he prepared bread in abundance: [21] For they ate of the sacrifices of the Lord, which he gave unto him and his seed. [22] Howbeit in the land of the people he had no inheritance, neither had he any portion among the people: for the Lord himself is his portion and inheritance. [23] The third in glory is Phinees the son of Eleazar, because he had zeal in the fear of the Lord, and stood up with good courage of heart when the people were turned back, and made reconciliation for Israel. [24] Therefore was there a covenant of peace made with him, that he should be the chief of the sanctuary and of his people, and that he and his posterity should have the dignity of the priesthood for ever: [25] According to the covenant made with David son of Jesse, of the tribe of Juda, that the inheritance of the king should be to his posterity alone: so the inheritance of Aaron should also be unto his seed. [26] God give you wisdom in your heart to judge his people in righteousness, that their good things be not abolished, and that their glory may endure for ever.

46 [1] Jesus the son a Nave was valiant in the wars, and was the successor of Moses in prophecies, who according to his name was made great for the saving of the elect of God, and taking vengeance of the enemies that rose up against them, that he might set Israel in their inheritance. [2] How great glory gat he, when he did lift up his hands, and stretched out his sword against the cities! [3] Who before him so stood to it? for the Lord himself brought his enemies unto him. [4] Did not the sun go back by his means? and was not one day as long as two? [5] He called upon the most high Lord, when the enemies pressed upon him on every side; and the great

Lord heard him. ⁶ And with hailstones of mighty power he made the battle to fall violently upon the nations, and in the descent [of Beth-horon] he destroyed them that resisted, that the nations might know all their strength, because he fought in the sight of the Lord, and he followed the Mighty One. ⁷ In the time of Moses also he did a work of mercy, he and Caleb the son of Jephunne, in that they withstood the congregation, and withheld the people from sin, and appeased the wicked murmuring. ⁸ And of six hundred thousand people on foot, they two were preserved to bring them in to the heritage, even unto the land that floweth with milk and honey. ⁹ The Lord gave strength also unto Caleb, which remained with him unto his old age: so that he entered upon the high places of the land, and his seed obtained it for an heritage: ¹⁰ that all the children of Israel might see that it is good to follow the Lord. ¹¹ And concerning the judges, every one by name, whose heart went not a whoring, nor departed from the Lord, let their memory be blessed. ¹² Let their bones flourish out of their place, and let the name of them that were honoured be continued upon their children. ¹³ Samuel, the prophet of the Lord, beloved of his Lord, established a kingdom, and anointed princes over his people. ¹⁴ By the law of the Lord he judged the congregation, and the Lord had respect unto Jacob. ¹⁵ By his faithfulness he was found a true prophet, and by his word he was known to be faithful in vision. ¹⁶ He called upon the mighty Lord, when his enemies pressed upon him on every side, when he offered the sucking lamb. ¹⁷ And the Lord thundered from heaven, and with a great noise made his voice to be heard. ¹⁸ And he destroyed the rulers of the Tyrians, and all the princes of the Philistines. ¹⁹ And before his long sleep he made protestations in the sight of the Lord and his anointed, I have not taken any man's goods, so much as a shoe: and no man did accuse him. [20] And after his death he prophesied, and shewed the king his end, and lifted up his voice from the earth in prophecy, to blot out the wickedness of the people.

47 [1] And after him rose up Nathan to prophesy in the time of David. [2] As is the fat taken away from the peace offering, so was David chosen out of the children of Israel. [3] He played with lions as with kids, and with bears as with lambs. [4] Slew he not a giant, when he was yet but young? and did he not take away reproach from the people, when he lifted up his hand with the stone in the sling, and beat down the boasting of Goliath? [5] For he called upon the most high Lord; and he gave him strength in his right hand to slay that mighty warrior, and set up the horn of his people. [6] So the people honoured him with ten thousands, and praised him in the blessings of the Lord, in that he gave him a crown of glory. [7] For he destroyed the enemies on every side, and brought to nought the Philistines his adversaries, and brake their horn in sunder unto this day. [8] In all his works he praised the Holy One most high with words of glory; with his whole heart he sung songs, and loved him that made him. [9] He set singers also before the altar, that by their voices they might make sweet melody, and daily sing praises in their songs. [10] He beautified their feasts, and set in order the solemn times until the end, that they might praise his holy name, and that the temple might sound from morning. [11] The Lord took away his sins, and exalted his horn for ever: he gave him a covenant of kings, and a throne of glory in Israel. [12] After him rose up a wise son, and for his sake he dwelt at large. ¹³ Solomon reigned in a peaceable time, and was honoured; for God made all quiet round about him, that he might build an house in his name, and prepare his sanctuary for ever. ¹⁴ How wise wast thou in thy youth and, as a flood, filled with understanding! ¹⁵ Thy soul covered the whole earth, and thou filledst it with dark parables. ¹⁶ Thy name went far unto the islands; and for thy peace thou wast beloved. ¹⁷ The countries marvelled at thee for thy songs, and proverbs, and parables, and interpretations. ¹⁸ By the name of the Lord God, which is called the Lord God of Israel, thou didst gather gold as tin and didst multiply silver as lead. ¹⁹ Thou didst bow thy loins unto women, and by thy body thou wast brought into subjection. ²⁰ Thou didst stain thy honour, and pollute thy seed: so that thou broughtest wrath upon thy children, and wast grieved for thy folly. ²¹ So the kingdom was divided, and out of Ephraim ruled a rebellious kingdom. ²² But the Lord will never leave off his mercy, neither shall any of his works perish, neither will he abolish the posterity of his elect, and the seed of him that loveth him he will not take away: wherefore he gave a remnant unto Jacob, and out of him a root unto David. ²³ Thus rested Solomon with his fathers, and of his seed he left behind him Roboam, even the foolishness of the people, and one that had no understanding, who turned away the people through his counsel. There was also Jeroboam the son of Nebat, who caused Israel to sin, and shewed Ephraim the way of sin: ²⁴ and their sins were multiplied exceedingly, that they were driven out of the land. ²⁵ For they sought out all wickedness, till the vengeance came upon them.

48 ¹ Then stood up Elias the prophet as fire, and his word burned like a lamp. ² He brought a sore famine upon them, and by his zeal he diminished their number. ³ By the word of the Lord he shut up the heaven, and also three times brought down fire. ⁴ O Elias, how wast thou honoured in thy wondrous deeds! and who may glory like unto thee! ⁵ Who didst raise up a dead man from death, and his soul from the place of the dead, by the word of the most High: ⁶ Who broughtest kings to destruction, and honourable men from their bed: ⁷ Who heardest the rebuke of the Lord in Sinai, and in Horeb the judgment of vengeance: ⁸ Who annointedst kings to take revenge, and prophets to succeed after him: ⁹ Who was taken up in a whirlwind of fire, and in a chariot of fiery horses: ¹⁰ Who wast ordained for reproofs in their times, to pacify the wrath of the Lord's judgment, before it brake forth into fury, and to turn the heart of the father unto the son, and to restore the tribes of Jacob. ¹¹ Blessed are they that saw thee, and slept in love; for we shall surely live. ¹² Elias it was, who was covered with a whirlwind: and Eliseus was filled with his spirit: whilst he lived, he was not moved with the presence of any prince, neither could any bring him into subjection. ¹³ No word could overcome him; and after his death his body prophesied. ¹⁴ He did wonders in his life, and at his death were his works marvellous. ¹⁵ For all this the people repented not, neither departed they from their sins, till they were spoiled and carried out of their land, and were scattered through all the earth: yet there remained a small people, and a ruler in the house of David: ¹⁶ of whom some did that which was pleasing to God, and some multiplied sins. ¹⁷ Ezekias fortified his city, and brought in water into the midst thereof: he digged the hard rock with iron,

and made wells for waters. ¹⁸ In his time Sennacherib came up, and sent Rabsaces, and lifted up his hand against Sion, and boasted proudly. ¹⁹ Then trembled their hearts and hands, and they were in pain, as women in travail. ²⁰ But they called upon the Lord which is merciful, and stretched out their hands toward him: and immediately the Holy One heard them out of heaven, and delivered them by the ministry of Esay. ²¹ He smote the host of the Assyrians, and his angel destroyed them. ²² For Ezekias had done the thing that pleased the Lord, and was strong in the ways of David his father, as Esay the prophet, who was great and faithful in his vision, had commanded him. ²³ In his time the sun went backward, and he lengthened the king's life. ²⁴ He saw by an excellent spirit what should come to pass at the last, and he comforted them that mourned in Sion. ²⁵ He shewed what should come to pass for ever, and secret things or ever they came.

49

¹ The remembrance of Josias is like the composition of the perfume that is made by the art of the apothecary: it is sweet as honey in all mouths, and as music at a banquet of wine. ² He behaved himself uprightly in the conversion of the people, and took away the abominations of iniquity. ³ He directed his heart unto the Lord, and in the time of the ungodly he established the worship of God. ⁴ All, except David and Ezekias and Josias, were defective: for they forsook the law of the most High, even the kings of Juda failed. ⁵ Therefore he gave their power unto others, and their glory to a strange nation. ⁶ They burnt the chosen city of the sanctuary, and made the streets desolate, according to the prophecy of Jeremias. ⁷ For they entreated him evil, who nevertheless was a prophet, sanctified in his mother's

womb, that he might root out, and afflict, and destroy; and that he might build up also, and plant. [8] It was Ezekiel who saw the glorious vision, which was shewed him upon the chariot of the cherubims. [9] For he made mention of the enemies under the figure of the rain, and directed them that went right. [10] And of the twelve prophets let the memorial be blessed, and let their bones flourish again out of their place: for they comforted Jacob, and delivered them by assured hope. [11] How shall we magnify Zorobabel? even he was as a signet on the right hand: [12] so was Jesus the son of Josedec: who in their time builded the house, and set up an holy temple to the Lord, which was prepared for everlasting glory. [13] And among the elect was Neemias, whose renown is great, who raised up for us the walls that were fallen, and set up the gates and the bars, and raised up our ruins again. [14] But upon the earth was no man created like Enoch; for he was taken from the earth. [15] Neither was there a young man born like Joseph, a governor of his brethren, a stay of the people, whose bones were regarded of the Lord. [16] Sem and Seth were in great honour among men, and so was Adam above every living thing in creation.

50 [1] Simon the high priest, the son of Onias, who in his life repaired the house again, and in his days fortified the temple: [2] and by him was built from the foundation the double height, the high fortress of the wall about the temple: [3] In his days the cistern to receive water, being in compass as the sea, was covered with plates of brass: [4] He took care of the temple that it should not fall, and fortified the city against besieging: [5] How was he honoured in the midst of the people in his coming out of the sanctuary! [6] He was as the morning star in

the midst of a cloud, and as the moon at the full: ⁷ as the sun shining upon the temple of the most High, and as the rainbow giving light in the bright clouds: ⁸ and as the flower of roses in the spring of the year, as lilies by the rivers of waters, and as the branches of the frankincense tree in the time of summer: ⁹ as fire and incense in the censer, and as a vessel of beaten gold set with all manner of precious stones: ¹⁰ and as a fair olive tree budding forth fruit, and as a cypress tree which groweth up to the clouds. ¹¹ When he put on the robe of honour, and was clothed with the perfection of glory, when he went up to the holy altar, he made the garment of holiness honourable. ¹² When he took the portions out of the priests' hands, he himself stood by the hearth of the altar, compassed with his brethren about, as a young cedar in Libanus; and as palm trees compassed they him round about. ¹³ So were all the sons of Aaron in their glory, and the oblations of the Lord in their hands, before all the congregation of Israel. ¹⁴ And finishing the service at the altar, that he might adorn the offering of the most high Almighty, ¹⁵ he stretched out his hand to the cup, and poured of the blood of the grape, he poured out at the foot of the altar a sweetsmelling savour unto the most high King of all. ¹⁶ Then shouted the sons of Aaron, and sounded the silver trumpets, and made a great noise to be heard, for a remembrance before the most High. ¹⁷ Then all the people together hasted, and fell down to the earth upon their faces to worship their Lord God Almighty, the most High. ¹⁸ The singers also sang praises with their voices, with great variety of sounds was there made sweet melody. ¹⁹ And the people besought the Lord, the most High, by prayer before him that is merciful, till the solemnity of the Lord was ended, and they had finished his service. [20] Then he went down, and lifted up his hands over the whole congregation of the children of Israel, to give the blessing of the Lord with his lips, and to rejoice in his name. [21] And they bowed themselves down to worship the second time, that they might receive a blessing from the most High. [22] Now therefore bless ye the God of all, which only doeth wondrous things every where, which exalteth our days from the womb, and dealeth with us according to his mercy. [23] He grant us joyfulness of heart, and that peace may be in our days in Israel for ever: [24] That he would confirm his mercy with us, and deliver us at his time! [25] There be two manner of nations which my heart abhorreth, and the third is no nation: [26] They that sit upon the mountain of Samaria, and they that dwell among the Philistines, and that foolish people that dwell in Sichem. [27] Jesus the son of Sirach of Jerusalem hath written in this book the instruction of understanding and knowledge, who out of his heart poured forth wisdom. [28] Blessed is he that shall be exercised in these things; and he that layeth them up in his heart shall become wise. [29] For if he do them, he shall be strong to all things: for the light of the Lord leadeth him, who giveth wisdom to the godly. Blessed be the name of the Lord for ever. Amen, Amen.

51

[1] I will thank thee, O Lord and King, and praise thee, O God my Saviour: I do give praise unto thy name: [2] For thou art my defender and helper, and has preserved my body from destruction, and from the snare of the slanderous tongue, and from the lips that forge lies, and has been mine helper against mine adversaries: [3] and hast delivered me, according to the multitude of thy mercies and greatness of thy name, from the teeth

of them that were ready to devour me, and out of the hands of such as sought after my life, and from the manifold afflictions which I had; ⁴ from the choking of fire on every side, and from the midst of the fire which I kindled not; ⁵ From the depth of the belly of hell, from an unclean tongue, and from lying words. ⁶ By an accusation to the king from an unrighteous tongue, my soul drew near even unto death, my life was near to the hell beneath. ⁷ They compassed me on every side, and there was no man to help me: I looked for the succour of men, but there was none. ⁸ Then thought I upon thy mercy, O Lord, and upon thine acts of old, how thou deliverest such as wait for thee, and savest them out of the hands of the enemies. ⁹ Then lifted I up my supplications from the earth, and prayed for deliverance from death. ¹⁰ I called upon the Lord, the Father of my Lord, that he would not leave me in the days of my trouble, and in the time of the proud, when there was no help. ¹¹ I will praise thy name continually, and will sing praises with thanksgiving; and so my prayer was heard: ¹² For thou savedst me from destruction, and deliveredst me from the evil time: therefore will I give thanks, and praise thee, and bless thy name, O Lord. ¹³ When I was yet young, or ever I went abroad, I desired wisdom openly in my prayer. ¹⁴ I prayed for her before the temple, and will seek her out even to the end. ¹⁵ Even from the flower till the grape was ripe hath my heart delighted in her: my foot went the right way, from my youth up sought I after her. ¹⁶ I bowed down mine ear a little, and received her, and gat much learning. ¹⁷ I profited therein, therefore will I ascribe glory unto him that giveth me wisdom. ¹⁸ For I purposed to do after her, and earnestly I followed that which is good; so shall I not be confounded. ¹⁹ My soul hath wrestled with her, and in my doings I was exact: I stretched forth my hands to the heaven above, and bewailed my ignorances of her. [20] I directed my soul unto her, and I found her in pureness: I have had my heart joined with her from the beginning, therefore shall I not be forsaken. [21] My heart was troubled in seeking her: therefore have I gotten a good possession. [22] The Lord hath given me a tongue for my reward, and I will praise him therewith. [23] Draw near unto me, ye unlearned, and dwell in the house of learning. [24] Wherefore are ye slow, and what say ye to these things, seeing your souls are very thirsty? [25] I opened my mouth, and said, Buy her for yourselves without money. [26] Put your neck under the yoke, and let your soul receive instruction: she is hard at hand to find. [27] Behold with your eyes, how that I have but little labour, and have gotten unto me much rest. [28] Get learning with a great sum of money, and get much gold by her. [29] Let your soul rejoice in his mercy, and be not ashamed of his praise. [30] Work your work betimes, and in his time he will give you your reward.

THE BOOK OF BARUCH

1 ¹ And these are the words of the book, which Baruch the son of Nerias, the son of Maasias, the son of Sedecias, the son of Asadias, the son of Chelcias, wrote in Babylon, ² in the fifth year, and in the seventh day of the month, what time as the Chaldeans took Jerusalem, and burnt it with fire. ³ And Baruch did read the words of this book in the hearing of Jechonias the son of Joachim king of Juda, and in the ears of all the people that came to hear the book, ⁴ and in the hearing of the nobles, and of the king's sons, and in the hearing of the elders, and of all the people, from the lowest unto the highest, even of all them that dwelt at Babylon by the river Sud. ⁵ Whereupon they wept, fasted, and prayed before the Lord. ⁶ They made also a collection of money according to every man's power: ⁷ and they sent it to Jerusalem unto Joachim the high priest, the son of Chelcias, son of Salom, and to the priests, and to all the people which were found with him at Jerusalem, ⁸ at the same time when he received the vessels of the house of the Lord, that were carried out of the temple, to return them into the land of Juda,

the tenth day of the month Sivan, namely, silver vessels, which Sedecias the son of Josias king of Juda had made, [9] after that Nabuchodonosor king of Babylon had carried away Jechonias, and the princes, and the captives, and the mighty men, and the people of the land, from Jerusalem, and brought them unto Babylon. [10] And they said, Behold, we have sent you money to buy you burnt offerings, and sin offerings, and incense, and prepare ye manna, and offer upon the altar of the Lord our God; [11] and pray for the life of Nabuchodonosor king of Babylon, and for the life of Balthasar his son, that their days may be upon earth as the days of heaven: [12] And the Lord will give us strength, and lighten our eyes, and we shall live under the shadow of Nabuchodonosor king of Babylon, and under the shadow of Balthasar his son, and we shall serve them many days, and find favour in their sight. [13] Pray for us also unto the Lord our God, for we have sinned against the Lord our God; and unto this day the fury of the Lord and his wrath is not turned from us. [14] And ye shall read this book which we have sent unto you, to make confession in the house of the Lord, upon the feasts and solemn days. [15] And ye shall say, To the Lord our God belongeth righteousness, but unto us the confusion of faces, as it is come to pass this day, unto them of Juda, and to the inhabitants of Jerusalem, [16] and to our kings, and to our princes, and to our priests, and to our prophets, and to our fathers: [17] For we have sinned before the Lord, [18] and disobeyed him, and have not hearkened unto the voice of the Lord our God, to walk in the commandments that he gave us openly: [19] Since the day that the Lord brought our forefathers out of the land of Egypt, unto this present day, we have been disobedient unto the Lord our God, and

we have been negligent in not hearing his voice.
²⁰ Wherefore the evils cleaved unto us, and the curse,
which the Lord appointed by Moses his servant at the
time that he brought our fathers out of the land of
Egypt, to give us a land that floweth with milk and
honey, like as it is to see this day. ²¹ Nevertheless we
have not hearkened unto the voice of the Lord our
God, according unto all the words of the prophets,
whom he sent unto us: ²² But every man followed the
imagination of his own wicked heart, to serve strange
gods, and to do evil in the sight of the Lord our God.

2 ¹ Therefore the Lord hath made good his word, which
he pronounced against us, and against our judges that
judged Israel, and against our kings, and against our
princes, and against the men of Israel and Juda, ² to
bring upon us great plagues, such as never happened
under the whole heaven, as it came to pass in
Jerusalem, according to the things that were written in
the law of Moses; ³ that a man should eat the flesh of
his own son, and the flesh of his own daughter.
⁴ Moreover he hath delivered them to be in subjection
to all the kingdoms that are round about us, to be as a
reproach and desolation among all the people round
about, where the Lord hath scattered them. ⁵ Thus we
were cast down, and not exalted, because we have
sinned against the Lord our God, and have not been
obedient unto his voice. ⁶ To the Lord our God appertaineth righteousness: but unto us and to our fathers
open shame, as appeareth this day. ⁷ For all these
plagues are come upon us, which the Lord hath pronounced against us. ⁸ Yet have we not prayed before the
Lord, that we might turn every one from the imagina-
tions of his wicked heart. ⁹ Wherefore the Lord

watched over us for evil, and the Lord hath brought it upon us: for the Lord is righteous in all his works which he hath commanded us. [10] Yet we have not hearkened unto his voice, to walk in the commandments of the Lord, that he hath set before us. [11] And now, O Lord God of Israel, that hast brought thy people out of the land of Egypt with a mighty hand, and high arm, and with signs, and with wonders, and with great power, and hast gotten thyself a name, as appeareth this day: [12] O Lord our God, we have sinned, we have done ungodly, we have dealt unrighteously in all thine ordinances. [13] Let thy wrath turn from us: for we are but a few left among the heathen, where thou hast scattered us. [14] Hear our prayers, O Lord, and our petitions, and deliver us for thine own sake, and give us favour in the sight of them which have led us away: [15] that all the earth may know that thou art the Lord our God, because Israel and his posterity is called by thy name. [16] O Lord, look down from thine holy house, and consider us: bow down thine ear, O Lord, to hear us. [17] Open thine eyes, and behold; for the dead that are in the graves, whose souls are taken from their bodies, will give unto the Lord neither praise nor righteousness: [18] but the soul that is greatly vexed, which goeth stooping and feeble, and the eyes that fail, and the hungry soul, will give thee praise and righteousness, O Lord. [19] Therefore we do not make our humble supplication before thee, O Lord our God, for the righteousness of our fathers, and of our kings. [20] For thou hast sent out thy wrath and indignation upon us, as thou hast spoken by thy servants the prophets, saying, [21] Thus saith the Lord, Bow down your shoulders to serve the king of Babylon: so shall ye remain in the land that I gave unto your fathers. [22] But if ye will not hear the voice of the

Lord, to serve the king of Babylon, 23 I will cause to cease out of the cities of Juda, and from without Jerusalem, the voice of mirth, and the voice of joy, the voice of the bridegroom, and the voice of the bride: and the whole land shall be desolate of inhabitants. 24 But we would not hearken unto thy voice, to serve the king of Babylon: therefore hast thou made good the words that thou spakest by thy servants the prophets, namely, that the bones of our kings, and the bones of our fathers, should be taken out of their places. 25 And, lo, they are cast out to the heat of the day, and to the frost of the night, and they died in great miseries by famine, by sword, and by pestilence. 26 And the house which is called by thy name hast thou laid waste, as it is to be seen this day, for the wickedness of the house of Israel and the house of Juda. 27 O Lord our God, thou hast dealt with us after all thy goodness, and according to all that great mercy of thine, 28 as thou spakest by thy servant Moses in the day when thou didst command him to write the law before the children of Israel, saying, 29 If ye will not hear my voice, surely this very great multitude shall be turned into a small number among the nations, where I will scatter them. 30 For I knew that they would not hear me, because it is a stiffnecked people: but in the land of their captivities they shall remember themselves. 31 And shall know that I am the Lord their God: for I will give them an heart, and ears to hear: 32 and they shall praise me in the land of their captivity, and think upon my name, 33 and return from their stiff neck, and from their wicked deeds: for they shall remember the way of their fathers, which sinned before the Lord. 34 And I will bring them again into the land which I promised with an oath unto their fathers, Abraham, Isaac, and Jacob, and they shall be lords of it:

and I will increase them, and they shall not be diminished. ³⁵ And I will make an everlasting covenant with them to be their God, and they shall be my people: and I will no more drive my people of Israel out of the land that I have given them.

3 ¹ O Lord Almighty, God of Israel, the soul in anguish the troubled spirit, crieth unto thee. ² Hear, O Lord, and have mercy; as thou art merciful: and have pity upon us, because we have sinned before thee. ³ For thou endurest for ever, and we perish utterly. ⁴ O Lord Almighty, thou God of Israel, hear now the prayers of the dead Israelites, and of their children, which have sinned before thee, and not hearkened unto the voice of thee, their God: for the which cause these plagues cleave unto us. ⁵ Remember not the iniquities of our forefathers: but think upon thy power and thy name now at this time. ⁶ For thou art the Lord our God, and thee, O Lord, will we praise. ⁷ And for this cause thou hast put thy fear in our hearts, to the intent that we should call upon thy name, and praise thee in our captivity: for we have called to mind all the iniquity of our forefathers, that sinned before thee. ⁸ Behold, we are yet this day in our captivity, where thou hast scattered us, for a reproach and a curse, and to be subject to payments, according to all the iniquities of our fathers, which departed from the Lord our God. ⁹ Hear, Israel, the commandments of life: give ear to understand wisdom. ¹⁰ How happeneth it, Israel, that thou art in thine enemies' land, that thou art waxen old in a strange country, that thou art defiled with the dead, ¹¹ that thou art counted with them that go down into the grave? ¹² Thou hast forsaken the fountain of wisdom. ¹³ For if thou hadst walked in the way of God, thou

shouldest have dwelled in peace for ever. ¹⁴ Learn
where is wisdom, where is strength, where is understanding; that thou mayest know also where is length of
days, and life, where is the light of the eyes, and peace.
¹⁵ Who hath found out her place? or who hath come
into her treasures? ¹⁶ Where are the princes of the heathen become, and such as ruled the beasts upon the
earth; ¹⁷ They that had their pastime with the fowls of
the air, and they that hoarded up silver and gold,
wherein men trust, and made no end of their getting?
¹⁸ For they that wrought in silver, and were so careful,
and whose works are unsearchable, ¹⁹ they are vanished
and gone down to the grave, and others are come up in
their steads. ²⁰ Young men have seen light, and dwelt
upon the earth: but the way of knowledge have they
not known, ²¹ nor understood the paths thereof, nor
laid hold of it: their children were far off from that way.
²² It hath not been heard of in Chanaan, neither hath
it been seen in Theman. ²³ The Agarenes that seek wisdom upon earth, the merchants of Meran and of
Theman, the authors of fables, and searchers out of
understanding; none of these have known the way of
wisdom, or remember her paths. ²⁴ O Israel, how great
is the house of God! and how large is the place of his
possession! ²⁵ Great, and hath none end; high, and
unmeasurable. ²⁶ There were the giants famous from
the beginning, that were of so great stature, and so
expert in war. ²⁷ Those did not the Lord choose, neither gave he the way of knowledge unto them: ²⁸ But
they were destroyed, because they had no wisdom, and
perished through their own foolishness. ²⁹ Who hath
gone up into heaven, and taken her, and brought her
down from the clouds? ³⁰ Who hath gone over the sea,
and found her, and will bring her for pure gold? ³¹ No

333

man knoweth her way, nor thinketh of her path. [32] But he that knoweth all things knoweth her, and hath found her out with his understanding: he that prepared the earth for evermore hath filled it with fourfooted beasts: [33] He that sendeth forth light, and it goeth, calleth it again, and it obeyeth him with fear. [34] The stars shined in their watches, and rejoiced: when he calleth them, they say, Here we be; and so with cheerfulness they shewed light unto him that made them. [35] This is our God, and there shall none other be accounted of in comparison of him. [36] He hath found out all the way of knowledge, and hath given it unto Jacob his servant, and to Israel his beloved. [37] Afterward did he shew himself upon earth, and conversed with men.

4 [1] This is the book of the commandments of God, and the law that endureth for ever: all they that keep it shall come to life; but such as leave it shall die. [2] Turn thee, O Jacob, and take hold of it: walk in the presence of the light thereof, that thou mayest be illuminated. [3] Give not thine honour to another, nor the things that are profitable unto thee to a strange nation. [4] O Israel, happy are we: for things that are pleasing to God are made known unto us. [5] Be of good cheer, my people, the memorial of Israel. [6] Ye were sold to the nations, not for [your] destruction: but because ye moved God to wrath, ye were delivered unto the enemies. [7] For ye provoked him that made you by sacrificing unto devils, and not to God. [8] Ye have forgotten the everlasting God, that brought you up; and ye have grieved Jerusalem, that nursed you. [9] For when she saw the wrath of God coming upon you, she said, Hearken, O ye that dwell about Sion: God hath brought upon me great mourning; [10] for I saw the captivity of my sons

and daughters, which the Everlasting brought upon them. [11] With joy did I nourish them; but sent them away with weeping and mourning. [12] Let no man rejoice over me, a widow, and forsaken of many, who for the sins of my children am left desolate; because they departed from the law of God. [13] They knew not his statutes, nor walked in the ways of his commandments, nor trod in the paths of discipline in his righteousness. [14] Let them that dwell about Sion come, and remember ye the captivity of my sons and daughters, which the Everlasting hath brought upon them. [15] For he hath brought a nation upon them from far, a shameless nation, and of a strange language, who neither reverenced old man, nor pitied child. [16] These have carried away the dear beloved children of the widow, and left her that was alone desolate without daughters. [17] But what can I help you? [18] For he that brought these plagues upon you will deliver you from the hands of your enemies. [19] Go your way, O my children, go your way: for I am left desolate. [20] I have put off the clothing of peace, and put upon me the sackcloth of my prayer: I will cry unto the Everlasting in my days. [21] Be of good cheer, O my children, cry unto the Lord, and he will deliver you from the power and hand of the enemies. [22] For my hope is in the Everlasting, that he will save you; and joy is come unto me from the Holy One, because of the mercy which shall soon come unto you from the Everlasting our Saviour. [23] For I sent you out with mourning and weeping: but God will give you to me again with joy and gladness for ever. [24] Like as now the neighbours of Sion have seen your captivity: so shall they see shortly your salvation from our God, which shall come upon you with great glory, and brightness of the Everlasting. [25] My children, suffer patiently the wrath that is come upon you from God: for thine enemy hath persecuted thee; but shortly thou shalt see his destruction, and shalt tread upon his neck. [26] My delicate ones have gone rough ways, and were taken away as a flock caught of the enemies. [27] Be of good comfort, O my children, and cry unto God: for ye shall be remembered of him that brought these things upon you. [28] For as it was your mind to go astray from God: so, being returned, seek him ten times more. [29] For he that hath brought these plagues upon you shall bring you everlasting joy with your salvation. [30] Take a good heart, O Jerusalem: for he that gave thee that name will comfort thee. [31] Miserable are they that afflicted thee, and rejoiced at thy fall. [32] Miserable are the cities which thy children served: miserable is she that received thy sons. [33] For as she rejoiced at thy ruin, and was glad of thy fall: so shall she be grieved for her own desolation. [34] For I will take away the rejoicing of her great multitude, and her pride shall be turned into mourning. [35] For fire shall come upon her from the Everlasting, long to endure; and she shall be inhabited of devils for a great time. [36] O Jerusalem, look about thee toward the east, and behold the joy that cometh unto thee from God. [37] Lo, thy sons come, whom thou sentest away, they come gathered together from the east to the west by the word of the Holy One, rejoicing in the glory of God.

5 [1] Put off, O Jerusalem, the garment of mourning and affliction, and put on the comeliness of the glory that cometh from God for ever. [2] Cast about thee a double garment of the righteousness which cometh from God; and set a diadem on thine head of the glory of the Everlasting. [3] For God will shew thy brightness unto

every country under heaven. [4] For thy name shall be called of God for ever, The peace of righteousness, and The glory of God's worship. [5] Arise, O Jerusalem, and stand on high, and look about toward the east, and behold thy children gathered from the west unto the east by the word of the Holy One, rejoicing in the remembrance of God. [6] For they departed from thee on foot, and were led away of their enemies: but God bringeth them unto thee exalted with glory, as children of the kingdom. [7] For God hath appointed that every high hill, and banks of long continuance, should be cast down, and valleys filled up, to make even the ground, that Israel may go safely in the glory of God. [8] Moreover even the woods and every sweet-smelling tree shall overshadow Israel by the commandment of God. [9] For God shall lead Israel with joy in the light of his glory with the mercy and righteousness that cometh from him.

THE EPISTLE OF JEREMY

¹ Because of the sins which ye have committed before God, ye shall be led away captives into Babylon by Nabuchodonosor king of the Babylonians. ² So when ye be come unto Babylon, ye shall remain there many years, and for a long season, namely, seven generations: and after that I will bring you away peaceably from thence. ³ Now shall ye see in Babylon gods of silver, and of gold, and of wood, borne upon shoulders, which cause the nations to fear. ⁴ Beware therefore that ye in no wise be like to strangers, neither be ye afraid of them, when ye see the multitude before them and behind them, worshipping them. ⁵ But say ye in your hearts, O Lord, we must worship thee. ⁶ For mine angel is with you, and I myself caring for your souls. ⁷ As for their tongue, it is polished by the workman, and they themselves are gilded and laid over with silver; yet are they but false, and cannot speak. ⁸ And taking gold, as it were for a virgin that loveth to go gay, they make crowns for the heads of their gods. ⁹ Sometimes also the priests convey from their gods gold and silver, and bestow it upon themselves. ¹⁰ Yea, they will give there-

of to the common harlots, and deck them as men with garments, [being] gods of silver, and gods of gold, and wood. [11] Yet cannot these gods save themselves from rust and moth, though they be covered with purple raiment. [12] They wipe their faces because of the dust of the temple, when there is much upon them. [13] And he that cannot put to death one that offendeth him holdeth a sceptre, as though he were a judge of the country. [14] He hath also in his right hand a dagger and an ax: but cannot deliver himself from war and thieves. [15] Whereby they are known not to be gods: therefore fear them not. [16] For like as a vessel that a man useth is nothing worth when it is broken; even so it is with their gods: when they be set up in the temple, their eyes be full of dust through the feet of them that come in. [17] And as the doors are made sure on every side upon him that offendeth the king, as being committed to suffer death: even so the priests make fast their temples with doors, with locks, and bars, lest their gods be spoiled with robbers. [18] They light them candles, yea, more than for themselves, whereof they cannot see one. [19] They are as one of the beams of the temple, yet they say their hearts are gnawed upon by things creeping out of the earth; and when they eat them and their clothes, they feel it not. [20] Their faces are blacked through the smoke that cometh out of the temple. [21] Upon their bodies and heads sit bats, swallows, and birds, and the cats also. [22] By this ye may know that they are no gods: therefore fear them not. [23] Notwithstanding the gold that is about them to make them beautiful, except they wipe off the rust, they will not shine: for neither when they were molten did they feel it. [24] The things wherein there is no breath are bought for a most high price. [25] They are borne upon shoulders, having no feet, whereby they declare unto men that they be nothing worth. 26 They also that serve them are ashamed: for if they fall to the ground at any time, they cannot rise up again of themselves: neither, if one set them upright, can they move of themselves: neither, if they be bowed down, can they make themselves straight: but they set gifts before them, as unto dead men. 27 As for the things that are sacrificed unto them, their priests sell and abuse; in like manner their wives lay up part thereof in salt; but unto the poor and impotent they give nothing of it. 28 Menstruous women and women in childbed eat their sacrifices: by these things ye may know that they are no gods: fear them not. 29 For how can they be called gods? because women set meat before the gods of silver, gold, and wood. 30 And the priests sit in their temples, having their clothes rent, and their heads and beards shaven, and nothing upon their heads. 31 They roar and cry before their gods, as men do at the feast when one is dead. 32 The priests also take off their garments, and clothe their wives and children. 33 Whether it be evil that one doeth unto them, or good, they are not able to recompense it: they can neither set up a king, nor put him down. 34 In like manner, they can neither give riches nor money: though a man make a vow unto them, and keep it not, they will not require it. 35 They can save no man from death, neither deliver the weak from the mighty. 36 They cannot restore a blind man to his sight, nor help any man in his distress. 37 They can shew no mercy to the widow, nor do good to the fatherless. 38 Their gods of wood, and which are overlaid with gold and silver, are like the stones that be hewn out of the mountain: they that worship them shall be confounded. 39 How should a man then think and say that they are gods, when even the Chaldeans themselves dishonour them? [40] Who, if they shall see one dumb that cannot speak, they bring him, and intreat Bel that he may speak, as though he were able to understand. [41] Yet they cannot understand this themselves, and leave them: for they have no knowledge. [42] The women also with cords about them, sitting in the ways, burn bran for perfume: but if any of them, drawn by some that passeth by, lie with him, she reproacheth her fellow, that she was not thought as worthy as herself, nor her cord broken. [43] Whatsoever is done among them is false: how may it then be thought or said that they are gods? [44] They are made of carpenters and goldsmiths: they can be nothing else than the workmen will have them to be. [45] And they themselves that made them can never continue long; how should then the things that are made of them be gods? [46] For they left lies and reproaches to them that come after. [47] For when there cometh any war or plague upon them, the priests consult with themselves, where they may be hidden with them. [48] How then cannot men perceive that they be no gods, which can neither save themselves from war, nor from plague? [49] For seeing they be but of wood, and overlaid with silver and gold, it shall be known hereafter that they are false: [50] And it shall manifestly appear to all nations and kings that they are no gods, but the works of men's hands, and that there is no work of God in them. [51] Who then may not know that they are no gods? [52] For neither can they set up a king in the land, nor give rain unto men. [53] Neither can they judge their own cause, nor redress a wrong, being unable: for they are as crows between heaven and earth. [54] Whereupon when fire falleth upon the house of gods of wood, or laid over with gold or silver, their priests will flee away, and escape; but they themselves shall be burned asunder like beams. ⁵⁵ Moreover they cannot withstand any king or enemies: how can it then be thought or said that they be gods? ⁵⁶ Neither are those gods of wood, and laid over with silver or gold, able to escape either from thieves or robbers. ⁵⁷ Whose gold, and silver, and garments wherewith they are clothed, they that are strong take, and go away withal: neither are they able to help themselves. ⁵⁸ Therefore it is better to be a king that sheweth his power, or else a profitable vessel in an house, which the owner shall have use of, than such false gods; or to be a door in an house, to keep such things therein, than such false gods; or a pillar of wood in a palace, than such false gods. ⁵⁹ For sun, moon, and stars, being bright and sent to do their offices, are obedient. ⁶⁰ In like manner the lightning when it breaketh forth is easy to be seen; and after the same manner the wind bloweth in every country. ⁶¹ And when God commandeth the clouds to go over the whole world, they do as they are bidden. ⁶² And the fire sent from above to consume hills and woods doeth as it is commanded: but these are like unto them neither in shew nor power. ⁶³ Wherefore it is neither to be supposed nor said that they are gods, seeing, they are able neither to judge causes, nor to do good unto men. ⁶⁴ Knowing therefore that they are no gods, fear them not, ⁶⁵ for they can neither curse nor bless kings: ⁶⁶ Neither can they shew signs in the heavens among the heathen, nor shine as the sun, nor give light as the moon. ⁶⁷ The beasts are better than they: for they can get under a cover and help themselves. ⁶⁸ It is then by no means manifest unto us that they are gods: therefore fear them not. ⁶⁹ For as a scarecrow in a garden of cucumbers keepeth nothing: so are their gods of wood, and laid over with silver and gold. [70] And likewise their gods of wood, and laid over with silver and gold, are like to a white thorn in an orchard, that every bird sitteth upon; as also to a dead body, that is cast into the dark. [71] And ye shall know them to be no gods by the bright purple that rotteth upon them: and they themselves afterward shall be eaten, and shall be a reproach in the country. [72] Better therefore is the just man that hath none idols: for he shall be far from reproach.

THE PRAYER OF AZARIAH

---

¹ And they walked in the midst of the fire, praising God, and blessing the Lord. ² Then Azarias stood up, and prayed in this manner; and opening his mouth in the midst of the fire said, ³ Blessed art thou, O Lord God of our fathers: thy name is worthy to be praised and glorified for evermore: ⁴ For thou art righteous in all the things that thou hast done to us: yea, true are all thy works, thy ways are right, and all thy judgments truth. ⁵ In all the things that thou hast brought upon us, and upon the holy city of our fathers, even Jerusalem, thou hast executed true judgment: for according to truth and judgment didst thou bring all these things upon us because of our sins. ⁶ For we have sinned and committed iniquity, departing from thee. ⁷ In all things have we trespassed, and not obeyed thy commandments, nor kept them, neither done as thou hast commanded us, that it might go well with us. ⁸ Wherefore all that thou hast brought upon us, and every thing that thou hast done to us, thou hast done in true judgment. ⁹ And thou didst deliver us into the hands of lawless enemies, most hateful forsakers of

God, and to an unjust king, and the most wicked in all the world. [10] And now we cannot open our mouths, we are become a shame and reproach to thy servants; and to them that worship thee. [11] Yet deliver us not up wholly, for thy name's sake, neither disannul thou thy covenant: [12] And cause not thy mercy to depart from us, for thy beloved Abraham's sake, for thy servant Issac's sake, and for thy holy Israel's sake; [13] to whom thou hast spoken and promised, that thou wouldest multiply their seed as the stars of heaven, and as the sand that lieth upon the seashore. [14] For we, O Lord, are become less than any nation, and be kept under this day in all the world because of our sins. [15] Neither is there at this time prince, or prophet, or leader, or burnt offering, or sacrifice, or oblation, or incense, or place to sacrifice before thee, and to find mercy. [16] Nevertheless in a contrite heart and an humble spirit let us be accepted. [17] Like as in the burnt offerings of rams and bullocks, and like as in ten thousands of fat lambs: so let our sacrifice be in thy sight this day, and grant that we may wholly go after thee: for they shall not be confounded that put their trust in thee. [18] And now we follow thee with all our heart, we fear thee, and seek thy face. [19] Put us not to shame: but deal with us after thy lovingkindness, and according to the multitude of thy mercies. [20] Deliver us also according to thy marvellous works, and give glory to thy name, O Lord: and let all them that do thy servants hurt be ashamed; [21] and let them be confounded in all their power and might, and let their strength be broken; [22] and let them know that thou art God, the only God, and glorious over the whole world. [23] And the king's servants, that put them in, ceased not to make the oven hot with rosin, pitch, tow, and small wood; [24] so that the flame streamed forth above the furnace forty and nine cubits. ²⁵ And it passed through, and burned those Chaldeans it found about the furnace. ²⁶ But the angel of the Lord came down into the oven together with Azarias and his fellows, and smote the flame of the fire out of the oven; ²⁷ and made the midst of the furnace as it had been a moist whistling wind, so that the fire touched them not at all, neither hurt nor troubled them. ²⁸ Then the three, as out of one mouth, praised, glorified, and blessed God in the furnace, saying, ²⁹ Blessed art thou, O Lord God of our fathers: and to be praised and exalted above all for ever. ³⁰ And blessed is thy glorious and holy name: and to be praised and exalted above all for ever. ³¹ Blessed art thou in the temple of thine holy glory: and to be praised and glorified above all for ever. ³² Blessed art thou that beholdest the depths, and sittest upon the cherubims: and to be praised and exalted above all for ever. ³³ Blessed art thou on the glorious throne of thy kingdom: and to be praised and glorified above all for ever. ³⁴ Blessed art thou in the firmament of heaven: and above all to be praised and glorified for ever. ³⁵ O all ye works of the Lord, bless ye the Lord: praise and exalt him above all for ever. ³⁶ O ye heavens, bless ye the Lord: praise and exalt him above all for ever. ³⁷ O ye angels of the Lord, bless ye the Lord: praise and exalt him above all for ever. ³⁸ O all ye waters that be above the heaven, bless ye the Lord: praise and exalt him above all for ever. ³⁹ O all ye powers of the Lord, bless ye the Lord: praise and exalt him above all for ever. ⁴⁰ O ye sun and moon, bless ye the Lord: praise and exalt him above all for ever. ⁴¹ O ye stars of heaven, bless ye the Lord: praise and exalt him above all for ever. ⁴² O every shower and dew, bless ye the Lord: praise and exalt him above all for ever. ⁴³ O all ye winds, bless ye the Lord: praise and exalt him above all for ever. 44 O ye fire and heat, bless ye the Lord: praise and exalt him above all for ever. 45 O ye winter and summer, bless ye the Lord: praise and exalt him above all for ever. 46 O ye dews and storms of snow, bless ye the Lord: praise and exalt him above all for ever. 47 O ye nights and days, bless ye the Lord: praise and exalt him above all for ever. 48 O ye light and darkness, bless ye the Lord: praise and exalt him above all for ever. 49 O ye ice and cold, bless ye the Lord: praise and exalt him above all for ever. 50 O ye frost and snow, bless ye the Lord: praise and exalt him above all for ever. 51 O ye lightnings and clouds, bless ye the Lord: praise and exalt him above all for ever. 52 O let the earth bless the Lord: praise and exalt him above all for ever. 53 O ye mountains and little hills, bless ye the Lord: praise and exalt him above all for ever. 54 O all ye things that grow in the earth, bless ye the Lord: praise and exalt him above all for ever. 55 O ye mountains, bless ye the Lord: praise and exalt him above all for ever. 56 O ye seas and rivers, bless ye the Lord: praise and exalt him above all for ever. 57 O ye whales, and all that move in the waters, bless ye the Lord: praise and exalt him above all for ever. 58 O all ye fowls of the air, bless ye the Lord: praise and exalt him above all for ever. 59 O all ye beasts and cattle, bless ye the Lord: praise and exalt him above all for ever. 60 O ye children of men, bless ye the Lord: praise and exalt him above all for ever. 61 O Israel, bless ye the Lord: praise and exalt him above all for ever. 62 O ye priests of the Lord, bless ye the Lord: praise and exalt him above all for ever. 63 O ye servants of the Lord, bless ye the Lord: praise and exalt him above all for ever. 64 O ye spirits and souls of the righteous, bless ye the Lord: praise and exalt him above all for ever. [65] O ye holy and humble men of heart, bless ye the Lord: praise and exalt him above all for ever. [66] O Ananias, Azarias, and Misael, bless ye the Lord: praise and exalt him above all for ever: for he hath delivered us from hell, and saved us from the hand of death, and delivered us out of the midst of the furnace and burning flame: even out of the midst of the fire hath he delivered us. [67] O give thanks unto the Lord, because he is gracious: for his mercy endureth for ever. [68] O all ye that worship the Lord, bless the God of gods, praise him, and give him thanks: for his mercy endureth for ever.

THE HISTORY OF SUSANNA

¹ There dwelt a man in Babylon, called Joacim: ² And he took a wife, whose name was Susanna, the daughter of Chelcias, a very fair woman, and one that feared the Lord. ³ Her parents also were righteous, and taught their daughter according to the law of Moses. ⁴ Now Joacim was a great rich man, and had a fair garden joining unto his house: and to him resorted the Jews; because he was more honourable than all others. ⁵ The same year were appointed two of the ancients of the people to be judges, such as the Lord spake of, that wickedness came from Babylon from ancient judges, who seemed to govern the people. ⁶ These kept much at Joacim's house: and all that had any suits in law came unto them. ⁷ Now when the people departed away at noon, Susanna went into her husband's garden to walk. ⁸ And the two elders saw her going in every day, and walking; so that their lust was inflamed toward her. ⁹ And they perverted their own mind, and turned away their eyes, that they might not look unto heaven, nor remember just judgments. ¹⁰ And albeit they both were wounded with her love, yet durst not one shew

another his grief. ¹¹ For they were ashamed to declare their lust, that they desired to have to do with her. ¹² Yet they watched diligently from day to day to see her. ¹³ And the one said to the other, Let us now go home: for it is dinner time. ¹⁴ So when they were gone out, they parted the one from the other, and turning back again they came to the same place; and after that they had asked one another the cause, they acknowledged their lust: then appointed they a time both together, when they might find her alone. ¹⁵ And it fell out, as they watched a fit time, she went in as before with two maids only, and she was desirous to wash herself in the garden: for it was hot. ¹⁶ And there was no body there save the two elders, that had hid themselves, and watched her. ¹⁷ Then she said to her maids, Bring me oil and washing balls, and shut the garden doors, that I may wash me. ¹⁸ And they did as she bade them, and shut the garden doors, and went out themselves at privy doors to fetch the things that she had commanded them: but they saw not the elders, because they were hid. ¹⁹ Now when the maids were gone forth, the two elders rose up, and ran unto her, saying, ²⁰ Behold, the garden doors are shut, that no man can see us, and we are in love with thee; therefore consent unto us, and lie with us. ²¹ If thou wilt not, we will bear witness against thee, that a young man was with thee: and therefore thou didst send away thy maids from thee. ²² Then Susanna sighed, and said, I am straitened on every side: for if I do this thing, it is death unto me: and if I do it not, I cannot escape your hands. ²³ It is better for me to fall into your hands, and not do it, than to sin in the sight of the Lord. ²⁴ With that Susanna cried with a loud voice: and the two elders cried out against her. ²⁵ Then ran the one, and opened the gar-

den door. ²⁶ So when the servants of the house heard
the cry in the garden, they rushed in at the privy door,
to see what was done unto her. ²⁷ But when the elders
had declared their matter, the servants were greatly
ashamed: for there was never such a report made of
Susanna. ²⁸ And it came to pass the next day, when the
people were assembled to her husband Joacim, the two
elders came also full of mischievous imagination
against Susanna to put her to death; ²⁹ and said before
the people, Send for Susanna, the daughter of Chelcias,
Joacim's wife. And so they sent. ³⁰ So she came with
her father and mother, her children, and all her kindred. ³¹ Now Susanna was a very delicate woman, and
beauteous to behold. ³² And these wicked men commanded to uncover her face (for she was covered,) that
they might be filled with her beauty. ³³ Therefore her
friends and all that saw her wept. ³⁴ Then the two
elders stood up in the midst of the people, and laid
their hands upon her head. ³⁵ And she weeping looked
up toward heaven: for her heart trusted in the Lord.
³⁶ And the elders said, As we walked in the garden
alone, this woman came in with two maids, and shut
the garden doors, and sent the maids away. ³⁷ Then a
young man, who there was hid, came unto her, and lay
with her. ³⁸ Then we that stood in a corner of the garden, seeing this wickedness, ran unto them. ³⁹ And
when we saw them together, the man we could not
hold: for he was stronger than we, and opened the door,
and leaped out. ⁴⁰ But having taken this woman, we
asked who the young man was, but she would not tell
us: these things do we testify. ⁴¹ Then the assembly
believed them as those that were the elders and judges
of the people: so they condemned her to death. ⁴² Then
Susanna cried out with a loud voice, and said, O ever-

lasting God, that knowest the secrets, and knowest all things before they be: [43] Thou knowest that they have borne false witness against me, and, behold, I must die; whereas I never did such things as these men have maliciously invented against me. [44] And the Lord heard her voice. [45] Therefore when she was led to be put to death, the Lord raised up the holy spirit of a young youth whose name was Daniel: [46] who cried with a loud voice, I am clear from the blood of this woman. [47] Then all the people turned them toward him, and said, What mean these words that thou hast spoken? [48] So he standing in the midst of them said, Are ye such fools, ye sons of Israel, that without examination or knowledge of the truth ye have condemned a daughter of Israel? [49] Return again to the place of judgment: for they have borne false witness against her. [50] Wherefore all the people turned again in haste, and the elders said unto him, Come, sit down among us, and shew it us, seeing God hath given thee the honour of an elder. [51] Then said Daniel unto them, Put these two aside one far from another, and I will examine them. [52] So when they were put asunder one from another, he called one of them, and said unto him, O thou that art waxen old in wickedness, now thy sins which thou hast committed aforetime are come to light. [53] For thou hast pronounced false judgment and hast condemned the innocent, and hast let the guilty go free; albeit the Lord saith, The innocent and righteous shalt thou not slay. [54] Now then, if thou hast seen her, tell me, Under what tree sawest thou them companying together? Who answered, Under a mastick tree. [55] And Daniel said, Very well; thou hast lied against thine own head; for even now the angel of God hath received the sentence of God to cut thee in two. [56] So he put him aside, and commanded to bring the other, and said unto him, O thou seed of Chanaan, and not of Juda, beauty hath deceived thee, and lust hath perverted thine heart. [57] Thus have ye dealt with the daughters of Israel, and they for fear companied with you: but the daughter of Juda would not abide your wickedness. [58] Now therefore tell me, Under what tree didst thou take them companying together? Who answered, Under an holm tree. [59] Then said Daniel unto him, Well; thou hast also lied against thine own head: for the angel of God waiteth with the sword to cut thee in two, that he may destroy you. [60] With that all the assembly cried out with a loud voice, and praised God, who saveth them that trust in him. [61] And they arose against the two elders, for Daniel had convicted them of false witness by their own mouth: [62] And according to the law of Moses they did unto them in such sort as they maliciously intended to do to their neighbour: and they put them to death. Thus the innocent blood was saved the same day. [63] Therefore Chelcias and his wife praised God for their daughter Susanna, with Joacim her husband, and all the kindred, because there was no dishonesty found in her. [64] From that day forth was Daniel had in great reputation in the sight of the people.

THE HISTORY OF THE DESTRUCTION OF BEL AND THE DRAGON

¹ And king Astyages was gathered to his fathers, and Cyrus of Persia received his kingdom. ² And Daniel conversed with the king, and was honoured above all his friends. ³ Now the Babylonians had an idol, called Bel, and there were spent upon him every day twelve great measures of fine flour, and forty sheep, and six vessels of wine. ⁴ And the king worshipped it and went daily to adore it: but Daniel worshipped his own God. And the king said unto him, Why dost thou not worship Bel? ⁵ Who answered and said, Because I may not worship idols made with hands, but the living God, who hath created the heaven and the earth, and hath sovereignty over all flesh. ⁶ Then said the king unto him, Thinkest thou not that Bel is a living God? seest thou not how much he eateth and drinketh every day?

7 Then Daniel smiled, and said, O king, be not deceived: for this is but clay within, and brass without, and did never eat or drink any thing. 8 So the king was wroth, and called for his priests, and said unto them, If ye tell me not who this is that devoureth these expenses, ye shall die. 9 But if ye can certify me that Bel devoureth them, then Daniel shall die: for he hath spoken blasphemy against Bel. And Daniel said unto the king, Let it be according to thy word. 10 Now the priests of Bel were threescore and ten, besides their wives and children. And the king went with Daniel into the temple of Bel. 11 So Bel's priests said, Lo, we go out: but thou, O king, set on the meat, and make ready the wine, and shut the door fast and seal it with thine own signet; 12 And tomorrow when thou comest in, if thou findest not that Bel hath eaten up all, we will suffer death: or else Daniel, that speaketh falsely against us. 13 And they little regarded it: for under the table they had made a privy entrance, whereby they entered in continually, and consumed those things. 14 So when they were gone forth, the king set meats before Bel. Now Daniel had commanded his servants to bring ashes, and those they strewed throughout all the temple in the presence of the king alone: then went they out, and shut the door, and sealed it with the king's signet, and so departed. 15 Now in the night came the priests with their wives and children, as they were wont to do, and did eat and drink up all. 16 In the morning betimes the king arose, and Daniel with him. 17 And the king said, Daniel, are the seals whole? And he said, Yea, O king, they be whole. 18 And as soon as he had opened the door, the king looked upon the table, and cried with a loud voice, Great art thou, O Bel, and with thee is no deceit at all. 19 Then laughed Daniel, and

held the king that he should not go in, and said, Behold now the pavement, and mark well whose footsteps are these. 20 And the king said, I see the footsteps of men, women, and children. And then the king was angry, 21 and took the priests with their wives and children, who shewed him the privy doors, where they came in, and consumed such things as were upon the table. 22 Therefore the king slew them, and delivered Bel into Daniel's power, who destroyed him and his temple. 23 And in that same place there was a great dragon, which they of Babylon worshipped. 24 And the king said unto Daniel, Wilt thou also say that this is of brass? lo, he liveth, he eateth and drinketh; thou canst not say that he is no living god: therefore worship him. 25 Then said Daniel unto the king, I will worship the Lord my God: for he is the living God. 26 But give me leave, O king, and I shall slay this dragon without sword or staff. The king said, I give thee leave. 27 Then Daniel took pitch, and fat, and hair, and did seethe them together, and made lumps thereof: this he put in the dragon's mouth, and so the dragon burst in sunder: and Daniel said, Lo, these are the gods ye worship. 28 When they of Babylon heard that, they took great indignation, and conspired against the king, saying, The king is become a Jew, and he hath destroyed Bel, he hath slain the dragon, and put the priests to death. 29 So they came to the king, and said, Deliver us Daniel, or else we will destroy thee and thine house. 30 Now when the king saw that they pressed him sore, being constrained, he delivered Daniel unto them: 31 who cast him into the lions' den: where he was six days. 32 And in the den there were seven lions, and they had given them every day two carcasses, and two sheep: which then were not given to them, to the intent they might devour Daniel. [33] Now there was in Jewry a prophet, called Habbacuc, who had made pottage, and had broken bread in a bowl, and was going into the field, for to bring it to the reapers. [34] But the angel of the Lord said unto Habbacuc, Go, carry the dinner that thou hast into Babylon unto Daniel, who is in the lions' den. [35] And Habbacuc said, Lord, I never saw Babylon; neither do I know where the den is. [36] Then the angel of the Lord took him by the crown, and bare him by the hair of his head, and through the vehemency of his spirit set him in Babylon over the den. [37] And Habbacuc cried, saying, O Daniel, Daniel, take the dinner which God hath sent thee. [38] And Daniel said, Thou hast remembered me, O God: neither hast thou forsaken them that seek thee and love thee. [39] So Daniel arose, and did eat: and the angel of the Lord set Habbacuc in his own place again immediately. [40] Upon the seventh day the king went to bewail Daniel: and when he came to the den, he looked in, and behold, Daniel was sitting. [41] Then cried the king with a loud voice, saying, Great art thou, Lord God of Daniel, and there is none other besides thee. [42] And he drew him out, and cast those that were the cause of his destruction into the den: and they were devoured in a moment before his face.

THE PRAYER OF MANASSES

1 O Lord, Almighty God of our fathers, Abraham, Isaac, and Jacob, and of their righteous seed; 2 who hast made heaven and earth, with all the ornament thereof; 3 who hast bound the sea by the word of thy commandment; who hast shut up the deep, and sealed it by thy terrible and glorious name; 4 whom all men fear, and tremble before thy power; 5 for the majesty of thy glory cannot be borne, and thine angry threatening toward sinners is importable; 6 but thy merciful promise is unmeasurable and unsearchable; 7 for thou art the most high Lord, of great compassion, long-suffering, very merciful, and repentest of the evils of men. Thou, O Lord, according to thy great goodness hast promised repentance and forgiveness to them that have sinned against thee: and of thine infinite mercies hast appointed repentance unto sinners, that they may be saved. 8 Thou therefore, O Lord, that art the God of the just, hast not appointed repentance to the just, as to Abraham, and Isaac, and Jacob, which have not sinned against thee; but thou hast appointed repentance unto me that am a sinner: 9 For I have sinned above the

number of the sands of the sea. My transgressions, O Lord, are multiplied: my transgressions are multiplied, and I am not worthy to behold and see the height of heaven for the multitude of mine iniquities. [10] I am bowed down with many iron bands, that I cannot lift-up mine head, neither have any release: for I have provoked thy wrath, and done evil before thee: I did not thy will, neither kept I thy commandments: I have set up abominations, and have multiplied offences. [11] Now therefore I bow the knee of mine heart, beseeching thee of grace. [12] I have sinned, O Lord, I have sinned, and I acknowledge mine iniquities: [13] Wherefore, I humbly beseech thee, forgive me, O Lord, forgive me, and destroy me not with mine iniquities. Be not angry with me for ever, by reserving evil for me; neither condemn me to the lower parts of the earth. For thou art the God, even the God of them that repent; [14] and in me thou wilt shew all thy goodness: for thou wilt save me, that am unworthy, according to thy great mercy. [15] Therefore I will praise thee for ever all the days of my life: for all the powers of the heavens do praise thee, and thine is the glory for ever and ever. Amen.

THE FIRST BOOK
OF MACCABEES

1 ¹ And it happened, after that Alexander son of Philip, the Macedonian, who came out of the land of Chettiim, had smitten Darius king of the Persians and Medes, that he reigned in his stead, the first over Greece, ² and made many wars, and won many strong holds, and slew the kings of the earth, ³ and went through to the ends of the earth, and took spoils of many nations, insomuch that the earth was quiet before him; whereupon he was exalted, and his heart was lifted up. ⁴ And he gathered a mighty strong host, and ruled over countries, and nations, and kings, who became tributaries unto him. ⁵ And after these things he fell sick, and perceived that he should die. ⁶ Wherefore he called his servants, such as were honourable, and had been brought up with him from his youth, and parted his kingdom among them while he was yet alive. ⁷ So Alexander reigned twelve years, and then died. ⁸ And his servants bare rule every one in his place. ⁹ And after his death they all put crowns upon themselves; so did their sons after them many years: and evils were multiplied in the earth. ¹⁰ And there came

out of them a wicked root, Antiochus surnamed Epiphanes, son of Antiochus the king, who had been an hostage at Rome, and he reigned in the hundred and thirty and seventh year of the kingdom of the Greeks. [11] In those days went there out of Israel wicked men, who persuaded many, saying, Let us go and make a covenant with the heathen that are round about us; for since we departed from them, we have had much sorrow. [12] So this device pleased them well. [13] Then certain of the people were so forward herein, that they went to the king, who gave them license to do after the ordinances of the heathen: [14] Whereupon they built a place of exercise at Jerusalem according to the customs of the heathen. [15] And made themselves uncircumcised, and forsook the holy covenant, and joined themselves to the heathen, and were sold to do mischief. [16] Now when the kingdom was established before Antiochus, he thought to reign over Egypt, that he might have the dominion of two realms. [17] Wherefore he entered into Egypt with a great multitude, with chariots, and elephants, and horsemen, and a great navy, [18] and made war against Ptolemee king of Egypt: but Ptolemee was afraid of him, and fled; and many were wounded to death. [19] Thus they got the strong cities in the land of Egypt, and he took the spoils thereof. [20] And after that Antiochus had smitten Egypt, he returned again in the hundred forty and third year, and went up against Israel and Jerusalem with a great multitude, [21] and entered proudly into the sanctuary, and took away the golden altar, and the candlestick of light, and all the vessels thereof. [22] And the table of the shew-bread, and the pouring vessels, and the vials, and the censers of gold, and the veil, and the crowns, and the golden ornaments that were before the temple, all which he pulled off. ²³ He took also the silver and the gold, and the precious vessels: also he took the hidden treasures which he found. ²⁴ And when he had taken all away, he went into his own land, having made a great massacre, and spoke very proudly. ²⁵ Therefore there was a great mourning in Israel, in every place where they were; ²⁶ so that the princes and elders mourned, the virgins and young men were made feeble, and the beauty of women was changed. ²⁷ Every bridegroom took up lamentation, and she that sat in the marriage chamber was in heaviness. ²⁸ The land also was moved for the inhabitants thereof, and all the house of Jacob was covered with confusion. ²⁹ And after two years fully expired, the king sent his chief collector of tribute unto the cities of Juda, who came unto Jerusalem with a great multitude; ³⁰ and spake peaceable words unto them, but all was deceit: for when they had given him credence, he fell suddenly upon the city, and smote it very sore, and destroyed much people of Israel. ³¹ And when he had taken the spoils of the city, he set it on fire, and pulled down the houses and walls thereof on every side. ³² But the women and children took they captive, and possessed the cattle. ³³ Then builded they the city of David with a great and strong wall, and with mighty towers, and made it a strong hold for them. ³⁴ And they put therein a sinful nation, wicked men, and fortified themselves therein. ³⁵ They stored it also with armour and victuals, and when they had gathered together the spoils of Jerusalem, they laid them up there, and so they became a sore snare: ³⁶ for it was a place to lie in wait against the sanctuary, and an evil adversary to Israel. ³⁷ Thus they shed innocent blood on every side of the sanctuary, and defiled it: ³⁸ insomuch that the inhabitants of Jerusalem fled because of them: whereupon the city was made an habitation of strangers, and became strange to those that were born in her; and her own children left her. [39] Her sanctuary was laid waste like a wilderness, her feasts were turned into mourning, her sabbaths into reproach her honour into contempt. [40] As had been her glory, so was her dishonour increased, and her excellency was turned into mourning. [41] Moreover king Antiochus wrote to his whole kingdom, that all should be one people, [42] and every one should leave his laws: so all the heathen agreed according to the commandment of the king. [43] Yea, many also of the Israelites consented to his religion and sacrificed unto idols, and profaned the sabbath. [44] For the king had sent letters by messengers unto Jerusalem and the cities of Juda that they should follow the strange laws of the land, [45] and forbid burnt offerings, and sacrifices, and drink offerings, in the temple; and that they should profane the sabbaths and festival days: [46] and pollute the sanctuary and holy people: [47] set up altars, and groves, and chapels of idols, and sacrifice swine's flesh, and unclean beasts: [48] That they should also leave their children uncircumcised, and make their souls abominable with all manner of uncleanness and profanation: [49] to the end they might forget the law, and change all the ordinances. [50] And whosoever would not do according to the commandment of the king, he said, he should die. [51] In the selfsame manner wrote he to his whole kingdom, and appointed overseers over all the people, commanding the cities of Juda to sacrifice, city by city. [52] Then many of the people were gathered unto them, to wit every one that forsook the law; and so they committed evils in the land; [53] and drove the Israelites into secret places, even wheresoever they could flee for succour. ⁵⁴ Now the fifteenth day of the month Casleu, in the hundred forty and fifth year, they set up the abomination of desolation upon the altar, and builded idol altars throughout the cities of Juda on every side; ⁵⁵ and burnt incense at the doors of their houses, and in the streets. ⁵⁶ And when they had rent in pieces the books of the law which they found, they burnt them with fire. ⁵⁷ And whosoever was found with any the book of the testament, or if any consented to the law, the king's commandment was, that they should put him to death. ⁵⁸ Thus did they by their authority unto the Israelites every month, to as many as were found in the cities. ⁵⁹ Now the five and twentieth day of the month they did sacrifice upon the idol altar, which was upon the altar of God. ⁶⁰ At which time according to the commandment they put to death certain women, that had caused their children to be circumcised. ⁶¹ And they hanged the infants about their necks, and rifled their houses, and slew them that had circumcised them. ⁶² Howbeit many in Israel were fully resolved and confirmed in themselves not to eat any unclean thing. ⁶³ Wherefore they chose to die, that they might not be defiled with meats, and that they might not profane the holy covenant: so then they died. ⁶⁴ And there was very great wrath upon Israel.

2 ¹ In those days arose Mattathias the son of John, the son of Simeon, a priest of the sons of Joarib, from Jerusalem, and dwelt in Modin. ² And he had five sons, Joannan, called Caddis: ³ Simon, called Thassi: ⁴ Judas, who was called Maccabeus: ⁵ Eleazar, called Avaran: and Jonathan, whose surname was Apphus. ⁶ And when he saw the blasphemies that were committed in Juda and Jerusalem, ⁷ he said, Woe is me! wherefore

was I born to see this misery of my people, and of the holy city, and to dwell there when it was delivered into the hand of the enemy, and the sanctuary into the hand of strangers? [8] Her temple is become as a man without glory. [9] Her glorious vessels are carried away into captivity, her infants are slain in the streets, her young men with the sword of the enemy. [10] What nation hath not had a part in her kingdom, and gotten of her spoils? [11] All her ornaments are taken away; of a free woman she is become a bondslave. [12] And, behold, our sanctuary, even our beauty and our glory, is laid waste, and the Gentiles have profaned it. [13] To what end therefore shall we live any longer? [14] Then Mattathias and his sons rent their clothes, and put on sackcloth, and mourned very sore. [15] In the mean while the king's officers, such as compelled the people to revolt, came into the city Modin, to make them sacrifice. [16] And when many of Israel came unto them, Mattathias also and his sons came together. [17] Then answered the king's officers, and said to Mattathias on this wise, Thou art a ruler, and an honourable and great man in this city, and strengthened with sons and brethren: [18] Now therefore come thou first, and fulfil the king's commandment, like as all the heathen have done, yea, and the men of Juda also, and such as remain at Jerusalem: so shalt thou and thy house be in the number of the king's friends, and thou and thy children shall be honoured with silver and gold, and many rewards. [19] Then Mattathias answered and spake with a loud voice, Though all the nations that are under the king's dominion obey him, and fall away every one from the religion of their fathers, and give consent to his commandments, [20] yet will I and my sons and my brethren walk in the covenant of our fathers. [21] God forbid that we should forsake the law and the ordinances. ²² We will not hearken to the king's words, to go from our religion, either on the right hand, or the left. ²³ Now when he had left speaking these words, there came one of the Jews in the sight of all to sacrifice on the altar which was at Modin, according to the king's commandment. ²⁴ Which thing when Mattathias saw, he was inflamed with zeal, and his reins trembled; neither could he forbear to shew his anger according to judgment: wherefore he ran, and slew him upon the altar. ²⁵ Also the king's commissioner, who compelled men to sacrifice, he killed at that time, and the altar he pulled down. ²⁶ Thus dealt he zealously for the law of God, like as Phinees did unto Zambri the son of Salom. ²⁷ And Mattathias cried throughout the city with a loud voice, saying, Whosoever is zealous of the law, and maintaineth the covenant, let him follow me. ²⁸ So he and his sons fled into the mountains, and left all that ever they had in the city. ²⁹ Then many that sought after justice and judgment went down into the wilderness, to dwell there: ³⁰ Both they, and their children, and their wives, and their cattle; because afflictions increased sore upon them. ³¹ Now when it was told the king's servants, and the host that was at Jerusalem, in the city of David, that certain men, who had broken the king's commandment, were gone down into the secret places in the wilderness, ³² they pursued after them a great number, and having overtaken them, they camped against them, and made war against them on the sabbath day. ³³ And they said unto them, Let that which ye have done hitherto suffice; come forth, and do according to the commandment of the king, and ye shall live. ³⁴ But they said, We will not come forth, neither will we do the king's commandment, to profane the sabbath day. [35] So then they gave them the battle with all speed. [36] Howbeit they answered them not, neither cast they a stone at them, nor stopped the places where they lay hid; [37] but said, Let us die all in our innocency: heaven and earth will testify for us, that ye put us to death wrongfully. [38] So they rose up against them in battle on the sabbath, and they slew them, with their wives and children, and their cattle, to the number of a thousand people. [39] Now when Mattathias and his friends understood hereof, they mourned for them right sore. [40] And one of them said to another, If we all do as our brethren have done, and fight not for our lives and laws against the heathen, they will now quickly root us out of the earth. [41] At that time therefore they decreed, saying, Whosoever shall come to make battle with us on the sabbath day, we will fight against him; neither will we die all, as our brethren that were murdered in the secret places. [42] Then came there unto him a company of Assideans, who were mighty men of Israel, even all such as were voluntarily devoted unto the law. [43] Also all they that fled for persecution joined themselves unto them, and were a stay unto them. [44] So they joined their forces, and smote sinful men in their anger, and wicked men in their wrath: but the rest fled to the heathen for succour. [45] Then Mattathias and his friends went round about, and pulled down the altars: [46] And what children soever they found within the coast of Israel uncircumcised, those they circumcised valiantly. [47] They pursued also after the proud men, and the work prospered in their hand. [48] So they recovered the law out of the hand of the Gentiles, and out of the hand of kings, neither suffered they the sinner to triumph. [49] Now when the time drew near that Mattathias should die, he said unto his sons, Now hath pride and rebuke gotten strength, and the time of destruction, and the wrath of indignation: [50] Now therefore, my sons, be ye zealous for the law, and give your lives for the covenant of your fathers. [51] Call to remembrance what acts our fathers did in their time; so shall ye receive great honour and an everlasting name. [52] Was not Abraham found faithful in temptation, and it was imputed unto him for righteousness? [53] Joseph in the time of his distress kept the commandment, and was made lord of Egypt. [54] Phinees our father in being zealous and fervent obtained the covenant of an everlasting priesthood. [55] Jesus for fulfilling the word was made a judge in Israel. [56] Caleb for bearing witness before the congregation received the heritage of the land. [57] David for being merciful possessed the throne of an everlasting kingdom. [58] Elias for being zealous and fervent for the law was taken up into heaven. [59] Ananias, Azarias, and Misael, by believing were saved out of the flame. [60] Daniel for his innocency was delivered from the mouth of lions. [61] And thus consider ye throughout all ages, that none that put their trust in him shall be overcome. [62] Fear not then the words of a sinful man: for his glory shall be dung and worms. [63] To day he shall be lifted up, and to morrow he shall not be found, because he is returned into his dust, and his thought is come to nothing. [64] Wherefore, ye my sons, be valiant, and shew yourselves men in the behalf of the law; for by it shall ye obtain glory. [65] And behold, I know that your brother Simon is a man of counsel, give ear unto him always: he shall be a father unto you. [66] As for Judas Maccabeus, he hath been mighty and strong, even from his youth up: let him be your captain, and fight the battle of the people. [67] Take also unto you all those that observe the law, and avenge ye the wrong of your people. [68] Recompense fully the heathen, and take heed to the commandments of the law. [69] So he blessed them, and was gathered to his fathers. [70] And he died in the hundred forty and sixth year, and his sons buried him in the sepulchres of his fathers at Modin, and all Israel made great lamentation for him.

3 [1] Then his son Judas, called Maccabeus, rose up in his stead. [2] And all his brethren helped him, and so did all they that held with his father, and they fought with cheerfulness the battle of Israel. [3] So he gat his people great honour, and put on a breastplate as a giant, and girt his warlike harness about him, and he made battles, protecting the host with his sword. [4] In his acts he was like a lion, and like a lion's whelp roaring for his prey. [5] For he pursued the wicked, and sought them out, and burnt up those that vexed his people. [6] Wherefore the wicked shrunk for fear of him, and all the workers of iniquity were troubled, because salvation prospered in his hand. [7] He grieved also many kings, and made Jacob glad with his acts, and his memorial is blessed for ever. [8] Moreover he went through the cities of Juda, destroying the ungodly out of them, and turning away wrath from Israel: [9] So that he was renowned unto the utmost part of the earth, and he received unto him such as were ready to perish. [10] Then Apollonius gathered the Gentiles together, and a great host out of Samaria, to fight against Israel. [11] Which thing when Judas perceived, he went forth to meet him, and so he smote him, and slew him: many also fell down slain, but the rest fled. [12] Wherefore Judas took their spoils, and Apollonius' sword also, and therewith he fought all his life long. [13] Now when Seron, a prince of the army of

Syria, heard say that Judas had gathered unto him a multitude and company of the faithful to go out with him to war; ¹⁴ he said, I will get me a name and honour in the kingdom; for I will go fight with Judas and them that are with him, who despise the king's commandment. ¹⁵ So he made him ready to go up, and there went with him a mighty host of the ungodly to help him, and to be avenged of the children of Israel. ¹⁶ And when he came near to the going up of Bethhoron, Judas went forth to meet him with a small company: ¹⁷ who, when they saw the host coming to meet them, said unto Judas, How shall we be able, being so few, to fight against so great a multitude and so strong, seeing we are ready to faint with fasting all this day? ¹⁸ Unto whom Judas answered, It is no hard matter for many to be shut up in the hands of a few; and with the God of heaven it is all one, to deliver with a great multitude, or a small company: ¹⁹ For the victory of battle standeth not in the multitude of an host; but strength cometh from heaven. ²⁰ They come against us in much pride and iniquity to destroy us, and our wives and children, and to spoil us: ²¹ But we fight for our lives and our laws. ²² Wherefore the Lord himself will overthrow them before our face: and as for you, be ye not afraid of them. ²³ Now as soon as he had left off speaking, he leapt suddenly upon them, and so Seron and his host was overthrown before him. ²⁴ And they pursued them from the going down of Bethhoron unto the plain, where were slain about eight hundred men of them; and the residue fled into the land of the Philistines. ²⁵ Then began the fear of Judas and his brethren, and an exceeding great dread, to fall upon the nations round about them: ²⁶ insomuch as his fame came unto the king, and all nations talked of the battles of Judas. ²⁷ Now when king

Antiochus heard these things, he was full of indignation: wherefore he sent and gathered together all the forces of his realm, even a very strong army. [28] He opened also his treasure, and gave his soldiers pay for a year, commanding them to be ready whensoever he should need them. [29] Nevertheless, when he saw that the money of his treasures failed, and that the tributes in the country were small, because of the dissension and plague, which he had brought upon the land in taking away the laws which had been of old time; [30] he feared that he should not be able to bear the charges any longer, nor to have such gifts to give so liberally as he did before: for he had abounded above the kings that were before him. [31] Wherefore, being greatly perplexed in his mind, he determined to go into Persia, there to take the tributes of the countries, and to gather much money. [32] So he left Lysias, a nobleman, and one of the blood royal, to oversee the affairs of the king from the river Euphrates unto the borders of Egypt: [33] and to bring up his son Antiochus, until he came again. [34] Moreover he delivered unto him the half of his forces, and the elephants, and gave him charge of all things that he would have done, as also concerning them that dwelt in Juda and Jerusalem: [35] To wit, that he should send an army against them to destroy and root out the strength of Israel, and the remnant of Jerusalem, and to take away their memorial from that place; [36] and that he should place strangers in all their quarters, and divide their land by lot. [37] So the king took the half of the forces that remained, and departed from Antioch, his royal city, the hundred forty and seventh year; and having passed the river Euphrates, he went through the high countries. [38] Then Lysias chose Ptolemee the son of Dorymenes, and Nicanor, and

Gorgias, mighty men of the king's friends: ³⁹ And with them he sent forty thousand footmen, and seven thousand horsemen, to go into the land of Juda, and to destroy it, as the king commanded. ⁴⁰ So they went forth with all their power, and came and pitched by Emmaus in the plain country. ⁴¹ And the merchants of the country, hearing the fame of them, took silver and gold very much, with servants, and came into the camp to buy the children of Israel for slaves: a power also of Syria and of the land of the Philistines joined themselves unto them. ⁴² Now when Judas and his brethren saw that miseries were multiplied, and that the forces did encamp themselves in their borders: for they knew how the king had given commandment to destroy the people, and utterly abolish them; ⁴³ they said one to another, Let us restore the decayed fortune of our people, and let us fight for our people and the sanctuary. ⁴⁴ Then was the congregation gathered together, that they might be ready for battle, and that they might pray, and ask mercy and compassion. ⁴⁵ Now Jerusalem lay void as a wilderness, there was none of her children that went in or out: the sanctuary also was trodden down, and aliens kept the strong hold; the heathen had their habitation in that place; and joy was taken from Jacob, and the pipe with the harp ceased. ⁴⁶ Wherefore the Israelites assembled themselves together, and came to Maspha, over against Jerusalem; for in Maspha was the place where they prayed aforetime in Israel. ⁴⁷ Then they fasted that day, and put on sackcloth, and cast ashes upon their heads, and rent their clothes, ⁴⁸ and laid open the book of the law, wherein the heathen had sought to paint the likeness of their images. ⁴⁹ They brought also the priests' garments, and the firstfruits, and the tithes: and the Nazarites they stirred up,

375

who had accomplished their days. ⁵⁰ Then cried they with a loud voice toward heaven, saying, What shall we do with these, and whither shall we carry them away? ⁵¹ For thy sanctuary is trodden down and profaned, and thy priests are in heaviness, and brought low. ⁵² And lo, the heathen are assembled together against us to destroy us: what things they imagine against us, thou knowest. ⁵³ How shall we be able to stand against them, except thou, O God, be our help? ⁵⁴ Then sounded they with trumpets, and cried with a loud voice. ⁵⁵ And after this Judas ordained captains over the people, even captains over thousands, and over hundreds, and over fifties, and over tens. ⁵⁶ But as for such as were building houses, or had betrothed wives, or were planting vineyards, or were fearful, those he commanded that they should return, every man to his own house, according to the law. ⁵⁷ So the camp removed, and pitched upon the south side of Emmaus. ⁵⁸ And Judas said, Arm yourselves, and be valiant men, and see that ye be in readiness against the morning, that ye may fight with these nations, that are assembled together against us to destroy us and our sanctuary: ⁵⁹ For it is better for us to die in battle, than to behold the calamities of our people and our sanctuary. ⁶⁰ Nevertheless, as the will of God is in heaven, so let him do.

4 ¹ Then took Gorgias five thousand footmen, and a thousand of the best horsemen, and removed out of the camp by night; ² to the end he might rush in upon the camp of the Jews, and smite them suddenly. And the men of the fortress were his guides. ³ Now when Judas heard thereof, he himself removed, and the valiant men with him, that he might smite the king's army

which was at Emmaus, ⁴ while as yet the forces were dispersed from the camp. ⁵ In the mean season came Gorgias by night into the camp of Judas: and when he found no man there, he sought them in the mountains: for, said he, These fellows flee from us. ⁶ But as soon as it was day, Judas shewed himself in the plain with three thousand men, who nevertheless had neither armour nor swords to their minds. ⁷ And they saw the camp of the heathen, that it was strong and well harnessed, and compassed round about with horsemen; and these were expert of war. ⁸ Then said Judas to the men that were with him, Fear ye not their multitude, neither be ye afraid of their assault. ⁹ Remember how our fathers were delivered in the Red Sea, when Pharaoh pursued them with an army. ¹⁰ Now therefore let us cry unto heaven, if peradventure the Lord will have mercy upon us, and remember the covenant of our fathers, and destroy this host before our face this day: ¹¹ that so all the heathen may know that there is one who delivereth and saveth Israel. ¹² Then the strangers lifted up their eyes, and saw them coming over against them. ¹³ Wherefore they went out of the camp to battle; but they that were with Judas sounded their trumpets. ¹⁴ So they joined battle, and the heathen being discomfited fled into the plain. ¹⁵ Howbeit all the hindmost of them were slain with the sword: for they pursued them unto Gazera, and unto the plains of Idumea, and Azotus, and Jamnia, so that there were slain of them about three thousand men. ¹⁶ This done, Judas returned again with his host from pursuing them, ¹⁷ and said to the people, Be not greedy of the spoils, inasmuch as there is a battle before us, ¹⁸ and Gorgias and his host are here by us in the mountains: but stand ye now against our enemies, and overcome them, and after this ye may boldly take the spoils. [19] As Judas was yet speaking these words, there appeared a part of them looking out of the mountain: [20] who when they perceived that the Jews had put their host to flight, and were burning the tents; for the smoke that was seen declared what was done: [21] When therefore they perceived these things, they were sore afraid, and seeing also the host of Judas in the plain ready to fight, [22] they fled every one into the land of strangers. [23] Then Judas returned to spoil the tents, where they got much gold and silver, and blue silk, and purple of the sea, and great riches. [24] After this they went home, and sung a song of thanksgiving, and praised the Lord in heaven: because it is good, because his mercy endureth forever. [25] Thus Israel had a great deliverance that day. [26] Now all the strangers that had escaped came and told Lysias what had happened: [27] Who, when he heard thereof, was confounded and discouraged, because neither such things as he would were done unto Israel, nor such things as the king commanded him were come to pass. [28] The next year therefore following, Lysias gathered together threescore thousand choice men of foot, and five thousand horsemen, that he might subdue them. [29] So they came into Idumea, and pitched their tents at Bethsura, and Judas met them with ten thousand men. [30] And when he saw that mighty army, he prayed, and said, Blessed art thou, O Saviour of Israel, who didst quell the violence of the mighty man by the hand of thy servant David, and gavest the host of strangers into the hands of Jonathan the son of Saul, and his armourbearer; [31] shut up this army in the hand of thy people Israel, and let them be confounded in their power and horsemen: [32] Make them to be of no courage, and cause the boldness of their strength to fall away, and let them quake at their

destruction: [33] Cast them down with the sword of them
that love thee, and let all those that know thy name
praise thee with thanksgiving. [34] So they joined battle;
and there were slain of the host of Lysias about five
thousand men, even before them were they slain.
[35] Now when Lysias saw his army put to flight, and the
manliness of Judas' soldiers, and how they were ready
either to live or die valiantly, he went into Antiochia,
and gathered together a company of strangers, and having made his army greater than it was, he purposed to
come again into Judea. [36] Then said Judas and his
brethren, Behold, our enemies are discomfited: let us go
up to cleanse and dedicate the sanctuary. [37] Upon this
all the host assembled themselves together, and went
up into mount Sion. [38] And when they saw the sanctuary desolate, and the altar profaned, and the gates
burned up, and shrubs growing in the courts as in a for-
est, or in one of the mountains, yea, and the priests'
chambers pulled down; [39] they rent their clothes, and
made great lamentation, and cast ashes upon their
heads, [40] and fell down flat to the ground upon their
faces, and blew an alarm with the trumpets, and cried
toward heaven. [41] Then Judas appointed certain men
to fight against those that were in the fortress, until he
had cleansed the sanctuary. [42] So he chose priests of
blameless conversation, such as had pleasure in the
law: [43] who cleansed the sanctuary, and bare out the
defiled stones into an unclean place. [44] And when as
they consulted what to do with the altar of burnt offerings, which was profaned; [45] they thought it best to pull
it down, lest it should be a reproach to them, because
the heathen had defiled it: wherefore they pulled it
down, [46] and laid up the stones in the mountain of the
temple in a convenient place, until there should come

a prophet to shew what should be done with them.
[47] Then they took whole stones according to the law,
and built a new altar according to the former; [48] and
made up the sanctuary, and the things that were within the temple, and hallowed the courts. [49] They made
also new holy vessels, and into the temple they brought
the candlestick, and the altar of burnt offerings, and of
incense, and the table. [50] And upon the altar they
burned incense, and the lamps that were upon the candlestick they lighted, that they might give light in the
temple. [51] Furthermore they set the loaves upon the
table, and spread out the veils, and finished all the
works which they had begun to make. [52] Now on the
five and twentieth day of the ninth month, which is
called the month Casleu, in the hundred forty and
eighth year, they rose up betimes in the morning, [53] and
offered sacrifice according to the law upon the new
altar of burnt offerings, which they had made. [54] Look,
at what time and what day the heathen had profaned
it, even in that was it dedicated with songs, and cith-
erns, and harps, and cymbals. [55] Then all the people fell
upon their faces, worshipping and praising the God of
heaven, who had given them good success. [56] And so
they kept the dedication of the altar eight days, and
offered burnt offerings with gladness, and sacrificed the
sacrifice of deliverance and praise. [57] They decked also
the forefront of the temple with crowns of gold, and
with shields; and the gates and the chambers they
renewed, and hanged doors upon them. [58] Thus was
there very great gladness among the people, for that the
reproach of the heathen was put away. [59] Moreover
Judas and his brethren with the whole congregation of
Israel ordained, that the days of the dedication of the
altar should be kept in their season from year to year by

the space of eight days, from the five and twentieth day of the month Casleu, with mirth and gladness. [60] At that time also they builded up the mount Sion with high walls and strong towers round about, lest the Gentiles should come and tread it down as they had done before. [61] And they set there a garrison to keep it, and fortified Bethsura to preserve it; that the people might have a defence against Idumea.

5 [1] Now when the nations round about heard that the altar was built, and the sanctuary renewed as before, it displeased them very much. [2] Wherefore they thought to destroy the generation of Jacob that was among them, and thereupon they began to slay and destroy the people. [3] Then Judas fought against the children of Esau in Idumea at Arabattine, because they besieged Israel: and he gave them a great overthrow, and abated their courage, and took their spoils. [4] Also he remembered the injury of the children of Bean, who had been a snare and an offence unto the people, in that they lay in wait for them in the ways. [5] He shut them up therefore in the towers, and encamped against them, and destroyed them utterly, and burned the towers of that place with fire, and all that were therein. [6] Afterward he passed over to the children of Ammon, where he found a mighty power, and much people, with Timotheus their captain. [7] So he fought many battles with them, till at length they were discomfited before him; and he smote them. [8] And when he had taken Jazar, with the towns belonging thereto, he returned into Judea. [9] Then the heathen that were at Galaad assembled themselves together against the Israelites that were in their quarters, to destroy them; but they fled to the fortress of Dathema, [10] and sent letters unto

Judas and his brethren, The heathen that are round about us are assembled together against us to destroy us: ¹¹ And they are preparing to come and take the fortress whereunto we are fled, Timotheus being captain of their host. ¹² Come now therefore, and deliver us from their hands, for many of us are slain: ¹³ Yea, all our brethren that were in the places of Tobie are put to death: their wives and their children also they have carried away captives, and borne away their stuff; and they have destroyed there about a thousand men. ¹⁴ While these letters were yet reading, behold, there came other messengers from Galilee with their clothes rent, who reported on this wise, ¹⁵ and said, They of Ptolemais, and of Tyrus, and Sidon, and all Galilee of the Gentiles, are assembled together against us to consume us. ¹⁶ Now when Judas and the people heard these words, there assembled a great congregation together, to consult what they should do for their brethren, that were in trouble, and assaulted of them. ¹⁷ Then said Judas unto Simon his brother, Choose thee out men, and go and deliver thy brethren that are in Galilee, for I and Jonathan my brother will go into the country of Galaad. ¹⁸ So he left Joseph the son of Zacharias, and Azarias, captains of the people, with the remnant of the host in Judea to keep it. ¹⁹ Unto whom he gave commandment, saying, Take ye the charge of this people, and see that ye make not war against the heathen until the time that we come again. ²⁰ Now unto Simon were given three thousand men to go into Galilee, and unto Judas eight thousand men for the country of Galaad. ²¹ Then went Simon into Galilee, where he fought many battles with the heathen, so that the heathen were discomfited by him. ²² And he pursued them unto the gate of Ptolemais; and there were slain of the heathen about three thousand men, whose spoils he took. ²³ And those that were in Galilee, and in Arbattis, with their wives and their children, and all that they had, took he away with him, and brought them into Judea with great joy. ²⁴ Judas Maccabeus also and his brother Jonathan went over Jordan, and travelled three days' journey in the wilderness, ²⁵ where they met with the Nabathites, who came unto them in a peaceable manner, and told them every thing that had happened to their brethren in the land of Galaad: ²⁶ and how that many of them were shut up in Bosora, and Bosor, and Alema, Casphor, Maked, and Carnaim; all these cities are strong and great: ²⁷ and that they were shut up in the rest of the cities of the country of Galaad, and that against to morrow they had appointed to bring their host against the forts, and to take them, and to destroy them all in one day. ²⁸ Hereupon Judas and his host turned suddenly by the way of the wilderness unto Bosora; and when he had won the city, he slew all the males with the edge of the sword, and took all their spoils, and burned the city with fire. ²⁹ From whence he removed by night, and went till he came to the fortress. ³⁰ And betimes in the morning they looked up, and, behold, there was an innumerable people bearing ladders and other engines of war, to take the fortress: for they assaulted them. ³¹ When Judas therefore saw that the battle was begun, and that the cry of the city went up to heaven, with trumpets, and a great sound, ³² he said unto his host, Fight this day for your brethren. ³³ So he went forth behind them in three companies, who sounded their trumpets, and cried with prayer. ³⁴ Then the host of Timotheus, knowing that it was Maccabeus, fled from him: wherefore he smote them with a great slaughter; so that there

were killed of them that day about eight thousand men.
³⁵ This done, Judas turned aside to Maspha; and after
he had assaulted it, he took it, and slew all the males
therein, and received the spoils thereof, and burnt it
with fire. ³⁶ From thence went he, and took Casphon,
Maged, Bosor, and the other cities of the country of
Galaad. ³⁷ After these things gathered Timotheus
another host, and encamped against Raphon beyond
the brook. ³⁸ So Judas sent men to espy the host, who
brought him word, saying, All the heathen that be
round about us are assembled unto them, even a very
great host. ³⁹ He hath also hired the Arabians to help
them, and they have pitched their tents beyond the
brook, ready to come and fight against thee. Upon this
Judas went to meet them. ⁴⁰ Then Timotheus said unto
the captains of his host, When Judas and his host come
near the brook, if he pass over first unto us, we shall not
be able to withstand him; for he will mightily prevail
against us: ⁴¹ But if he be afraid, and camp beyond the
river, we shall go over unto him, and prevail against
him. ⁴² Now when Judas came near the brook, he
caused the scribes of the people to remain by the brook:
unto whom he gave commandment, saying, Suffer no
man to remain in the camp, but let all come to the battle. ⁴³ So he went first over unto them, and all the people after him: then all the heathen, being discomfited
before him, cast away their weapons, and fled unto the
temple that was at Carnaim. ⁴⁴ But they took the city,
and burned the temple with all that were therein. Thus
was Carnaim subdued, neither could they stand any
longer before Judas. ⁴⁵ Then Judas gathered together all
the Israelites that were in the country of Galaad, from
the least unto the greatest, even their wives, and their
children, and their stuff, a very great host, to the end

they might come into the land of Judea. ⁴⁶ Now when they came unto Ephron, (this was a great city in the way as they should go, very well fortified) they could not turn from it, either on the right hand or the left, but must needs pass through the midst of it. ⁴⁷ Then they of the city shut them out, and stopped up the gates with stones. ⁴⁸ Whereupon Judas sent unto them in peaceable manner, saying, Let us pass through your land to go into our own country, and none shall do you any hurt; we will only pass through on foot: howbeit they would not open unto him. ⁴⁹ Wherefore Judas commanded a proclamation to be made throughout the host, that every man should pitch his tent in the place where he was. ⁵⁰ So the soldiers pitched, and assaulted the city all that day and all that night, till at length the city was delivered into his hands: ⁵¹ Who then slew all the males with the edge of the sword, and rased the city, and took the spoils thereof, and passed through the city over them that were slain. ⁵² After this went they over Jordan into the great plain before Bethsan. ⁵³ And Judas gathered together those that came behind, and exhorted the people all the way through, till they came into the land of Judea. ⁵⁴ So they went up to mount Sion with joy and gladness, where they offered burnt offerings, because not one of them were slain until they had returned in peace. ⁵⁵ Now what time as Judas and Jonathan were in the land of Galaad, and Simon his brother in Galilee before Ptolemais, ⁵⁶ Joseph the son of Zacharias, and Azarias, captains of the garrisons, heard of the valiant acts and warlike deeds which they had done. ⁵⁷ Wherefore they said, Let us also get us a name, and go fight against the heathen that are round about us. ⁵⁸ So when they had given charge unto the garrison that was with them, they went toward Jamnia. [59] Then came Gorgias and his men out of the city to fight against them. [60] And so it was, that Joseph and Azarias were put to flight, and pursued unto the borders of Judea: and there were slain that day of the people of Israel about two thousand men. [61] Thus was there a great overthrow among the children of Israel, because they were not obedient unto Judas and his brethren, but thought to do some valiant act. [62] Moreover these men came not of the seed of those, by whose hand deliverance was given unto Israel. [63] Howbeit the man Judas and his brethren were greatly renowned in the sight of all Israel, and of all the heathen, wheresoever their name was heard of; [64] insomuch as the people assembled unto them with joyful acclamations. [65] Afterward went Judas forth with his brethren and fought against the children of Esau in the land towards the south, where he smote Hebron, and the towns thereof, and pulled down the fortress of it, and burned the towers thereof round about. [66] From thence he removed to go into the land of the Philistines, and passed through Samaria. [67] At that time certain priests, desirous to shew their valour, were slain in battle, for that they went out to fight unadvisedly. [68] So Judas turned to Azotus in the land of the Philistines, and when he had pulled down their altars, and burned their carved images with fire, and spoiled their cities, he returned into the land of Judea.

6 [1] About that time king Antiochus travelling through the high countries heard say, that Elymais in the country of Persia was a city greatly renowned for riches, silver, and gold; [2] and that there was in it a very rich temple, wherein were coverings of gold, and breastplates, and shields, which Alexander, son of Philip, the

Macedonian king, who reigned first among the Grecians, had left there. ³ Wherefore he came and sought to take the city, and to spoil it; but he was not able, because they of the city, having had warning thereof, ⁴ rose up against him in battle: so he fled, and departed thence with great heaviness, and returned to Babylon. ⁵ Moreover there came one who brought him tidings into Persia, that the armies, which went against the land of Judea, were put to flight: ⁶ And that Lysias, who went forth first with a great power, was driven away of the Jews; and that they were made strong by the armour, and power, and store of spoils, which they had gotten of the armies, whom they had destroyed: ⁷ Also that they had pulled down the abomination, which he had set up upon the altar in Jerusalem, and that they had compassed about the sanctuary with high walls, as before, and his city Bethsura. ⁸ Now when the king heard these words, he was astonished and sore moved: whereupon he laid him down upon his bed, and fell sick for grief, because it had not befallen him as he looked for. ⁹ And there he continued many days: for his grief was ever more and more, and he made account that he should die. ¹⁰ Wherefore he called for all his friends, and said unto them, The sleep is gone from mine eyes, and my heart faileth for very care. ¹¹ And I thought with myself, Into what tribulation am I come, and how great a flood of misery is it, wherein now I am! for I was bountiful and beloved in my power. ¹² But now I remember the evils that I did at Jerusalem, and that I took all the vessels of gold and silver that were therein, and sent to destroy the inhabitants of Judea without a cause. ¹³ I perceive therefore that for this cause these troubles are come upon me, and, behold, I perish through great grief in a strange land. ¹⁴ Then called he for Philip, one of his friends, who he made ruler over all his realm, [15] and gave him the crown, and his robe, and his signet, to the end he should bring up his son Antiochus, and nourish him up for the kingdom. [16] So king Antiochus died there in the hundred forty and ninth year. [17] Now when Lysias knew that the king was dead, he set up Antiochus his son, whom he had brought up, being young, to reign in his stead, and his name he called Eupator. [18] About this time they that were in the tower shut up the Israelites round about the sanctuary, and sought always their hurt, and the strengthening of the heathen. [19] Wherefore Judas, purposing to destroy them, called all the people together to besiege them. [20] So they came together, and besieged them in the hundred and fiftieth year, and he made mounts for shot against them, and other engines. [21] Howbeit, certain of them that were besieged got forth, unto whom some ungodly men of Israel joined themselves: [22] And they went unto the king, and said, How long will it be ere thou execute judgment, and avenge our brethren? [23] We have been willing to serve thy father, and to do as he would have us, and to obey his commandments; [24] for which cause they of our nation besiege the tower, and are alienated from us: moreover as many of us as they could light on they slew, and spoiled our inheritance. [25] Neither have they stretched out their hand against us only, but also against their borders. [26] And, behold, this day are they besieging the tower at Jerusalem, to take it: the sanctuary also and Bethsura have they fortified. [27] Wherefore, if thou dost not prevent them quickly, they will do greater things than these, neither shalt thou be able to rule them. [28] Now when the king heard this, he was angry, and gathered together all his friends, and the captains of his army, and those that had charge of the horse. [29] There came also unto him from other kingdoms, and from isles of the sea, bands of hired soldiers. [30] So that the number of his army was an hundred thousand footmen, and twenty thousand horsemen, and two and thirty elephants exercised in battle. [31] These went through Idumea, and pitched against Bethsura, which they assaulted many days, making engines of war; but they of Bethsura came out, and burned them with fire, and fought valiantly. [32] Upon this Judas removed from the tower, and pitched in Bathzacharias, over against the king's camp. [33] Then the king rising very early marched fiercely with his host toward Bathzacharias, where his armies made them ready to battle, and sounded the trumpets. [34] And to the end they might provoke the elephants to fight, they shewed them the blood of grapes and mulberries. [35] Moreover they divided the beasts among the armies, and for every elephant they appointed a thousand men, armed with coats of mail, and with helmets of brass on their heads; and besides this, for every beast were ordained five hundred horsemen of the best. [36] These were ready at every occasion: wheresoever the beast was, and whithersoever the beast went, they went also, neither departed they from him. [37] And upon the beasts were there strong towers of wood, which covered every one of them, and were girt fast unto them with devices: there were also upon every one two and thirty strong men, that fought upon them, besides the Indian that ruled him. [38] As for the remnant of the horsemen, they set them on this side and that side at the two parts of the host, giving them signs what to do, and being harnessed all over amidst the ranks. [39] Now when the sun shone upon the shields of gold and brass, the mountains glistened therewith, and shined like lamps of fire. [40] So part of the king's army being spread upon the high mountains, and part on the valleys below, they marched on safely and in order. [41] Wherefore all that heard the noise of their multitude, and the marching of the company, and the rattling of the harness, were moved: for the army was very great and mighty. [42] Then Judas and his host drew near, and entered into battle, and there were slain of the king's army six hundred men. [43] Eleazar also, surnamed Savaran, perceiving that one of the beasts, armed with royal harness, was higher than all the rest, and supposing that the king was upon him, [44] put himself in jeopardy, to the end that he might deliver his people, and get him a perpetual name: [45] Wherefore he ran upon him courageously through the midst of the battle, slaying on the right hand and on the left, so that they were divided from him on both sides. [46] Which done, he crept under the elephant, and thrust him under, and slew him: whereupon the elephant fell down upon him, and there he died. [47] Howbeit the rest of the Jews seeing the strength of the king, and the violence of his forces, turned away from them. [48] Then the king's army went up to Jerusalem to meet them, and the king pitched his tents against Judea, and against mount Sion. [49] But with them that were in Bethsura he made peace: for they came out of the city, because they had no victuals there to endure the siege, it being a year of rest to the land. [50] So the king took Bethsura, and set a garrison there to keep it. [51] As for the sanctuary, he besieged it many days: and set there artillery with engines and instruments to cast fire and stones, and pieces to cast darts and slings. [52] Whereupon they also made engines against their engines, and held them to battle a long season. [53] Yet at the last, their vessels being without victuals, (for that it was the seventh year, and they in Judea that were delivered from the Gentiles, had eaten up the residue of the store;) [54] there were but a few left in the sanctuary, because the famine did so prevail against them, that they were fain to disperse themselves, every man to his own place. [55] At that time Lysias heard say, that Philip, whom Antiochus the king, while he lived, had appointed to bring up his son Antiochus, that he might be king, [56] was returned out of Persia and Media, and the king's host also that went with him, and that he sought to take unto him the ruling of the affairs. [57] Wherefore he went in all haste, and said to the king and the captains of the host and the company, We decay daily, and our victuals are but small, and the place we lay siege unto is strong, and the affairs of the kingdom lie upon us: [58] Now therefore let us be friends with these men, and make peace with them, and with all their nation; [59] and covenant with them, that they shall live after their laws, as they did before: for they are therefore displeased, and have done all these things, because we abolished their laws. [60] So the king and the princes were content: wherefore he sent unto them to make peace; and they accepted thereof. [61] Also the king and the princes made an oath unto them: whereupon they went out of the strong hold. [62] Then the king entered into mount Sion; but when he saw the strength of the place, he broke his oath that he had made, and gave commandment to pull down the wall round about. [63] Afterward departed he in all haste, and returned unto Antiochia, where he found Philip to be master of the city: so he fought against him, and took the city by force.

7 [1] In the hundred and one and fiftieth year Demetrius the son of Seleucus departed from Rome, and came up with a few men unto a city of the sea coast, and reigned

there. [2] And as he entered into the palace of his ancestors, so it was, that his forces had taken Antiochus and Lysias, to bring them unto him. [3] Wherefore, when he knew it, he said, Let me not see their faces. [4] So his host slew them. Now when Demetrius was set upon the throne of his kingdom, [5] there came unto him all the wicked and ungodly men of Israel, having Alcimus, who was desirous to be high priest, for their captain: [6] And they accused the people to the king, saying, Judas and his brethren have slain all thy friends, and driven us out of our own land. [7] Now therefore send some man whom thou trustest, and let him go and see what havock he hath made among us, and in the king's land, and let him punish them with all them that aid them. [8] Then the king chose Bacchides, a friend of the king, who ruled beyond the flood, and was a great man in the kingdom, and faithful to the king. [9] And him he sent with that wicked Alcimus, whom he made high priest, and commanded that he should take vengeance of the children of Israel. [10] So they departed, and came with a great power into the land of Judea, where they sent messengers to Judas and his brethren with peaceable words deceitfully. [11] But they gave no heed to their words; for they saw that they were come with a great power. [12] Then did there assemble unto Alcimus and Bacchides a company of scribes, to require justice. [13] Now the Assideans were the first among the children of Israel that sought peace of them: [14] For said they, One that is a priest of the seed of Aaron is come with this army, and he will do us no wrong. [15] So he spake unto them, peaceably, and sware unto them, saying, We will procure the harm neither of you nor your friends. [16] Whereupon they believed him: howbeit he took of them threescore men, and slew them in one day, according to the words which he wrote, [17] The flesh of thy saints have they cast out, and their blood have they shed round about Jerusalem, and there was none to bury them. [18] Wherefore the fear and dread of them fell upon all the people, who said, There is neither truth nor righteousness in them; for they have broken the covenant and oath that they made. [19] After this, removed Bacchides from Jerusalem, and pitched his tents in Bezeth, where he sent and took many of the men that had forsaken him, and certain of the people also, and when he had slain them, he cast them into the great pit. [20] Then committed he the country to Alcimus, and left with him a power to aid him: so Bacchides went to the king. [21] But Alcimus contended for the high priesthood. [22] And unto him resorted all such as troubled the people, who, after they had gotten the land of Juda into their power, did much hurt in Israel. [23] Now when Judas saw all the mischief that Alcimus and his company had done among the Israelites, even above the heathen, [24] he went out into all the coasts of Judea round about, and took vengeance of them that had revolted from him, so that they durst no more go forth into the country. [25] On the other side, when Alcimus saw that Judas and his company had gotten the upper hand, and knew that he was not able to abide their force, he went again to the king, and said all the worst of them that he could. [26] Then the king sent Nicanor, one of his honourable princes, a man that bare deadly hate unto Israel, with commandment to destroy the people. [27] So Nicanor came to Jerusalem with a great force; and sent unto Judas and his brethren deceitfully with friendly words, saying, [28] Let there be no battle between me and you; I will come with a few men, that I may see you in peace. [29] He came therefore to Judas, and they saluted one another peaceably. Howbeit the enemies were prepared to take away Judas by violence. 30 Which thing after it was known to Judas, to wit, that he came unto him with deceit, he was sore afraid of him, and would see his face no more. 31 Nicanor also, when he saw that his counsel was discovered, went out to fight against Judas beside Capharsalama: 32 where there were slain of Nicanor's side about five thousand men, and the rest fled into the city of David. 33 After this went Nicanor up to mount Sion, and there came out of the sanctuary certain of the priests and certain of the elders of the people, to salute him peaceably, and to shew him the burnt sacrifice that was offered for the king. 34 But he mocked them, and laughed at them, and abused them shamefully, and spake proudly, 35 and sware in his wrath, saying, Unless Judas and his host be now delivered into my hands, if ever I come again in safety, I will burn up this house: and with that he went out in a great rage. 36 Then the priests entered in, and stood before the altar and the temple, weeping, and saying, 37 Thou, O Lord, didst choose this house to be called by thy name, and to be a house of prayer and petition for thy people: 38 Be avenged of this man and his host, and let them fall by the sword: remember their blasphemies, and suffer them not to continue any longer. 39 So Nicanor went out of Jerusalem, and pitched his tents in Bethhoron, where an host out of Syria met him. 40 But Judas pitched in Adasa with three thousand men, and there he prayed, saying, 41 O Lord, when they that were sent from the king of the Assyrians blasphemed, thine angel went out, and smote an hundred fourscore and five thousand of them. 42 Even so destroy thou this host before us this day, that the rest may know that he hath spoken blasphemously against thy sanctuary, and judge thou him according to his wickedness. [43] So the thirteenth day of the month Adar the hosts joined battle: but Nicanor's host was discomfited, and he himself was first slain in the battle. [44] Now when Nicanor's host saw that he was slain, they cast away their weapons, and fled. [45] Then they pursued after them a day's journey, from Adasa unto Gazera, sounding an alarm after them with their trumpets. [46] Whereupon they came forth out of all the towns of Judea round about, and closed them in; so that they, turning back upon them that pursued them, were all slain with the sword, and not one of them was left. [47] Afterwards they took the spoils, and the prey, and smote off Nicanor's head, and his right hand, which he stretched out so proudly, and brought them away, and hanged them up toward Jerusalem. [48] For this cause the people rejoiced greatly, and they kept that day a day of great gladness. [49] Moreover, they ordained to keep yearly this day, being the thirteenth of Adar. [50] Thus the land of Juda was in rest a little while.

8 [1] Now Judas had heard of the fame of the Romans, that they were mighty and valiant men, and such as would lovingly accept all that joined themselves unto them, and make a league of amity with all that came unto them; [2] and that they were men of great valour. It was told him also of their wars and noble acts which they had done among the Galatians, and how they had conquered them, and brought them under tribute; [3] and what they had done in the country of Spain, for the winning of the mines of the silver and gold which is there; [4] and that by their policy and patience they had conquered all the place, though it were very far from them; and the kings also that came against them from

the uttermost part of the earth, till they had discomfited them, and given them a great overthrow, so that the rest did give them tribute every year: [5] Besides this, how they had discomfited in battle Philip, and Perseus, king of the Citims, with others that lifted up themselves against them, and had overcome them: [6] How also Antiochus, the great king of Asia, that came against them in battle, having an hundred and twenty elephants, with horsemen, and chariots, and a very great army, was discomfited by them; [7] and how they took him alive, and covenanted that he and such as reigned after him should pay a great tribute, and give hostages, and that which was agreed upon, [8] and the country of India, and Media, and Lydia, and of the goodliest countries, which they took of him, and gave to king Eumenes: [9] Moreover how the Grecians had determined to come and destroy them; [10] and that they, having knowledge thereof, sent against them a certain captain, and fighting with them slew many of them, and carried away captives their wives and their children, and spoiled them, and took possession of their lands, and pulled down their strong holds, and brought them to be their servants unto this day: [11] It was told him besides, how they destroyed and brought under their dominion all other kingdoms and isles that at any time resisted them; [12] but with their friends and such as relied upon them they kept amity: and that they had conquered kingdoms both far and nigh, insomuch as all that heard of their name were afraid of them: [13] Also that, whom they would help to a kingdom, those reign; and whom again they would, they displace: finally, that they were greatly exalted: [14] Yet for all this none of them wore a crown or was clothed in purple, to be magnified thereby: [15] Moreover how they had made for themselves a senate house, wherein three hundred and twenty men sat in council daily, consulting always for the people, to the end they might be well ordered: [16] And that they committed their government to one man every year, who ruled over all their country, and that all were obedient to that one, and that there was neither envy nor emulation among them. [17] In consideration of these things, Judas chose Eupolemus the son of John, the son of Accos, and Jason the son of Eleazar, and sent them to Rome, to make a league of amity and confederacy with them, [18] and to intreat them that they would take the yoke from them; for they saw that the kingdom of the Grecians did oppress Israel with servitude. [19] They went therefore to Rome, which was a very great journey, and came into the senate, where they spake and said, [20] Judas Maccabeus with his brethren, and the people of the Jews, have sent us unto you, to make a confederacy and peace with you, and that we might be registered your confederates and friends. [21] So that matter pleased the Romans well. [22] And this is the copy of the epistle which the senate wrote back again on tables of brass, and sent to Jerusalem, that there they might have by them a memorial of peace and confederacy: [23] Good success be to the Romans, and to the people of the Jews, by sea and by land for ever: the sword also and enemy be far from them. [24] If there come first any war upon the Romans or any of their confederates throughout all their dominion, [25] the people of the Jews shall help them, as the time shall be appointed, with all their heart: [26] Neither shall they give any thing unto them that make war upon them, or aid them with victuals, weapons, money, or ships, as it hath seemed good unto the Romans; but they shall keep their covenants without taking any thing therefore. ²⁷ In the same manner also, if war come first upon the nation of the Jews, the Romans shall help them with all their heart, according as the time shall be appointed them: ²⁸ Neither shall victuals be given to them that take part against them, or weapons, or money, or ships, as it hath seemed good to the Romans; but they shall keep their covenants, and that without deceit. ²⁹ According to these articles did the Romans make a covenant with the people of the Jews. ³⁰ Howbeit, if hereafter the one party or the other shall think meet to add or diminish any thing, they may do it at their pleasures, and whatsoever they shall add or take away shall be ratified. ³¹ And as touching the evils that Demetrius doeth to the Jews, we have written unto him, saying, Wherefore hast thou made thy yoke heavy upon our friends and confederates the Jews? ³² If therefore they complain any more against thee, we will do them justice, and fight with thee by sea and by land.

9 ¹ Furthermore, when Demetrius heard that Nicanor and his host were slain in battle, he sent Bacchides and Alcimus into the land of Judea the second time, and with them the chief strength of his host: ² who went forth by the way that leadeth to Galgala, and pitched their tents before Masaloth, which is in Arbela, and after they had won it, they slew much people. ³ also the first month of the hundred fifty and second year they encamped before Jerusalem: ⁴ from whence they removed, and went to Berea, with twenty thousand footmen and two thousand horsemen. ⁵ Now Judas had pitched his tents at Eleasa, and three thousand chosen men with him: ⁶ who seeing the multitude of the other army to be so great were sore afraid; whereupon many

conveyed themselves out of the host, insomuch as there abode of them no more but eight hundred men. ⁷ When Judas therefore saw that his host slipped away, and that the battle pressed upon him, he was sore troubled in mind, and much distressed, for that he had no time to gather them together. ⁸ Nevertheless, unto them that remained he said, Let us arise and go up against our enemies, if peradventure we may be able to fight with them. ⁹ But they dehorted him, saying, We shall never be able: let us now rather save our lives, and hereafter we will return with our brethren, and fight against them: for we are but few. ¹⁰ Then Judas said, God forbid that I should do this thing, and flee away from them; if our time be come, let us die manfully for our brethren, and let us not stain our honour. ¹¹ With that the host of Bacchides removed out of their tents, and stood over against them, their horsemen being divided into two troops, and their slingers and archers going before the host, and they that marched in the foreward were all mighty men. ¹² As for Bacchides, he was in the right wing: so the host drew near on the two parts, and sounded their trumpets. ¹³ They also of Judas' side, even they sounded their trumpets also, so that the earth shook at the noise of the armies, and the battle continued from morning till night. ¹⁴ Now when Judas perceived that Bacchides and the strength of his army were on the right side, he took with him all the hardy men, ¹⁵ who discomfited the right wing, and pursued them unto the mount Azotus. ¹⁶ But when they of the left wing saw that they of the right wing were discomfited, they followed upon Judas and those that were with him hard at the heels from behind. ¹⁷ Whereupon there was a sore battle, insomuch as many were slain on both parts. ¹⁸ Judas also was killed, and the remnant fled. 19 Then Jonathan and Simon took Judas their brother, and buried him in the sepulchre of his fathers in Modin. 20 Moreover they bewailed him, and all Israel made great lamentation for him, and mourned many days, saying, 21 How is the valiant man fallen, that delivered Israel! 22 As for the other things concerning Judas and his wars, and the noble acts which he did, and his greatness, they are not written: for they were very many. 23 Now after the death of Judas the wicked began to put forth their heads in all the coasts of Israel, and there arose up all such as wrought iniquity. 24 In those days also was there a very great famine, by reason whereof the country revolted, and went with them. 25 Then Bacchides chose the wicked men, and made them lords of the country. 26 And they made enquiry and search for Judas' friends, and brought them unto Bacchides, who took vengeance of them, and used them despitefully. 27 So was there a great affliction in Israel, the like whereof was not since the time that a prophet was not seen among them. 28 For this cause all Judas' friends came together, and said unto Jonathan, 29 Since thy brother Judas died, we have no man like him to go forth against our enemies, and Bacchides, and against them of our nation that are adversaries to us. 30 Now therefore we have chosen thee this day to be our prince and captain in his stead, that thou mayest fight our battles. 31 Upon this Jonathan took the governance upon him at that time, and rose up instead of his brother Judas. 32 But when Bacchides gat knowledge thereof, he sought for to slay him. 33 Then Jonathan, and Simon his brother, and all that were with him, perceiving that, fled into the wilderness of Thecoe, and pitched their tents by the water of the pool Asphar. 34 Which when Bacchides understood, he came near to

Jordan with all his host upon the sabbath day. ³⁵ Now Jonathan had sent his brother John, a captain of the people, to pray his friends the Nabathites, that they might leave with them their carriage, which was much. ³⁶ But the children of Jambri came out of Medaba, and took John, and all that he had, and went their way with it. ³⁷ After this came word to Jonathan and Simon his brother, that the children of Jambri made a great marriage, and were bringing the bride from Nadabatha with a great train, as being the daughter of one of the great princes of Chanaan. ³⁸ Therefore they remembered John their brother, and went up, and hid themselves under the covert of the mountain: ³⁹ where they lifted up their eyes, and looked, and, behold, there was much ado and great carriage: and the bridegroom came forth, and his friends and brethren, to meet them with drums, and instruments of music, and many weapons. ⁴⁰ Then Jonathan and they that were with him rose up against them from the place where they lay in ambush, and made a slaughter of them in such sort, as many fell down dead, and the remnant fled into the mountain, and they took all their spoils. ⁴¹ Thus was the marriage turned into mourning, and the noise of their melody into lamentation. ⁴² So when they had avenged fully the blood of their brother, they turned again to the marsh of Jordan. ⁴³ Now when Bacchides heard thereof, he came on the sabbath day unto the banks of Jordan with a great power. ⁴⁴ Then Jonathan said to his company, Let us go up now and fight for our lives, for it standeth not with us to day, as in time past: ⁴⁵ For, behold, the battle is before us and behind us, and the water of Jordan on this side and that side, the marsh likewise and wood, neither is there place for us to turn aside. ⁴⁶ Wherefore cry ye now unto heaven, that ye may be delivered from the hand of your enemies. [47] With that they joined battle, and Jonathan stretched forth his hand to smite Bacchides, but he turned back from him. [48] Then Jonathan and they that were with him leapt into Jordan, and swam over unto the other bank: howbeit the other passed not over Jordan unto them. [49] So there were slain of Bacchides' side that day about a thousand men. [50] Afterward returned Bacchides to Jerusalem, and repaired the strong cites in Judea; the fort in Jericho, and Emmaus, and Bethhoron, and Bethel, and Thamnatha, Pharathoni, and Taphon, these did he strengthen with high walls, with gates and with bars. [51] And in them he set a garrison, that they might work malice upon Israel. [52] He fortified also the city Bethsura, and Gazara, and the tower, and put forces in them, and provision of victuals. [53] Besides, he took the chief men's sons in the country for hostages, and put them into the tower at Jerusalem to be kept. [54] Moreover in the hundred fifty and third year, in the second month, Alcimus commanded that the wall of the inner court of the sanctuary should be pulled down; he pulled down also the works of the prophets. [55] And as he began to pull down, even at that time was Alcimus plagued, and his enterprizes hindered: for his mouth was stopped, and he was taken with a palsy, so that he could no more speak any thing, nor give order concerning his house. [56] So Alcimus died at that time with great torment. [57] Now when Bacchides saw that Alcimus was dead, he returned to the king: whereupon the land of Judea was in rest two years. [58] Then all the ungodly men held a council, saying, Behold, Jonathan and his company are at ease, and dwell without care: now therefore we will bring Bacchides hither, who shall take them all in one night.

⁵⁹ So they went and consulted with him. ⁶⁰ Then removed he, and came with a great host, and sent letters privily to his adherents in Judea, that they should take Jonathan and those that were with him: howbeit they could not, because their counsel was known unto them. ⁶¹ Wherefore they took of the men of the country, that were authors of that mischief, about fifty persons, and slew them. ⁶² Afterward Jonathan, and Simon, and they that were with him, got them away to Bethbasi, which is in the wilderness, and they repaired the decays thereof, and made it strong. ⁶³ Which thing when Bacchides knew, he gathered together all his host, and sent word to them that were of Judea. ⁶⁴ Then went he and laid siege against Bethbasi; and they fought against it a long season and made engines of war. ⁶⁵ But Jonathan left his brother Simon in the city, and went forth himself into the country, and with a certain number went he forth. ⁶⁶ And he smote Odonarkes and his brethren, and the children of Phasiron in their tent. ⁶⁷ And when he began to smite them, and came up with his forces, Simon and his company went out of the city, and burned up the engines of war, ⁶⁸ and fought against Bacchides, who was discomfited by them, and they afflicted him sore: for his counsel and travail was in vain. ⁶⁹ Wherefore he was very wroth at the wicked men that gave him counsel to come into the country, inasmuch as he slew many of them, and purposed to return into his own country. ⁷⁰ Whereof when Jonathan had knowledge, he sent ambassadors unto him, to the end he should make peace with him, and deliver them the prisoners. ⁷¹ Which thing he accepted, and did according to his demands, and sware unto him that he would never do him harm all the days of his life. ⁷² When therefore he had restored unto him the pris-

oners that he had taken aforetime out of the land of Judea, he returned and went his way into his own land, neither came he any more into their borders. ⁷³ Thus the sword ceased from Israel: but Jonathan dwelt at Machmas, and began to govern the people; and he destroyed the ungodly men out of Israel.

10 ¹ In the hundred and sixtieth year, Alexander, the son of Antiochus surnamed Epiphanes, went up and took Ptolemais: for the people had received him, by means whereof he remained there. ² Now when king Demetrius heard thereof, he gathered together an exceeding great host, and went forth against him to fight. ³ Moreover, Demetrius sent letters unto Jonathan with loving words, so as he magnified him. ⁴ For, said he, Let us first make peace with him, before he join with Alexander against us: ⁵ else he will remember all the evils that we have done against him, and against his brethren and his people. ⁶ Wherefore he gave him authority to gather together an host, and to provide weapons, that he might aid him in battle: he commanded also that the hostages that were in the tower should be delivered him. ⁷ Then came Jonathan to Jerusalem, and read the letters in the audience of all the people, and of them that were in the tower: ⁸ who were sore afraid, when they heard that the king had given him authority to gather together an host. ⁹ Whereupon they of the tower delivered their hostages unto Jonathan, and he delivered them unto their parents. ¹⁰ This done, Jonathan settled himself in Jerusalem, and began to build and repair the city. ¹¹ And he commanded the workmen to build the walls and the mount Sion round about with square stones for fortification; and they did so. ¹² Then the strangers, that were in the fortresses which Bacchides had built, fled away; [13] insomuch as every man left his place, and went into his own country. [14] Only at Bethsura certain of those that had forsaken the law and the commandments remained still: for it was their place of refuge. [15] Now when king Alexander had heard what promises Demetrius had sent unto Jonathan: when also it was told him of the battles and noble acts which he and his brethren had done, and of the pains that they had endured, [16] he said, Shall we find such another man? now therefore we will make him our friend and confederate. [17] Upon this he wrote a letter, and sent it unto him, according to these words, saying, [18] King Alexander to his brother Jonathan sendeth greeting: [19] We have heard of thee, that thou art a man of great power, and meet to be our friend. [20] Wherefore now this day we ordain thee to be the high priest of thy nation, and to be called the king's friend; (and therewithal he sent him a purple robe and a crown of gold:) and require thee to take our part, and keep friendship with us. [21] So in the seventh month of the hundred and sixtieth year, at the feast of the tabernacles, Jonathan put on the holy robe, and gathered together forces, and provided much armour. [22] Whereof when Demetrius heard, he was very sorry, and said, [23] What have we done, that Alexander hath prevented us in making amity with the Jews to strengthen himself? [24] I also will write unto them words of encouragement, and promise them dignities and gifts, that I may have their aid. [25] He sent unto them therefore to this effect: King Demetrius unto the people of the Jews sendeth greeting: [26] Whereas ye have kept covenants with us, and continued in our friendship, not joining yourselves with our enemies, we have heard hereof, and are glad. [27] Wherefore now continue ye still to be faithful unto us, and we will well recompense you for the things ye do in our behalf, [28] and will grant you many immunities, and give you rewards. [29] And now do I free you, and for your sake I release all the Jews, from tributes, and from the customs of salt, and from crown taxes, [30] and from that which appertaineth unto me to receive for the third part of the seed, and the half of the fruit of the trees, I release it from this day forth, so that they shall not be taken of the land of Judea, nor of the three governments which are added thereunto out of the country of Samaria and Galilee, from this day forth for evermore. [31] Let Jerusalem also be holy and free, with the borders thereof, both from tenths and tributes. [32] And as for the tower which is at Jerusalem, I yield up authority over it, and give it to the high priest, that he may set in it such men as he shall choose to keep it. [33] Moreover I freely set at liberty every one of the Jews that were carried captives out of the land of Judea into any part of my kingdom, and I will that all my officers remit the tributes even of their cattle. [34] Furthermore I will that all the feasts, and sabbaths, and new moons, and solemn days, and the three days before the feast, and the three days after the feast, shall be all days of immunity and freedom for all the Jews in my realm. [35] Also, no man shall have authority to meddle with or to molest any of them in any matter. [36] I will further, that there be enrolled among the king's forces about thirty thousand men of the Jews, unto whom pay shall be given, as belongeth to all the king's forces. [37] And of them some shall be placed in the king's strong holds, of whom also some shall be set over the affairs of the kingdom, which are of trust: and I will that their overseers and governors be of themselves, and that they live after their own laws, even as the king hath commanded in the land of Judea.

³⁸ And concerning the three governments that are added to Judea from the country of Samaria, let them be joined with Judea, that they may be reckoned to be under one, nor bound to obey other authority than the high priest's. ³⁹ As for Ptolemais, and the land pertaining thereto, I give it as a free gift to the sanctuary at Jerusalem for the necessary expences of the sanctuary. ⁴⁰ Moreover I give every year fifteen thousand shekels of silver out of the king's accounts from the places appertaining. ⁴¹ And all the overplus, which the officers paid not in as in former time, from henceforth shall be given toward the works of the temple. ⁴² And besides this, the five thousand shekels of silver, which they took from the uses of the temple out of the accounts year by year, even those things shall be released, because they appertain to the priests that minister. ⁴³ And whosoever they be that flee unto the temple at Jerusalem, or be within the liberties thereof, being indebted unto the king, or for any other matter, let them be at liberty, and all that they have in my realm. ⁴⁴ For the building also and repairing of the works of the sanctuary, expences shall be given of the king's accounts. ⁴⁵ Yea, and for the building of the walls of Jerusalem, and the fortifying thereof round about, expences shall be given out of the king's accounts, as also for the building of the walls in Judea. ⁴⁶ Now when Jonathan and the people heard these words, they gave no credit unto them, nor received them, because they remembered the great evil that he had done in Israel; for he had afflicted them very sore. ⁴⁷ But with Alexander they were well pleased, because he was the first that entreated of true peace with them, and they were confederate with him always. ⁴⁸ Then gathered king Alexander great forces, and camped over against

Demetrius. [49] And after the two kings had joined battle, Demetrius' host fled: but Alexander followed after him, and prevailed against them. [50] And he continued the battle very sore until the sun went down: and that day was Demetrius slain. [51] Afterward Alexander sent ambassadors to Ptolemee king of Egypt with a message to this effect: [52] Forasmuch as I am come again to my realm, and am set in the throne of my progenitors, and have gotten the dominion, and overthrown Demetrius, and recovered our country; [53] for after I had joined battle with him, both he and his host was discomfited by us, so that we sit in the throne of his kingdom: [54] Now therefore let us make a league of amity together, and give me now thy daughter to wife: and I will be thy son in law, and will give both thee and her gifts according to thy dignity. [55] Then Ptolemee the king gave answer, saying, Happy be the day wherein thou didst return into the land of thy fathers, and sattest in the throne of their kingdom. [56] And now will I do to thee, as thou hast written: meet me therefore at Ptolemais, that we may see one another; for I will marry my daughter to thee according to thy desire. [57] So Ptolemee went out of Egypt with his daughter Cleopatra, and they came unto Ptolemais in the hundred threescore and second year: [58] Where king Alexander meeting him, gave unto him his daughter Cleopatra, and celebrated her marriage at Ptolemais with great glory, as the manner of kings is. [59] Now king Alexander had written unto Jonathan, that he should come and meet him. [60] Who thereupon went honourably to Ptolemais, where he met the two kings, and gave them and their friends silver and gold, and many presents, and found favour in their sight. [61] At that time certain pestilent fellows of Israel, men of a wicked life, assembled themselves against him, to accuse him: but the king would not hear them. ⁶² Yea more than that, the king commanded to take off his garments, and clothe him in purple: and they did so. ⁶³ And he made him sit by himself, and said unto his princes, Go with him into the midst of the city, and make proclamation, that no man complain against him of any matter, and that no man trouble him for any manner of cause. ⁶⁴ Now when his accusers saw that he was honored according to the proclamation, and clothed in purple, they fled all away. ⁶⁵ So the king honoured him, and wrote him among his chief friends, and made him a duke, and partaker of his dominion. ⁶⁶ Afterward Jonathan returned to Jerusalem with peace and gladness. ⁶⁷ Furthermore in the hundred threescore and fifth year came Demetrius son of Demetrius out of Crete into the land of his fathers: ⁶⁸ Whereof when king Alexander heard tell, he was right sorry, and returned into Antioch. ⁶⁹ Then Demetrius made Apollonius the governor of Celosyria his general, who gathered together a great host, and camped in Jamnia, and sent unto Jonathan the high priest, saying, ⁷⁰ Thou alone liftest up thyself against us, and I am laughed to scorn for thy sake, and reproached: and why dost thou vaunt thy power against us in the mountains? ⁷¹ Now therefore, if thou trustest in thine own strength, come down to us into the plain field, and there let us try the matter together: for with me is the power of the cities. ⁷² Ask and learn who I am, and the rest that take our part, and they shall tell thee that thy foot is not able to stand before our face; for thy fathers have been twice put to flight in their own land. ⁷³ Wherefore now thou shalt not be able to abide the horsemen and so great a power in the plain, where is neither stone nor flint, nor place to flee unto. ⁷⁴ So when Jonathan heard these words of Apollonius, he was moved in his mind, and choosing ten thousand men he went out of Jerusalem, where Simon his brother met him for to help him. [75] And he pitched his tents against Joppa: but they of Joppa shut him out of the city, because Apollonius had a garrison there. [76] Then Jonathan laid siege unto it: whereupon they of the city let him in for fear: and so Jonathan won Joppa. [77] Whereof when Apollonius heard, he took three thousand horsemen, with a great host of footmen, and went to Azotus as one that journeyed, and therewithal drew him forth into the plain, because he had a great number of horsemen, in whom he put his trust. [78] Then Jonathan followed after him to Azotus, where the armies joined battle. [79] Now Apollonius had left a thousand horsemen in ambush. [80] And Jonathan knew that there was an ambushment behind him; for they had compassed in his host, and cast darts at the people from morning till evening. [81] But the people stood still, as Jonathan had commanded them: and so the enemies' horses were tired. [82] Then brought Simon forth his host, and set them against the footmen (for the horsemen were spent), who were discomfited by him, and fled. [83] The horsemen also, being scattered in the field, fled to Azotus, and went into Bethdagon, their idol's temple, for safety. [84] But Jonathan set fire on Azotus, and the cities round about it, and took their spoils; and the temple of Dagon, with them that were fled into it, he burned with fire. [85] Thus there were burned and slain with the sword well nigh eight thousand men. [86] And from thence Jonathan removed his host, and camped against Ascalon, where the men of the city came forth, and met him with great pomp. [87] After this returned Jonathan and his host unto Jerusalem, having many spoils. ⁸⁸ Now when king Alexander heard these things, he honoured Jonathan yet more. ⁸⁹ And sent him a buckle of gold, as the use is to be given to such as are of the king's blood: he gave him also Accaron with the borders thereof in possession.

11 ¹ And the king of Egypt gathered together a great host, like the sand that lieth upon the sea shore, and many ships, and went about through deceit to get Alexander's kingdom, and join it to his own. ² Whereupon he took his journey into Syria in peaceable manner, so as they of the cities opened unto him, and met him: for king Alexander had commanded them so to do, because he was his father in law. ³ Now as Ptolemee entered into the cities, he set in every one of them a garrison of soldiers to keep it. ⁴ And when he came near to Azotus, they shewed him the temple of Dagon that was burnt, and Azotus and the suburbs thereof that were destroyed, and the bodies that were cast abroad and them that he had burnt in the battle; for they had made heaps of them by the way where he should pass. ⁵ Also they told the king whatsoever Jonathan had done, to the intent he might blame him: but the king held his peace. ⁶ Then Jonathan met the king with great pomp at Joppa, where they saluted one another, and lodged. ⁷ Afterward Jonathan, when he had gone with the king to the river called Eleutherus, returned again to Jerusalem. ⁸ King Ptolemee therefore, having gotten the dominion of the cities by the sea unto Seleucia upon the sea coast, imagined wicked counsels against Alexander. ⁹ Whereupon he sent ambassadors unto king Demetrius, saying, Come, let us make a league betwixt us, and I will give thee my daughter whom Alexander hath, and thou shalt reign in thy

father's kingdom: [10] For I repent that I gave my daughter unto him, for he sought to slay me. [11] Thus did he slander him, because he was desirous of his kingdom. [12] Wherefore he took his daughter from him, and gave her to Demetrius, and forsook Alexander, so that their hatred was openly known. [13] Then Ptolemee entered into Antioch, where he set two crowns upon his head, the crown of Asia, and of Egypt. [14] In the mean season was king Alexander in Cilicia, because those that dwelt in those parts had revolted from him. [15] But when Alexander heard of this, he came to war against him: whereupon king Ptolemee brought forth his host, and met him with a mighty power, and put him to flight. [16] So Alexander fled into Arabia, there to be defended; but king Ptolemee was exalted: [17] For Zabdiel the Arabian took off Alexander's head, and sent it unto Ptolemee. [18] King Ptolemee also died the third day after, and they that were in the strong holds were slain one of another. [19] By this means Demetrius reigned in the hundred threescore and seventh year. [20] At the same time Jonathan gathered together them that were in Judea to take the tower that was in Jerusalem: and he made many engines of war against it. [21] Then certain ungodly persons, who hated their own people, went unto the king, and told him that Jonathan besieged the tower. [22] Whereof when he heard, he was angry, and immediately removing, he came to Ptolemais, and wrote unto Jonathan, that he should not lay siege to the tower, but come and speak with him at Ptolemais in great haste. [23] Nevertheless Jonathan, when he heard this, commanded to besiege it still: and he chose certain of the elders of Israel and the priests, and put himself in peril; [24] and took silver and gold, and raiment, and divers presents besides, and went to

Ptolemais unto the king, where he found favour in his sight. ²⁵ And though certain ungodly men of the people had made complaints against him, ²⁶ yet the king entreated him as his predecessors had done before, and promoted him in the sight of all his friends, ²⁷ and confirmed him in the high priesthood, and in all the honours that he had before, and gave him preeminence among his chief friends. ²⁸ Then Jonathan desired the king, that he would make Judea free from tribute, as also the three governments, with the country of Samaria; and he promised him three hundred talents. ²⁹ So the king consented, and wrote letters unto Jonathan of all these things after this manner: ³⁰ King Demetrius unto his brother Jonathan, and unto the nation of the Jews, sendeth greeting: ³¹ We send you here a copy of the letter which we did write unto our cousin Lasthenes concerning you, that ye might see it. ³² King Demetrius unto his father Lasthenes sendeth greeting: ³³ We are determined to do good to the people of the Jews, who are our friends, and keep covenants with us, because of their good will toward us. ³⁴ Wherefore we have ratified unto them the borders of Judea, with the three governments of Apherema and Lydda and Ramathem, that are added unto Judea from the country of Samaria, and all things appertaining unto them, for all such as do sacrifice in Jerusalem, instead of the payments which the king received of them yearly aforetime out of the fruits of the earth and of trees. ³⁵ And as for other things that belong unto us, of the tithes and customs pertaining unto us, as also the salt pits, and the crown taxes, which are due unto us, we discharge them of them all for their relief. ³⁶ And nothing hereof shall be revoked from this time forth for ever. ³⁷ Now therefore see that thou make a copy of these things, and let it be delivered unto Jonathan, and set upon the holy mount in a conspicuous place. [38] After this, when king Demetrius saw that the land was quiet before him, and that no resistance was made against him, he sent away all his forces, every one to his own place, except certain bands of strangers, whom he had gathered from the isles of the heathen: wherefore all the forces of his fathers hated him. [39] Moreover, there was one Tryphon, that had been of Alexander's part afore, who, seeing that all the host murmured against Demetrius, went to Simalcue the Arabian that brought up Antiochus the young son of Alexander, [40] and lay sore upon him to deliver him this young Antiochus, that he might reign in his father's stead: he told him therefore all that Demetrius had done, and how his men of war were at enmity with him, and there he remained a long season. [41] In the mean time Jonathan sent unto king Demetrius, that he would cast those of the tower out of Jerusalem, and those also in the fortresses: for they fought against Israel. [42] So Demetrius sent unto Jonathan, saying, I will not only do this for thee and thy people, but I will greatly honour thee and thy nation, if opportunity serve. [43] Now therefore thou shalt do well, if thou send me men to help me; for all my forces are gone from me. [44] Upon this Jonathan sent him three thousand strong men unto Antioch: and when they came to the king, the king was very glad of their coming. [45] Howbeit they that were of the city gathered themselves together into the midst of the city, to the number of an hundred and twenty thousand men, and would have slain the king. [46] Wherefore the king fled into the court, but they of the city kept the passages of the city, and began to fight. [47] Then the king called to the Jews for help, who came unto him all at once, and dispersing themselves through the city slew that day in the city to the number of an hundred thousand. ⁴⁸ Also they set fire on the city, and gat many spoils that day, and delivered the king. ⁴⁹ So when they of the city saw that the Jews had got the city as they would, their courage was abated: wherefore they made supplication to the king, and cried, saying, ⁵⁰ Grant us peace, and let the Jews cease from assaulting us and the city. ⁵¹ With that they cast away their weapons, and made peace; and the Jews were honoured in the sight of the king, and in the sight of all that were in his realm; and they returned to Jerusalem, having great spoils. ⁵² So king Demetrius sat on the throne of his kingdom, and the land was quiet before him. ⁵³ Nevertheless he dissembled in all that ever he spake, and estranged himself from Jonathan, neither rewarded he him according to the benefits which he had received of him, but troubled him very sore. ⁵⁴ After this returned Tryphon, and with him the young child Antiochus, who reigned, and was crowned. ⁵⁵ Then there gathered unto him all the men of war, whom Demetrius had put away, and they fought against Demetrius, who turned his back and fled. ⁵⁶ Moreover Tryphon took the elephants, and won Antioch. ⁵⁷ At that time young Antiochus wrote unto Jonathan, saying, I confirm thee in the high priesthood, and appoint thee ruler over the four governments, and to be one of the king's friends. ⁵⁸ Upon this he sent him golden vessels to be served in, and gave him leave to drink in gold, and to be clothed in purple, and to wear a golden buckle. ⁵⁹ His brother Simon also he made captain from the place called the ladder of Tyrus unto the borders of Egypt. ⁶⁰ Then Jonathan went forth, and passed through the cities beyond the water, and all the forces of Syria gathered themselves unto him for to help him: and when he came to Ascalon, they of the city met him honourably. 61 From whence he went to Gaza, but they of Gaza shut him out; wherefore he laid siege unto it, and burned the suburbs thereof with fire, and spoiled them. 62 Afterward, when they of Gaza made supplication unto Jonathan, he made peace with them, and took the sons of their chief men for hostages, and sent them to Jerusalem, and passed through the country unto Damascus. 63 Now when Jonathan heard that Demetrius' princes were come to Cades, which is in Galilee, with a great power, purposing to remove him out of the country, 64 he went to meet them, and left Simon his brother in the country. 65 Then Simon encamped against Bethsura and fought against it a long season, and shut it up: 66 But they desired to have peace with him, which he granted them, and then put them out from thence, and took the city, and set a garrison in it. 67 As for Jonathan and his host, they pitched at the water of Gennesar, from whence betimes in the morning they gat them to the plain of Nasor. 68 And, behold, the host of strangers met them in the plain, who, having laid men in ambush for him in the mountains, came themselves over against him. 69 So when they that lay in ambush rose out of their places and joined battle, all that were of Jonathan's side fled; 70 insomuch as there was not one of them left, except Mattathias the son of Absalom, and Judas the son of Calphi, the captains of the host. 71 Then Jonathan rent his clothes, and cast earth upon his head, and prayed. 72 Afterwards turning again to battle, he put them to flight, and so they ran away. 73 Now when his own men that were fled saw this, they turned again unto him, and with him pursued them to Cades, even unto their own tents, and there they camped. ⁷⁴ So there were slain of the heathen that day about three thousand men: but Jonathan returned to Jerusalem.

12

¹ Now when Jonathan saw that the time served him, he chose certain men, and sent them to Rome, for to confirm and renew the friendship that they had with them. ² He sent letters also to the Lacedemonians, and to other places, for the same purpose. ³ So they went unto Rome, and entered into the senate, and said, Jonathan the high priest, and the people of the Jews, sent us unto you, to the end ye should renew the friendship, which ye had with them, and league, as in former time. ⁴ Upon this the Romans gave them letters unto the governors of every place, that they should bring them into the land of Judea peaceably. ⁵ And this is the copy of the letters which Jonathan wrote to the Lacedemonians: ⁶ Jonathan the high priest, and the elders of the nation, and the priests, and the other people of the Jews, unto the Lacedemonians their brethren send greeting: ⁷ There were letters sent in times past unto Onias the high priest from Darius, who reigned then among you, to signify that ye are our brethren, as the copy here underwritten doth specify. ⁸ At which time Onias entreated the ambassador that was sent honourably, and received the letters, wherein declaration was made of the league and friendship. ⁹ Therefore we also, albeit we need none of these things, for that we have the holy books of scripture in our hands to comfort us, ¹⁰ have nevertheless attempted to send unto you for the renewing of brotherhood and friendship, lest we should become strangers unto you altogether: for there is a long time passed since ye sent unto us. ¹¹ We therefore at all times without ceasing, both in our feasts, and

other convenient days, do remember you in the sacrifices which we offer, and in our prayers, as reason is, and as it becometh us to think upon our brethren: [12] And we are right glad of your honour. [13] As for ourselves, we have had great troubles and wars on every side, forsomuch as the kings that are round about us have fought against us. [14] Howbeit we would not be troublesome unto you, nor to others of our confederates and friends, in these wars: [15] For we have help from heaven that succoureth us, so as we are delivered from our enemies, and our enemies are brought under foot. [16] For this cause we chose Numenius the son of Antiochus, and Antipater the son of Jason, and sent them unto the Romans, to renew the amity that we had with them, and the former league. [17] We commanded them also to go unto you, and to salute you, and to deliver you our letters concerning the renewing of our brotherhood. [18] Wherefore now ye shall do well to give us an answer thereto. [19] And this is the copy of the letters which Oniares sent. [20] Areus king of the Lacedemonians to Onias the high priest, greeting: [21] It is found in writing, that the Lacedemonians and Jews are brethren, and that they are of the stock of Abraham: [22] Now therefore, since this is come to our knowledge, ye shall do well to write unto us of your prosperity. [23] We do write back again to you, that your cattle and goods are ours, and ours are yours. We do command therefore our ambassadors to make report unto you on this wise. [24] Now when Jonathan heard that Demetrius' princes were come to fight against him with a greater host than afore, [25] he removed from Jerusalem, and met them in the land of Amathis: for he gave them no respite to enter his country. [26] He sent spies also unto their tents, who came again, and told them that they were appointed to come upon them in the night season. ²⁷ Wherefore so soon as the sun was down, Jonathan commanded his men to watch, and to be in arms, that all the night long they might be ready to fight: also he sent forth sentinels round about the host. ²⁸ But when the adversaries heard that Jonathan and his men were ready for battle, they feared, and trembled in their hearts, and they kindled fires in their camp. ²⁹ Howbeit Jonathan and his company knew it not till the morning: for they saw the lights burning. ³⁰ Then Jonathan pursued after them, but overtook them not: for they were gone over the river Eleutherus. ³¹ Wherefore Jonathan turned to the Arabians, who were called Zabadeans, and smote them, and took their spoils. ³² And removing thence, he came to Damascus, and so passed through all the country. ³³ Simon also went forth, and passed through the country unto Ascalon, and the holds there adjoining from whence he turned aside to Joppa, and won it. ³⁴ For he had heard that they would deliver the hold unto them that took Demetrius' part; wherefore he set a garrison there to keep it. ³⁵ After this came Jonathan home again, and calling the elders of the people together, he consulted with them about building strong holds in Judea, ³⁶ and making the walls of Jerusalem higher, and raising a great mount between the tower and the city, for to separate it from the city, that so it might be alone, that men might neither sell nor buy in it. ³⁷ Upon this they came together to build up the city, forasmuch as part of the wall toward the brook on the east side was fallen down, and they repaired that which was called Caphenatha. ³⁸ Simon also set up Adida in Sephela, and made it strong with gates and bars. ³⁹ Now Tryphon went about to get the kingdom of Asia, and to kill

Antiochus the king, that he might set the crown upon his own head. [40] Howbeit he was afraid that Jonathan would not suffer him, and that he would fight against him; wherefore he sought a way how to take Jonathan, that he might kill him. So he removed, and came to Bethsan. [41] Then Jonathan went out to meet him with forty thousand men chosen for the battle, and came to Bethsan. [42] Now when Tryphon saw that Jonathan came with so great a force, he durst not stretch his hand against him; [43] but received him honourably, and commended him unto all his friends, and gave him gifts, and commanded his men of war to be as obedient unto him, as to himself. [44] Unto Jonathan also he said, Why hast thou brought all this people to so great trouble, seeing there is no war betwixt us? [45] Therefore send them now home again, and choose a few men to wait on thee, and come thou with me to Ptolemais, for I will give it thee, and the rest of the strong holds and forces, and all that have any charge: as for me, I will return and depart: for this is the cause of my coming. [46] So Jonathan, believing him, did as he bade him, and sent away his host, who went into the land of Judea. [47] And with himself he retained but three thousand men, of whom he sent two thousand into Galilee, and one thousand went with him. [48] Now as soon as Jonathan entered into Ptolemais, they of Ptolemais shut the gates and took him, and all them that came with him they slew with the sword. [49] Then sent Tryphon an host of footmen and horsemen into Galilee, and into the great plain, to destroy all Jonathan's company. [50] But when they knew that Jonathan and they that were with him were taken and slain, they encouraged one another; and went close together, prepared to fight. [51] They therefore that followed upon them, perceiving that they were ready to fight for their lives, turned back again. [52] Whereupon they all came into the land of Judea peaceably, and there they bewailed Jonathan, and them that were with him, and they were sore afraid; wherefore all Israel made great lamentation. [53] Then all the heathen that were round about then sought to destroy them: for said they, They have no captain, nor any to help them: now therefore let us make war upon them, and take away their memorial from among men.

13

[1] Now when Simon heard that Tryphon had gathered together a great host to invade the land of Judea, and destroy it, [2] and saw that the people was in great trembling and fear, he went up to Jerusalem, and gathered the people together, [3] and gave them exhortation, saying, Ye yourselves know what great things I, and my brethren, and my father's house, have done for the laws and the sanctuary, the battles also and troubles which we have seen. [4] By reason whereof all my brethren are slain for Israel's sake, and I am left alone. [5] Now therefore be it far from me, that I should spare mine own life in any time of trouble: for I am no better than my brethren. [6] Doubtless I will avenge my nation, and the sanctuary, and our wives, and our children: for all the heathen are gathered to destroy us of very malice. [7] Now as soon as the people heard these words, their spirit revived. [8] And they answered with a loud voice, saying, Thou shalt be our leader instead of Judas and Jonathan thy brother. [9] Fight thou our battles, and whatsoever thou commandest us, that will we do. [10] So then he gathered together all the men of war, and made haste to finish the walls of Jerusalem, and he fortified it round about. [11] Also he sent Jonathan the son of Absalom, and with him a great power, to Joppa: who casting out

them that were therein, remained there in it. [12] So Tryphon removed from Ptolemais with a great power to invade the land of Judea, and Jonathan was with him in ward. [13] But Simon pitched his tents at Adida, over against the plain. [14] Now when Tryphon knew that Simon was risen up instead of his brother Jonathan, and meant to join battle with him, he sent messengers unto him, saying, [15] Whereas we have Jonathan thy brother in hold, it is for money that he is owing unto the king's treasure, concerning the business that was committed unto him. [16] Wherefore now send an hundred talents of silver, and two of his sons for hostages, that when he is at liberty he may not revolt from us, and we will let him go. [17] Hereupon Simon, albeit he perceived that they spake deceitfully unto him, yet sent he the money and the children, lest peradventure he should procure to himself great hatred of the people, [18] who might have said, Because I sent him not the money and the children, therefore is Jonathan dead. [19] So he sent them the children and the hundred talents: howbeit Tryphon dissembled, neither would he let Jonathan go. [20] And after this came Tryphon to invade the land, and destroy it, going round about by the way that leadeth unto Adora: but Simon and his host marched against him in every place, wheresoever he went. [21] Now they that were in the tower sent messengers unto Tryphon, to the end that he should hasten his coming unto them by the wilderness, and send them victuals. [22] Wherefore Tryphon made ready all his horsemen to come that night: but there fell a very great snow, by reason whereof he came not. So he departed, and came into the country of Galaad. [23] And when he came near to Bascama he slew Jonathan, who was buried there. [24] Afterward Tryphon returned and went into his own land. ²⁵ Then sent Simon, and took the bones of Jonathan his brother, and buried them in Modin, the city of his fathers. ²⁶ And all Israel made great lamentation for him, and bewailed him many days. ²⁷ Simon also built a monument upon the sepulchre of his father and his brethren, and raised it aloft to the sight, with hewn stone behind and before. ²⁸ Moreover he set up seven pyramids, one against another, for his father, and his mother, and his four brethren. ²⁹ And in these he made cunning devices, about the which he set great pillars, and upon the pillars he made all their armour for a perpetual memory, and by the armour ships carved, that they might be seen of all that sail on the sea. ³⁰ This is the sepulchre which he made at Modin, and it standeth yet unto this day. ³¹ Now Tryphon dealt deceitfully with the young king Antiochus, and slew him. ³² And he reigned in his stead, and crowned himself king of Asia, and brought a great calamity upon the land. ³³ Then Simon built up the strong holds in Judea, and fenced them about with high towers, and great walls, and gates, and bars, and laid up victuals therein. ³⁴ Moreover Simon chose men, and sent to king Demetrius, to the end he should give the land an immunity, because all that Tryphon did was to spoil. ³⁵ Unto whom king Demetrius answered and wrote after this manner: ³⁶ King Demetrius unto Simon the high priest, and friend of kings, as also unto the elders and nation of the Jews, sendeth greeting: ³⁷ The golden crown, and the scarlet robe, which ye sent unto us, we have received: and we are ready to make a stedfast peace with you, yea, and to write unto our officers, to confirm the immunities which we have granted. ³⁸ And whatsoever covenants we have made with you shall stand; and the strong holds, which ye have builded, shall be your own. ³⁹ As for any oversight or fault committed unto this day, we forgive it, and the crown tax also, which ye owe us: and if there were any other tribute paid in Jerusalem, it shall no more be paid. ⁴⁰ And look who are meet among you to be in our court, let them be enrolled, and let there be peace betwixt us. ⁴¹ Thus the yoke of the heathen was taken away from Israel in the hundred and seventieth year. ⁴² Then the people of Israel began to write in their instruments and contracts, In the first year of Simon the high priest, the governor and leader of the Jews. ⁴³ In those days Simon camped against Gaza and besieged it round about; he made also an engine of war, and set it by the city, and battered a certain tower, and took it. ⁴⁴ And they that were in the engine leaped into the city; whereupon there was a great uproar in the city: ⁴⁵ insomuch as the people of the city rent their clothes, and climbed upon the walls with their wives and children, and cried with a loud voice, beseeching Simon to grant them peace. ⁴⁶ And they said, Deal not with us according to our wickedness, but according to thy mercy. ⁴⁷ So Simon was appeased toward them, and fought no more against them, but put them out of the city, and cleansed the houses wherein the idols were, and so entered into it with songs and thanksgiving. ⁴⁸ Yea, he put all uncleanness out of it, and placed such men there as would keep the law, and made it stronger than it was before, and built therein a dwellingplace for himself. ⁴⁹ They also of the tower in Jerusalem were kept so strait that they could neither come forth, nor go into the country, nor buy, nor sell: wherefore they were in great distress for want of victuals, and a great number of them perished through famine. ⁵⁰ Then cried they to Simon, beseeching him to be at one with them:

which thing he granted them; and when he had put them out from thence, he cleansed the tower from pollutions: [51] and entered into it the three and twentieth day of the second month in the hundred seventy and first year, with thanksgiving, and branches of palm trees, and with harps, and cymbals, and with viols, and hymns, and songs: because there was destroyed a great enemy out of Israel. [52] He ordained also that that day should be kept every year with gladness. Moreover the hill of the temple that was by the tower he made stronger than it was, and there he dwelt himself with his company. [53] And when Simon saw that John his son was a valiant man, he made him captain of all the hosts; and he dwelt in Gazara.

14 [1] Now in the hundred threescore and twelfth year king Demetrius gathered his forces together, and went into Media to get him help to fight against Tryphone. [2] But when Arsaces, the king of Persia and Media, heard that Demetrius was entered within his borders, he sent one of his princes to take him alive: [3] who went and smote the host of Demetrius, and took him, and brought him to Arsaces, by whom he was put in ward. [4] As for the land of Judea, that was quiet all the days of Simon; for he sought the good of his nation in such wise, as that evermore his authority and honour pleased them well. [5] And as he was honourable in all his acts, so in this, that he took Joppa for an haven, and made an entrance to the isles of the sea, [6] and enlarged the bounds of his nation, and recovered the country, [7] and gathered together a great number of captives, and had the dominion of Gazara, and Bethsura, and the tower, out of the which he took all uncleanness, neither was there any that resisted him. [8] Then did they till their ground in peace, and the earth gave her increase, and the trees of the field their fruit. ⁹ The ancient men sat all in the streets, communing together of good things, and the young men put on glorious and warlike apparel. ¹⁰ He provided victuals for the cities, and set in them all manner of munition, so that his honourable name was renowned unto the end of the world. ¹¹ He made peace in the land, and Israel rejoiced with great joy: ¹² For every man sat under his vine and his fig tree, and there was none to fray them: ¹³ Neither was there any left in the land to fight against them: yea, the kings themselves were overthrown in those days. ¹⁴ Moreover he strengthened all those of his people that were brought low: the law he searched out; and every contemner of the law and wicked person he took away. ¹⁵ He beautified the sanctuary, and multiplied the vessels of the temple. ¹⁶ Now when it was heard at Rome, and as far as Sparta, that Jonathan was dead, they were very sorry. ¹⁷ But as soon as they heard that his brother Simon was made high priest in his stead, and ruled the country, and the cities therein: ¹⁸ They wrote unto him in tables of brass, to renew the friendship and league which they had made with Judas and Jonathan his brethren: ¹⁹ Which writings were read before the congregation at Jerusalem. ²⁰ And this is the copy of the letters that the Lacedemonians sent; The rulers of the Lacedemonians, with the city, unto Simon the high priest, and the elders, and priests, and residue of the people of the Jews, our brethren, send greeting: ²¹ The ambassadors that were sent unto our people certified us of your glory and honour: wherefore we were glad of their coming, ²² and did register the things that they spake in the council of the people in this manner; Numenius son of Antiochus, and Antipater son of Jason, the Jews' ambassadors, came unto us to renew the friendship they had with us. ²³ And it pleased the people to entertain the men honourably, and to put the copy of their ambassage in public records, to the end the people of the Lacedemonians might have a memorial thereof: furthermore we have written a copy thereof unto Simon the high priest. ²⁴ After this, Simon sent Numenius to Rome with a great shield of gold of a thousand pound weight to confirm the league with them. ²⁵ Whereof when the people heard, they said, What thanks shall we give to Simon and his sons? ²⁶ For he and his brethren and the house of his father have established Israel, and chased away in fight their enemies from them, and confirmed their liberty. ²⁷ So then they wrote it in tables of brass, which they set upon pillars in mount Sion: and this is the copy of the writing; The eighteenth day of the month Elul, in the hundred threescore and twelfth year, being the third year of Simon the high priest, ²⁸ at Saramel in the great congregation of the priests, and people, and rulers of the nation, and elders of the country, were these things notified unto us. ²⁹ Forasmuch as oftentimes there have been wars in the country, wherein for the maintenance of their sanctuary, and the law, Simon the son of Mattathias, of the posterity of Jarib, together with his brethren, put themselves in jeopardy, and resisting the enemies of their nation, did their nation great honour: ³⁰ (For after that Jonathan, having gathered his nation together, and been their high priest, was added to his people, ³¹ their enemies prepared to invade their country, that they might destroy it, and lay hands on the sanctuary: ³² At which time Simon rose up, and fought for his nation, and spent much of his own substance, and armed the valiant men of his nation, and gave them wages, [33] and fortified the cities of Judea, together with Bethsura, that lieth upon the borders of Judea, where the armour of the enemies had been before; but he set a garrison of Jews there: [34] Moreover, he fortified Joppa, which lieth upon the sea, and Gazara, that bordereth upon Azotus, where the enemies had dwelt before: but he placed Jews there, and furnished them with all things convenient for the reparation thereof.) [35] The people therefore, seeing the acts of Simon, and unto what glory he thought to bring his nation, made him their governor and chief priest, because he had done all these things, and for the justice and faith which he kept to his nation, and for that he sought by all means to exalt his people. [36] For in his time things prospered in his hands, so that the heathen were taken out of their country, and they also that were in the city of David in Jerusalem, who had made themselves a tower, out of which they issued, and polluted all about the sanctuary, and did much hurt in the holy place: [37] But he placed Jews therein, and fortified it for the safety of the country and the city, and raised up the walls of Jerusalem. [38] King Demetrius also confirmed him in the high priesthood according to those things, [39] and made him one of his friends, and honoured him with great honour. [40] For he had heard say, that the Romans had called the Jews their friends and confederates and brethren; and that they had entertained the ambassadors of Simon honourably; [41] also that the Jews and priests were well pleased that Simon should be their governor and high priest for ever, until there should arise a faithful prophet; [42] moreover, that he should be their captain, and should take charge of the sanctuary, to set them over their works, and over the country, and over the armour, and over the fortresses, that, I say, he should take charge of the sanctuary; ⁴³ besides this, that he should be obeyed of every man, and that all the writings in the country should be made in his name, and that he should be clothed in purple, and wear gold: ⁴⁴ Also that it should be lawful for none of the people or priests to break any of these things, or to gainsay his words, or to gather an assembly in the country without him, or to be clothed in purple, or wear a buckle of gold; ⁴⁵ and whosoever should do otherwise, or break any of these things, he should be punished. ⁴⁶ Thus it liked all the people to deal with Simon, and do as hath been said. ⁴⁷ Then Simon accepted hereof, and was well pleased to be high priest, and captain and governor of the Jews and priests, and to defend them all. ⁴⁸ So they commanded that this writing should be put in tables of brass, and that they should be set up within the compass of the sanctuary in a conspicuous place; ⁴⁹ also that the copies thereof should be laid up in the treasury, to the end that Simon and his sons might have them.

15 ¹ Moreover Antiochus, son of Demetrius the king, sent letters from the isles of the sea unto Simon the priest and prince of the Jews, and to all the people; ² the contents whereof were these: King Antiochus to Simon the high priest and prince of his nation, and to the people of the Jews, greeting: ³ Forasmuch as certain pestilent men have usurped the kingdom of our fathers, and my purpose is to challenge it again, that I may restore it to the old estate, and to that end have gathered a multitude of foreign soldiers together, and prepared ships of war; ⁴ my meaning also being to go through the country, that I may be avenged of them that have destroyed it, and made many cities in the kingdom des-

olate: [5] Now therefore I confirm unto thee all the oblations which the kings before me granted thee, and whatsoever gifts besides they granted. [6] I give thee leave also to coin money for thy country with thine own stamp. [7] And as concerning Jerusalem and the sanctuary, let them be free; and all the armour that thou hast made, and fortresses that thou hast built, and keepest in thine hands, let them remain unto thee. [8] And if anything be, or shall be, owing to the king, let it be forgiven thee from this time forth for evermore. [9] Furthermore, when we have obtained our kingdom, we will honour thee, and thy nation, and thy temple, with great honour, so that your honour shall be known throughout the world. [10] In the hundred threescore and fourteenth year went Antiochus into the land of his fathers: at which time all the forces came together unto him, so that few were left with Tryphon. [11] Wherefore being pursued by king Antiochus, he fled unto Dora, which lieth by the sea side: [12] For he saw that troubles came upon him all at once, and that his forces had forsaken him. [13] Then camped Antiochus against Dora, having with him an hundred and twenty thousand men of war, and eight thousand horsemen. [14] And when he had compassed the city round about, and joined ships close to the town on the sea side, he vexed the city by land and by sea, neither suffered he any to go out or in. [15] In the mean season came Numenius and his company from Rome, having letters to the kings and countries; wherein were written these things: [16] Lucius, consul of the Romans unto king Ptolemee, greeting: [17] The Jews' ambassadors, our friends and confederates, came unto us to renew the old friendship and league, being sent from Simon the high priest, and from the people of the Jews: [18] And they brought a shield of gold of a thousand pound. [19] We thought it good therefore to write unto the kings and countries, that they should do them no harm, nor fight against them, their cities, or countries, nor yet aid their enemies against them. [20] It seemed also good to us to receive the shield of them. [21] If therefore there be any pestilent fellows, that have fled from their country unto you, deliver them unto Simon the high priest, that he may punish them according to their own law. [22] The same things wrote he likewise unto Demetrius the king, and Attalus, to Ariarathes, and Arsaces, [23] and to all the countries and to Sampsames, and the Lacedemonians, and to Delus, and Myndus, and Sicyon, and Caria, and Samos, and Pamphylia, and Lycia, and Halicarnassus, and Rhodus, and Phaselis, and Cos, and Side, and Aradus, and Gortyna, and Cnidus, and Cyprus, and Cyrene. [24] And the copy hereof they wrote to Simon the high priest. [25] So Antiochus the king camped against Dora the second day, assaulting it continually, and making engines, by which means he shut up Tryphon, that he could neither go out nor in. [26] At that time Simon sent him two thousand chosen men to aid him; silver also, and gold, and much armour. [27] Nevertheless he would not receive them, but brake all the covenants which he had made with him afore, and became strange unto him. [28] Furthermore he sent unto him Athenobius, one of his friends, to commune with him, and say, Ye withhold Joppa and Gazara; with the tower that is in Jerusalem, which are cities of my realm. [29] The borders thereof ye have wasted, and done great hurt in the land, and got the dominion of many places within my kingdom. [30] Now therefore deliver the cities which ye have taken, and the tributes of the places whereof ye have gotten dominion without the borders of Judea: [31] or else give me for them five hundred talents of silver; and for the harm that ye have done, and the tributes of the cities, other five hundred talents: if not, we will come and fight against you. [32] So Athenobius the king's friend came to Jerusalem: and when he saw the glory of Simon, and the cupboard of gold and silver plate, and his great attendance, he was astonished, and told him the king's message. [33] Then answered Simon, and said unto him, We have neither taken other men's land, nor holden that which appertaineth to others, but the inheritance of our fathers, which our enemies had wrongfully in possession a certain time. [34] Wherefore we, having opportunity, hold the inheritance of our fathers. [35] And whereas thou demandest Joppa and Gazara, albeit they did great harm unto the people in our country, yet will we give thee an hundred talents for them. Hereunto Athenobius answered him not a word; [36] but returned in a rage to the king, and made report unto him of these speeches, and of the glory of Simon, and of all that he had seen: whereupon the king was exceeding wroth. [37] In the mean time fled Tryphon by ship unto Orthosias. [38] Then the king made Cendebeus captain of the sea coast, and gave him an host of footmen and horsemen, [39] and commanded him to remove his host toward Judea; also he commanded him to build up Cedron, and to fortify the gates, and to war against the people; but as for the king himself, he pursued Tryphon. [40] So Cendebeus came to Jamnia and began to provoke the people and to invade Judea, and to take the people prisoners, and slay them. [41] And when he had built up Cedron, he set horsemen there, and an host of footmen, to the end that issuing out they might make outroads upon the ways of Judea, as the king had commanded them.

16 ¹ Then came up John from Gazara, and told Simon his father what Cendebeus had done. ² Wherefore Simon called his two eldest sons, Judas and John, and said unto them, I, and my brethren, and my father's house, have ever from my youth unto this day fought against the enemies of Israel; and things have prospered so well in our hands, that we have delivered Israel oftentimes. ³ But now I am old, and ye, by God's mercy, are of a sufficient age: be ye instead of me and my brother, and go and fight for our nation, and the help from heaven be with you. ⁴ So he chose out of the country twenty thousand men of war with horsemen, who went out against Cendebeus, and rested that night at Modin. ⁵ And when as they rose in the morning, and went into the plain, behold, a mighty great host both of footmen and horsemen came against them: howbeit there was a water brook betwixt them. ⁶ So he and his people pitched over against them: and when he saw that the people were afraid to go over the water brook, he went first over himself, and then the men seeing him passed through after him. ⁷ That done, he divided his men, and set the horsemen in the midst of the footmen: for the enemies' horsemen were very many. ⁸ Then sounded they with the holy trumpets: whereupon Cendebeus and his host were put to flight, so that many of them were slain, and the remnant gat them to the strong hold. ⁹ At that time was Judas, John's brother, wounded; but John still followed after them, until he came to Cedron, which Cendebeus had built. ¹⁰ So they fled even unto the towers in the fields of Azotus; wherefore he burned it with fire: so that there were slain of them about two thousand men. Afterward he returned into the land of Judea in peace. ¹¹ Moreover in the plain of Jericho was Ptolemeus the son of Abubus made captain, and he had abundance of silver and gold: [12] For he was the high priest's son in law. [13] Wherefore his heart being lifted up, he thought to get the country to himself, and thereupon consulted deceitfully against Simon and his sons to destroy them. [14] Now Simon was visiting the cities that were in the country, and taking care for the good ordering of them; at which time he came down himself to Jericho with his sons, Mattathias and Judas, in the hundred threescore and seventeenth year, in the eleventh month, called Sabat: [15] Where the son of Abubus receiving them deceitfully into a little hold, called Docus, which he had built, made them a great banquet: howbeit he had hid men there. [16] So when Simon and his sons had drunk largely, Ptolemee and his men rose up, and took their weapons, and came upon Simon into the banqueting place, and slew him, and his two sons, and certain of his servants. [17] In which doing he committed a great treachery, and recompensed evil for good. [18] Then Ptolemee wrote these things, and sent to the king, that he should send him an host to aid him, and he would deliver him the country and cities. [19] He sent others also to Gazara to kill John: and unto the tribunes he sent letters to come unto him, that he might give them silver, and gold, and rewards. [20] And others he sent to take Jerusalem, and the mountain of the temple. [21] Now one had run afore to Gazara and told John that his father and brethren were slain, and, quoth he, Ptolemee hath sent to slay thee also. [22] Hereof when he heard, he was sore astonished: so he laid hands on them that were come to destroy him, and slew them; for he knew that they sought to make him away. [23] As concerning the rest of the acts of John, and his wars, and worthy deeds which he did, and the building of the walls which he made, and his doings, [24] behold, these are written in the chronicles of his priesthood, from the time he was made high priest after his father.

THE SECOND
BOOK OF
MACCABEES

1 ¹ The brethren, the Jews that be at Jerusalem and in the land of Judea, wish unto the brethren, the Jews that are throughout Egypt health and peace: ² God be gracious unto you, and remember his covenant that he made with Abraham, Isaac, and Jacob, his faithful servants; ³ and give you all an heart to serve him, and to do his will, with a good courage and a willing mind; ⁴ and open your hearts in his law and commandments, and send you peace, ⁵ and hear your prayers, and be at one with you, and never forsake you in time of trouble. ⁶ And now we be here praying for you. ⁷ What time as Demetrius reigned, in the hundred threescore and ninth year, we the Jews wrote unto you in the extremity of trouble that came upon us in those years, from the time that Jason and his company revolted from the holy land and kingdom, ⁸ and burned the porch, and shed innocent blood: then we prayed unto the Lord, and were heard; we offered also sacrifices and fine flour, and lighted the lamps, and set forth the loaves. ⁹ And

now see that ye keep the feast of tabernacles in the month Casleu. [10] In the hundred fourscore and eighth year, the people that were at Jerusalem and in Judea, and the council, and Judas, sent greeting and health unto Aristobulus, king Ptolemeus' master, who was of the stock of the anointed priests, and to the Jews that were in Egypt: [11] Insomuch as God hath delivered us from great perils, we thank him highly, as having been in battle against a king. [12] For he cast them out that fought within the holy city. [13] For when the leader was come into Persia, and the army with him that seemed invincible, they were slain in the temple of Nanea by the deceit of Nanea's priests. [14] For Antiochus, as though he would marry her, came into the place, and his friends that were with him, to receive money in name of a dowry. [15] Which when the priests of Nanea had set forth, and he was entered with a small company into the compass of the temple, they shut the temple as soon as Antiochus was come in: [16] And opening a privy door of the roof, they threw stones like thunderbolts, and struck down the captain, hewed them in pieces, smote off their heads and cast them to those that were without. [17] Blessed be our God in all things, who hath delivered up the ungodly. [18] Therefore whereas we are now purposed to keep the purification of the temple upon the five and twentieth day of the month Casleu, we thought it necessary to certify ye thereof, that ye also might keep it, as the feast of the tabernacles, and of the fire, which was given us when Neemias offered sacrifice, after that he had builded the temple and the altar. [19] For when our fathers were led into Persia, the priests that were then devout took the fire of the altar privily, and hid it in an hollow place of a pit without water, where they kept it sure, so that the place was unknown to all men. [20] Now after many years, when it pleased God, Neemias, being sent from the king of Persia, did send of the posterity of those priests that had hid it to the fire: but when they told us they found no fire, but thick water; [21] then commanded he them to draw it up, and to bring it; and when the sacrifices were laid on, Neemias commanded the priests to sprinkle the wood and the things laid thereupon with the water. [22] When this was done, and the time came that the sun shone, which afore was hid in the cloud, there was a great fire kindled, so that every man marvelled. [23] And the priests made a prayer whilst the sacrifice was consuming, I say, both the priests, and all the rest, Jonathan beginning, and the rest answering thereunto, as Neemias did. [24] And the prayer was after this manner; O Lord, Lord God, Creator of all things, who art fearful and strong, and righteous, and merciful, and the only and gracious King, [25] the only giver of all things, the only just, almighty, and everlasting, thou that deliverest Israel from all trouble, and didst choose the fathers, and sanctify them: [26] Receive the sacrifice for thy whole people Israel, and preserve thine own portion, and sanctify it. [27] Gather those together that are scattered from us, deliver them that serve among the heathen, look upon them that are despised and abhorred, and let the heathen know that thou art our God. [28] Punish them that oppress us, and with pride do us wrong. [29] Plant thy people again in thy holy place, as Moses hath spoken. [30] And the priests sung psalms of thanksgiving. [31] Now when the sacrifice was consumed, Neemias commanded the water that was left to be poured on the great stones. [32] When this was done, there was kindled a flame: but it was consumed by the light that shined from the altar. [33] So when this matter was known, it was told the king of Persia, that in the place, where the priests that were led away had hid the fire, there appeared water, and that Neemias had purified the sacrifices therewith. ³⁴ Then the king, enclosing the place, made it holy, after he had tried the matter. ³⁵ And the king took many gifts, and bestowed thereof on those whom he would gratify. ³⁶ And Neemias called this thing Naphthar, which is as much as to say, a cleansing: but many men call it Nephi.

2 ¹ It is also found in the records, that Jeremy the prophet commanded them that were carried away to take of the fire, as it hath been signified: ² And how that the prophet, having given them the law, charged them not to forget the commandments of the Lord, and that they should not err in their minds, when they see images of silver and gold, with their ornaments. ³ And with other such speeches exhorted he them, that the law should not depart from their hearts. ⁴ It was also contained in the same writing, that the prophet, being warned of God, commanded the tabernacle and the ark to go with him, as he went forth into the mountain, where Moses climbed up, and saw the heritage of God. ⁵ And when Jeremy came thither, he found an hollow cave, wherein he laid the tabernacle, and the ark, and the altar of incense, and so stopped the door. ⁶ And some of those that followed him came to mark the way, but they could not find it. ⁷ Which when Jeremy perceived, he blamed them, saying, As for that place, it shall be unknown until the time that God gather his people again together, and receive them unto mercy. ⁸ Then shall the Lord shew them these things, and the glory of the Lord shall appear, and the cloud also, as it was

shewed unto Moses, and as when Solomon desired that the place might be honourably sanctified. ⁹ It was also declared, that he being wise offered the sacrifice of dedication, and of the finishing of the temple. ¹⁰ And as when Moses prayed unto the Lord, the fire came down from heaven, and consumed the sacrifices: even so prayed Solomon also, and the fire came down from heaven, and consumed the burnt offerings. ¹¹ And Moses said, Because the sin offering was not to be eaten, it was consumed. ¹² So Solomon kept those eight days. ¹³ The same things also were reported in the writings and commentaries of Neemias; and how he founding a library gathered together the acts of the kings, and the prophets, and of David, and the epistles of the kings concerning the holy gifts. ¹⁴ In like manner also Judas gathered together all those things that were lost by reason of the war we had, and they remain with us. ¹⁵ Wherefore if ye have need thereof, send some to fetch them unto you. ¹⁶ Whereas we then are about to celebrate the purification, we have written unto you, and ye shall do well, if ye keep the same days. ¹⁷ We hope also, that the God that delivered all his people, and gave them all an heritage, and the kingdom, and the priesthood, and the sanctuary, ¹⁸ as he promised in the law, will shortly have mercy upon us, and gather us together out of every land under heaven into the holy place: for he hath delivered us out of great troubles, and hath purified the place. ¹⁹ Now as concerning Judas Maccabeus, and his brethren, and the purification of the great temple, and the dedication of the altar, ²⁰ and the wars against Antiochus Epiphanes, and Eupator his son, ²¹ and the manifest signs that came from heaven unto those that behaved themselves manfully to their honour for Judaism: so that, being but a few, they overcame the whole country, and chased barbarous multitudes, [22] and recovered again the temple renowned all the world over, and freed the city, and upheld the laws which were going down, the Lord being gracious unto them with all favour: [23] All these things, I say, being declared by Jason of Cyrene in five books, we will assay to abridge in one volume. [24] For considering the infinite number, and the difficulty which they find that desire to look into the narrations of the story, for the variety of the matter, [25] we have been careful, that they that will read may have delight, and that they that are desirous to commit to memory might have ease, and that all into whose hands it comes might have profit. [26] Therefore to us, that have taken upon us this painful labour of abridging, it was not easy, but a matter of sweat and watching; [27] even as it is no ease unto him that prepareth a banquet, and seeketh the benefit of others: yet for the pleasuring of many we will undertake gladly this great pains; [28] leaving to the author the exact handling of every particular, and labouring to follow the rules of an abridgement. [29] For as the master builder of a new house must care for the whole building; but he that undertaketh to set it out, and paint it, must seek out fit things for the adorning thereof: even so I think it is with us. [30] To stand upon every point, and go over things at large, and to be curious in particulars, belongeth to the first author of the story: [31] But to use brevity, and avoid much labouring of the work, is to be granted to him that will make an abridgment. [32] Here then will we begin the story: only adding thus much to that which hath been said, that it is a foolish thing to make a long prologue, and to be short in the story itself.

3 ¹ Now when the holy city was inhabited with all peace, and the laws were kept very well, because of the godliness of Onias the high priest, and his hatred of wickedness, ² it came to pass that even the kings themselves did honour the place, and magnify the temple with their best gifts; ³ insomuch that Seleucus, king of Asia, of his own revenues, bare all the costs belonging to the service of the sacrifices. ⁴ But one Simon, of the tribe of Benjamin, who was made governor of the temple, fell out with the high priest about disorder in the city. ⁵ And when he could not overcome Onias, he gat him to Apollonius the son of Thraseas, who then was governor of Celosyria and Phenice, ⁶ and told him that the treasury in Jerusalem was full of infinite sums of money, so that the multitude of their riches, which did not pertain to the account of the sacrifices, was innumerable, and that it was possible to bring all into the king's hand. ⁷ Now when Apollonius came to the king, and had shewed him of the money whereof he was told, the king chose out Heliodorus his treasurer, and sent him with a commandment to bring him the aforesaid money. ⁸ So forthwith Heliodorus took his journey; under a colour of visiting the cities of Celosyria and Phenice, but indeed to fulfil the king's purpose. ⁹ And when he was come to Jerusalem, and had been courteously received of the high priest of the city, he told him what intelligence was given of the money, and declared wherefore he came, and asked if these things were so indeed. ¹⁰ Then the high priest told him that there was such money laid up for the relief of widows and fatherless children: ¹¹ and that some of it belonged to Hircanus son of Tobias, a man of great dignity, and not as that wicked Simon had misinformed: the sum whereof in all was four hundred talents of silver, and two

hundred of gold: [12] And that it was altogether impossible that such wrongs should be done unto them, that had committed it to the holiness of the place, and to the majesty and inviolable sanctity of the temple, honoured over all the world. [13] But Heliodorus, because of the king's commandment given him, said, That in any wise it must be brought into the king's treasury. [14] So at the day which he appointed he entered in to order this matter: wherefore there was no small agony throughout the whole city. [15] But the priests, prostrating themselves before the altar in their priests' vestments, called unto heaven upon him that made a law concerning things given to be kept, that they should safely be preserved for such as had committed them to be kept. [16] Then whoso had looked the high priest in the face, it would have wounded his heart: for his countenance and the changing of his colour declared the inward agony of his mind. [17] For the man was so compassed with fear and horror of the body, that it was manifest to them that looked upon him, what sorrow he had now in his heart. [18] Others ran flocking out of their houses to the general supplication, because the place was like to come into contempt. [19] And the women, girt with sackcloth under their breasts, abounded in the streets, and the virgins that were kept in ran, some to the gates, and some to the walls, and others looked out of the windows. [20] And all, holding their hands toward heaven, made supplication. [21] Then it would have pitied a man to see the falling down of the multitude of all sorts, and the fear of the high priest being in such an agony. [22] They then called upon the Almighty Lord to keep the things committed of trust safe and sure for those that had committed them. [23] Nevertheless Heliodorus executed that which was decreed. [24] Now as he was there present himself with his guard about the treasury, the Lord of spirits, and the Prince of all power, caused a great apparition, so that all that presumed to come in with him were astonished at the power of God, and fainted, and were sore afraid. ²⁵ For there appeared unto them an horse with a terrible rider upon him, and adorned with a very fair covering, and he ran fiercely, and smote at Heliodorus with his forefeet, and it seemed that he that sat upon the horse had complete harness of gold. ²⁶ Moreover two other young men appeared before him, notable in strength, excellent in beauty, and comely in apparel, who stood by him on either side; and scourged him continually, and gave him many sore stripes. ²⁷ And Heliodorus fell suddenly unto the ground, and was compassed with great darkness: but they that were with him took him up, and put him into a litter. ²⁸ Thus him, that lately came with a great train and with all his guard into the said treasury, they carried out, being unable to help himself with his weapons: and manifestly they acknowledged the power of God. ²⁹ For he by the hand of God was cast down, and lay speechless without all hope of life. ³⁰ But they praised the Lord, that had miraculously honoured his own place: for the temple, which a little afore was full of fear and trouble, when the Almighty Lord appeared, was filled with joy and gladness. ³¹ Then straightways certain of Heliodorus' friends prayed Onias, that he would call upon the most High to grant him his life, who lay ready to give up the ghost. ³² So the high priest, suspecting lest the king should misconceive that some treachery had been done to Heliodorus by the Jews, offered a sacrifice for the health of the man. ³³ Now as the high priest was making an atonement, the same young men in the same clothing appeared and stood beside Heliodorus, saying, Give Onias the high priest great thanks, insomuch as for his sake the Lord hath granted thee life: [34] And seeing that thou hast been scourged from heaven, declare unto all men the mighty power of God. And when they had spoken these words, they appeared no more. [35] So Heliodorus, after he had offered sacrifice unto the Lord, and made great vows unto him that had saved his life, and saluted Onias, returned with his host to the king. [36] Then testified he to all men the works of the great God, which he had seen with his eyes. [37] And when the king asked Heliodorus, who might be a fit man to be sent yet once again to Jerusalem, he said, [38] If thou hast any enemy or traitor, send him thither, and thou shalt receive him well scourged, if he escape with his life: for in that place, no doubt; there is an especial power of God. [39] For he that dwelleth in heaven hath his eye on that place, and defendeth it; and he beateth and destroyeth them that come to hurt it. [40] And the things concerning Heliodorus, and the keeping of the treasury, fell out on this sort.

4 [1] This Simon now, of whom we spake afore, having been a betrayer of the money, and of his country, slandered Onias, as if he had terrified Heliodorus, and been the worker of these evils. [2] Thus was he bold to call him a traitor, that had deserved well of the city, and tendered his own nation, and was so zealous of the laws. [3] But when their hatred went so far, that by one of Simon's faction murders were committed, [4] Onias seeing the danger of this contention, and that Apollonius, as being the governor of Celosyria and Phenice, did rage, and increase Simon's malice, [5] he went to the king, not to be an accuser of his countrymen, but seeking the

good of all, both public and private: [6] For he saw that it was impossible that the state should continue quiet, and Simon leave his folly, unless the king did look thereunto. [7] But after the death of Seleucus, when Antiochus, called Epiphanes, took the kingdom, Jason the brother of Onias laboured underhand to be high priest, [8] promising unto the king by intercession three hundred and threescore talents of silver, and of another revenue eighty talents: [9] Besides this, he promised to assign an hundred and fifty more, if he might have licence to set him up a place for exercise, and for the training up of youth in the fashions of the heathen, and to write them of Jerusalem by the name of Antiochians. [10] Which when the king had granted, and he had gotten into his hand the rule, he forthwith brought his own nation to Greekish fashion. [11] And the royal privileges granted of special favour to the Jews by the means of John the father of Eupolemus, who went ambassador to Rome for amity and aid, he took away; and putting down the governments which were according to the law, he brought up new customs against the law: [12] For he built gladly a place of exercise under the tower itself, and brought the chief young men under his subjection, and made them wear a hat. [13] Now such was the height of Greek fashions, and increase of heathenish manners, through the exceeding profaneness of Jason, that ungodly wretch, and no high priest; [14] that the priests had no courage to serve any more at the altar, but despising the temple, and neglecting the sacrifices, hastened to be partakers of the unlawful allowance in the place of exercise, after the game of Discus called them forth; [15] not setting by the honours of their fathers, but liking the glory of the Grecians best of all. [16] By reason whereof sore calamity came upon them: for they had them to be their enemies and avengers, whose custom they followed so earnestly, and unto whom they desired to be like in all things. [17] For it is not a light thing to do wickedly against the laws of God: but the time following shall declare these things. [18] Now when the game that was used every fifth year was kept at Tyrus, the king being present, [19] this ungracious Jason sent special messengers from Jerusalem, who were Antiochians, to carry three hundred drachms of silver to the sacrifice of Hercules, which even the bearers thereof thought fit not to bestow upon the sacrifice, because it was not convenient, but to be reserved for other charges. [20] This money then, in regard of the sender, was appointed to Hercules' sacrifice; but because of the bearers thereof, it was employed to the making of gallies. [21] Now when Apollonius the son of Menestheus was sent into Egypt for the coronation of king Ptolemeus Philometor, Antiochus, understanding him not to be well affected to his affairs, provided for his own safety: whereupon he came to Joppa, and from thence to Jerusalem: [22] where he was honourably received of Jason, and of the city, and was brought in with torch alight, and with great shoutings: and so afterward went with his host unto Phenice. [23] Three years afterward Jason sent Menelaus, the aforesaid Simon's brother, to bear the money unto the king, and to put him in mind of certain necessary matters. [24] But he being brought to the presence of the king, when he had magnified him for the glorious appearance of his power, got the priesthood to himself, offering more than Jason by three hundred talents of silver. [25] So he came with the king's mandate, bringing nothing worthy the high priesthood, but having the fury of a cruel tyrant, and the rage of a savage beast. [26] Then Jason, who had undermined his own brother, being undermined by another, was compelled to flee into the country of the Ammonites. [27] So Menelaus got the principality: but as for the money that he had promised unto the king, he took no good order for it, albeit Sostratus the ruler of the castle required it: [28] For unto him appertained the gathering of the customs. Wherefore they were both called before the king. [29] Now Menelaus left his brother Lysimachus in his stead in the priesthood; and Sostratus left Crates, who was governor of the Cyprians. [30] While those things were in doing, they of Tarsus and Mallos made insurrection, because they were given to the king's concubine, called Antiochus. [31] Then came the king in all haste to appease matters, leaving Andronicus, a man in authority, for his deputy. [32] Now Menelaus, supposing that he had gotten a convenient time, stole certain vessels of gold out of the temple, and gave some of them to Andronicus, and some he sold into Tyrus and the cities round about. [33] Which when Onias knew of a surety, he reproved him, and withdrew himself into a sanctuary at Daphne, that lieth by Antiochia. [34] Wherefore Menelaus, taking Andronicus apart, prayed, him to get Onias into his hands; who being persuaded thereunto, and coming to Onias in deceit, gave him his right hand with oaths; and though he were suspected by him, yet persuaded he him to come forth of the sanctuary: whom forthwith he shut up without regard of justice. [35] For the which cause not only the Jews, but many also of other nations, took great indignation, and were much grieved for the unjust murder of the man. [36] And when the king was come again from the places about Cilicia, the Jews that were in the city, and certain of the Greeks that abhorred the fact also, complained because Onias was slain without cause. [37] Therefore Antiochus was heartily sorry, and moved to pity, and wept, because of the sober and modest behaviour of him that was dead. [38] And being kindled with anger, forthwith he took away Andronicus his purple, and rent off his clothes, and leading him through the whole city unto that very place where he had committed impiety against Onias, there slew he the cursed murderer. Thus the Lord rewarded him his punishment, as he had deserved. [39] Now when many sacrileges had been committed in the city by Lysimachus with the consent of Menelaus, and the fruit thereof was spread abroad, the multitude gathered themselves together against Lysimachus, many vessels of gold being already carried away. [40] Whereupon the common people rising, and being filled with rage, Lysimachus armed about three thousand men, and began first to offer violence; one Auranus being the leader, a man far gone in years, and no less in folly. [41] They then seeing the attempt of Lysimachus, some of them caught stones, some clubs, others taking handfuls of dust, that was next at hand, cast them all together upon Lysimachus, and those that set upon them. [42] Thus many of them they wounded, and some they struck to the ground, and all of them they forced to flee: but as for the churchrobber himself, him they killed beside the treasury. [43] Of these matters therefore there was an accusation laid against Menelaus. [44] Now when the king came to Tyrus, three men that were sent from the senate pleaded the cause before him: [45] But Menelaus, being now convicted, promised Ptolemee the son of Dorymenes to give him much money, if he would pacify the king toward him. [46] Whereupon Ptolemee taking the king aside into a certain gallery, as it were to take the air, brought him to be of another mind: ⁴⁷ insomuch that he discharged Menelaus from the accusations, who notwithstanding was cause of all the mischief: and those poor men, who, if they had told their cause, yea, before the Scythians, should have been judged innocent, them he condemned to death. ⁴⁸ Thus they that followed the matter for the city, and for the people, and for the holy vessels, did soon suffer unjust punishment. ⁴⁹ Wherefore even they of Tyrus, moved with hatred of that wicked deed, caused them to be honourably buried. ⁵⁰ And so through the covetousness of them that were of power, Menelaus remained still in authority, increasing in malice, and being a great traitor to the citizens.

5 ¹ About the same time Antiochus prepared his second voyage into Egypt: ² And then it happened, that through all the city, for the space almost of forty days, there were seen horsemen running in the air, in cloth of gold, and armed with lances, like a band of soldiers, ³ and troops of horsemen in array, encountering and running one against another, with shaking of shields, and multitude of pikes, and drawing of swords, and casting of darts, and glittering of golden ornaments, and harness of all sorts. ⁴ Wherefore every man prayed that that apparition might turn to good. ⁵ Now when there was gone forth a false rumour, as though Antiochus had been dead, Jason took at the least a thousand men, and suddenly made an assault upon the city; and they that were upon the walls being put back, and the city at length taken, Menelaus fled into the castle: ⁶ But Jason slew his own citizens without mercy, not considering that to get the day of them of his own nation would be a most unhappy day for him; but thinking they had been his enemies, and not his coun-

trymen, whom he conquered. ⁷ Howbeit for all this he obtained not the principality, but at the last received shame for the reward of his treason, and fled again into the country of the Ammonites. ⁸ In the end therefore he had an unhappy return, being accused before Aretas the king of the Arabians, fleeing from city to city, pursued of all men, hated as a forsaker of the laws, and being had in abomination as an open enemy of his country and countrymen, he was cast out into Egypt. ⁹ Thus he that had driven many out of their country perished in a strange land, retiring to the Lacedemonians, and thinking there to find succour by reason of his kindred: ¹⁰ And he that had cast out many unburied had none to mourn for him, nor any solemn funerals at all, nor sepulchre with his fathers. ¹¹ Now when this that was done came to the king's ear, he thought that Judea had revolted: whereupon removing out of Egypt in a furious mind, he took the city by force of arms, ¹² and commanded his men of war not to spare such as they met, and to slay such as went up upon the houses. ¹³ Thus there was killing of young and old, making away of men, women, and children, slaying of virgins and infants. ¹⁴ And there were destroyed within the space of three whole days fourscore thousand, whereof forty thousand were slain in the conflict; and no fewer sold than slain. ¹⁵ Yet was he not content with this, but presumed to go into the most holy temple of all the world; Menelaus, that traitor to the laws, and to his own country, being his guide: ¹⁶ And taking the holy vessels with polluted hands, and with profane hands pulling down the things that were dedicated by other kings to the augmentation and glory and honour of the place, he gave them away. ¹⁷ And so haughty was Antiochus in mind, that he considered not that the Lord was angry for a while for the sins of them that dwelt in the city, and therefore his eye was not upon the place. [18] For had they not been formerly wrapped in many sins, this man, as soon as he had come, had forthwith been scourged, and put back from his presumption, as Heliodorus was, whom Seleucus the king sent to view the treasury. [19] Nevertheless God did not choose the people for the place's sake, but the place for the people's sake. [20] And therefore the place itself, that was partaker with them of the adversity that happened to the nation, did afterward communicate in the benefits sent from the Lord: and as it was forsaken in the wrath of the Almighty, so again, the great Lord being reconciled, it was set up with all glory. [21] So when Antiochus had carried out of the temple a thousand and eight hundred talents, he departed in all haste unto Antiochia, weening in his pride to make the land navigable, and the sea passable by foot: such was the haughtiness of his mind. [22] And he left governors to vex the nation: at Jerusalem, Philip, for his country a Phrygian, and for manners more barbarous than he that set him there; [23] and at Garizim, Andronicus; and besides, Menelaus, who worse than all the rest bare an heavy hand over the citizens, having a malicious mind against his countrymen the Jews. [24] He sent also that detestable ringleader Apollonius with an army of two and twenty thousand, commanding him to slay all those that were in their best age, and to sell the women and the younger sort: [25] who coming to Jerusalem, and pretending peace, did forbear till the holy day of the sabbath, when taking the Jews keeping holy day, he commanded his men to arm themselves. [26] And so he slew all them that were gone to the celebrating of the sabbath, and running through the city with weapons slew great multitudes. [27] But Judas Maccabeus with nine others, or thereabout, withdrew himself into the wilderness, and lived in the mountains after the manner of beasts, with his company, who fed on herbs continually, lest they should be partakers of the pollution.

6 [1] Not long after this the king sent an old man of Athens to compel the Jews to depart from the laws of their fathers, and not to live after the laws of God: [2] and to pollute also the temple in Jerusalem, and to call it the temple of Jupiter Olympius; and that in Garizim, of Jupiter the Defender of strangers, as they did desire that dwelt in the place. [3] The coming in of this mischief was sore and grievous to the people: [4] For the temple was filled with riot and revelling by the Gentiles, who dallied with harlots, and had to do with women within the circuit of the holy places, and besides that brought in things that were not lawful. [5] The altar also was filled with profane things, which the law forbiddeth. [6] Neither was it lawful for a man to keep sabbath days or ancient feasts, or to profess himself at all to be a Jew. [7] And in the day of the king's birth, every month they were brought by bitter constraint to eat of the sacrifices; and when the feast of Bacchus was kept, the Jews were compelled to go in procession to Bacchus, carrying ivy. [8] Moreover there went out a decree to the neighbour cities of the heathen, by the suggestion of Ptolemee, against the Jews, that they should observe the same fashions, and be partakers of their sacrifices: [9] And whoso would not conform themselves to the manners of the Gentiles should be put to death. Then might a man have seen the present misery. [10] For there were two women brought, who had circumcised their children; whom when they had

openly led round about the city, the babes hanging at their breasts, they cast them down headlong from the wall. [11] And others, that had run together into caves near by, to keep the sabbath day secretly, being discovered by Philip, were all burnt together, because they made a conscience to help themselves for the honour of the most sacred day. [12] Now I beseech those that read this book, that they be not discouraged for these calamities, but that they judge those punishments not to be for destruction, but for a chastening of our nation. [13] For it is a token of his great goodness, when wicked doers are not suffered any long time, but forthwith punished. [14] For not as with other nations, whom the Lord patiently forbeareth to punish, till they be come to the fulness of their sins, so dealeth he with us, [15] lest that, being come to the height of sin, afterwards he should take vengeance of us. [16] And therefore he never withdraweth his mercy from us: and though he punish with adversity, yet doth he never forsake his people. [17] But let this that we have spoken be for a warning unto us. And now will we come to the declaring of the matter in a few words. [18] Eleazar, one of the principal scribes, an aged man, and of a well favoured countenance, was constrained to open his mouth, and to eat swine's flesh. [19] But he, choosing rather to die gloriously, than to live stained with such an abomination, spit it forth, and came of his own accord to the torment, [20] as it behooved them to come, that are resolute to stand out against such things as are not lawful for love of life to be tasted. [21] But they that had the charge of that wicked feast, for the old acquaintance they had with the man, taking him aside, besought him to bring flesh of his own provision, such as was lawful for him to use, and make as if he did eat of the flesh taken from the sacrifice commanded by the king; [22] that in so doing he might be delivered from death, and for the old friendship with them find favour. [23] But he began to consider discreetly, and as became his age, and the excellency of his ancient years, and the honour of his gray head, whereon was come, and his most honest education from a child, or rather the holy law made and given by God: therefore he answered accordingly, and willed them straightways to send him to the grave. [24] For it becometh not our age, said he, in any wise to dissemble, whereby many young persons might think that Eleazar, being fourscore years old and ten, were now gone to a strange religion; [25] and so they through mine hypocrisy, and desire to live a little time and a moment longer, should be deceived by me, and I get a stain to mine old age, and make it abominable. [26] For though for the present time I should be delivered from the punishment of men: yet should I not escape the hand of the Almighty, neither alive, nor dead. [27] Wherefore now, manfully changing this life, I will shew myself such an one as mine age requireth, [28] and leave a notable example to such as be young to die willingly and courageously for the honourable and holy laws. And when he had said these words, immediately he went to the torment: [29] They that led him changing the good will they bare him a little before into hatred, because the foresaid speeches proceeded, as they thought, from a desperate mind. [30] But when he was ready to die with stripes, he groaned, and said, It is manifest unto the Lord, that hath the holy knowledge, that whereas I might have been delivered from death, I now endure sore pains in body by being beaten: but in soul am well content to suffer these things, because I fear him. [31] And thus this man died, leaving his death for an example of a noble courage, and a memorial of virtue, not only unto young men, but unto all his nation.

7 ¹ It came to pass also, that seven brethren with their mother were taken, and compelled by the king against the law to taste swine's flesh, and were tormented with scourges and whips. ² But one of them that spake first said thus, What wouldest thou ask or learn of us? we are ready to die, rather than to transgress the laws of our fathers. ³ Then the king, being in a rage, commanded pans and caldrons to be made hot: ⁴ Which forthwith being heated, he commanded to cut out the tongue of him that spake first, and to cut off the utmost parts of his body, the rest of his brethren and his mother looking on. ⁵ Now when he was thus maimed in all his members, he commanded him, being yet alive, to be brought to the fire, and to be fried in the pan: and as the vapour of the pan was for a good space dispersed, they exhorted one another with the mother to die manfully, saying thus, ⁶ The Lord God looketh upon us, and in truth hath comfort in us, as Moses in his song, which witnessed to their faces, declared, saying, And he shall be comforted in his servants. ⁷ So when the first was dead after this manner, they brought the second to make him a mocking stock: and when they had pulled off the skin of his head with the hair, they asked him, Wilt thou eat, before thou be punished throughout every member of thy body? ⁸ But he answered in his own language, and said, No. Wherefore he also received the next torment in order, as the former did. ⁹ And when he was at the last gasp, he said, Thou like a fury takest us out of this present life, but the King of the world shall raise us up, who have died for his laws, unto everlasting life. ¹⁰ After him was the third made a

mocking stock: and when he was required, he put out his tongue, and that right soon, holding forth his hands manfully. [11] And said courageously, These I had from heaven; and for his laws I despise them; and from him I hope to receive them again. [12] Insomuch that the king, and they that were with him, marvelled at the young man's courage, for that he nothing regarded the pains. [13] Now when this man was dead also, they tormented and mangled the fourth in like manner. [14] So when he was ready to die he said thus, It is good, being put to death by men, to look for hope from God to be raised up again by him: as for thee, thou shalt have no resurrection to life. [15] Afterward they brought the fifth also, and mangled him. [16] Then looked he unto the king, and said, Thou hast power over men, thou art corruptible, thou doest what thou wilt; yet think not that our nation is forsaken of God; [17] but abide a while, and behold his great power, how he will torment thee and thy seed. [18] After him also they brought the sixth, who being ready to die said, Be not deceived without cause: for we suffer these things for ourselves, having sinned against our God: therefore marvellous things are done unto us. [19] But think not thou, that takest in hand to strive against God, that thou shalt escape unpunished. [20] But the mother was marvellous above all, and worthy of honourable memory: for when she saw her seven sons slain within the space of one day, she bare it with a good courage, because of the hope that she had in the Lord. [21] Yea, she exhorted every one of them in her own language, filled with courageous spirits; and stirring up her womanish thoughts with a manly stomach, she said unto them, [22] I cannot tell how ye came into my womb: for I neither gave you breath nor life, neither was it I that formed the members of every one of you; [23] but doubtless the Creator of the world, who formed the generation of man, and found out the beginning of all things, will also of his own mercy give you breath and life again, as ye now regard not your own selves for his laws' sake. [24] Now Antiochus, thinking himself despised, and suspecting it to be a reproachful speech, whilst the youngest was yet alive, did not only exhort him by words, but also assured him with oaths, that he would make him both a rich and a happy man, if he would turn from the laws of his fathers; and that also he would take him for his friend, and trust him with affairs. [25] But when the young man would in no case hearken unto him, the king called his mother, and exhorted her that she would counsel the young man to save his life. [26] And when he had exhorted her with many words, she promised him that she would counsel her son. [27] But she bowing herself toward him, laughing the cruel tyrant to scorn, spake in her country language on this manner; O my son, have pity upon me that bare thee nine months in my womb, and gave thee suck three years, and nourished thee, and brought thee up unto this age, and endured the troubles of education. [28] I beseech thee, my son, look upon the heaven and the earth, and all that is therein, and consider that God made them of things that were not; and so was mankind made likewise. [29] Fear not this tormentor, but, being worthy of thy brethren, take thy death that I may receive thee again in mercy with thy brethren. [30] While she was yet speaking these words, the young man said, Whom wait ye for? I will not obey the king's commandment: but I will obey the commandment of the law that was given unto our fathers by Moses. [31] And thou, that hast been the author of all mischief against the Hebrews, shalt not escape the hands of God. [32] For we suffer because of our sins. [33] And though the living Lord be angry with us a little while for our chastening and correction, yet shall he be at one again with his servants. [34] But thou, O godless man, and of all other most wicked, be not lifted up without a cause, nor puffed up with uncertain hopes, lifting up thy hand against the servants of God: [35] For thou hast not yet escaped the judgment of Almighty God, who seeth all things. [36] For our brethren, who now have suffered a short pain, are dead under God's covenant of everlasting life: but thou, through the judgment of God, shalt receive just punishment for thy pride. [37] But I, as my brethren, offer up my body and life for the laws of our fathers, beseeching God that he would speedily be merciful unto our nation; and that thou by torments and plagues mayest confess, that he alone is God; [38] And that in me and my brethren the wrath of the Almighty, which is justly brought upon our nation, may cease. [39] Then the king, being in a rage, handled him worse than all the rest, and took it grievously that he was mocked. [40] So this man died undefiled, and put his whole trust in the Lord. [41] Last of all, after the sons, the mother died. [42] Let this be enough now to have spoken concerning the idolatrous feasts, and the extreme tortures.

8 [1] Then Judas Maccabeus, and they that were with him, went privily into the towns, and called their kinsfolks together, and took unto them all such as continued in the Jews' religion, and assembled about six thousand men. [2] And they called upon the Lord, that he would look upon the people that was trodden down of all; and also pity the temple profaned of ungodly men; [3] and that he would have compassion upon the city, sore

defaced, and ready to be made even with the ground; and hear the blood that cried unto him, [4] and remember the wicked slaughter of harmless infants, and the blasphemies committed against his name; and that he would shew his hatred against the wicked. [5] Now when Maccabeus had his company about him, he could not be withstood by the heathen: for the wrath of the Lord was turned into mercy. [6] Therefore he came at unawares, and burnt up towns and cities, and got into his hands the most commodious places, and overcame and put to flight no small number of his enemies. [7] But specially took he advantage of the night for such privy attempts, insomuch that the fruit of his holiness was spread every where. [8] So when Philip saw that this man increased by little and little, and that things prospered with him still more and more, he wrote unto Ptolemeus, the governor of Celosyria and Phenice, to yield more aid to the king's affairs. [9] Then forthwith choosing Nicanor the son of Patroclus, one of his special friends, he sent him with no fewer than twenty thousand of all nations under him, to root out the whole generation of the Jews; and with him he joined also Gorgias a captain, who in matters of war had great experience. [10] So Nicanor undertook to make so much money of the captive Jews, as should defray the tribute of two thousand talents, which the king was to pay to the Romans. [11] Wherefore immediately he sent to the cities upon the sea coast, proclaiming a sale of the captive Jews, and promising that they should have fourscore and ten bodies for one talent, not expecting the vengeance that was to follow upon him from the Almighty God. [12] Now when word was brought unto Judas of Nicanor's coming, and he had imparted unto those that were with him that the army was at hand,

[13] they that were fearful, and distrusted the justice of God, fled, and conveyed themselves away. [14] Others sold all that they had left, and withal besought the Lord to deliver them, sold by the wicked Nicanor before they met together: [15] And if not for their own sakes, yet for the covenants he had made with their fathers, and for his holy and glorious name's sake, by which they were called. [16] So Maccabeus called his men together unto the number of six thousand, and exhorted them not to be stricken with terror of the enemy, nor to fear the great multitude of the heathen, who came wrongly against them; but to fight manfully, [17] and to set before their eyes the injury that they had unjustly done to the holy place, and the cruel handling of the city, whereof they made a mockery, and also the taking away of the government of their forefathers: [18] For they, said he, trust in their weapons and boldness; but our confidence is in the Almighty God, who at a beck can cast down both them that come against us, and also all the world. [19] Moreover, he recounted unto them what helps their forefathers had found, and how they were delivered, when under Sennacherib an hundred fourscore and five thousand perished. [20] And he told them of the battle that they had in Babylon with the Galatians, how they came but eight thousand in all to the business, with four thousand Macedonians, and that the Macedonians being perplexed, the eight thousand destroyed an hundred and twenty thousand because of the help that they had from heaven, and so received a great booty. [21] Thus when he had made them bold with these words, and ready to die for the law and the country, he divided his army into four parts; [22] and joined with himself his own brethren, leaders of each band, to wit, Simon, and Joseph, and Jonathan, giving each one fifteen hundred

men. ²³ Also he appointed Eleazar to read the holy book: and when he had given them this watchword, The help of God; himself leading the first band, he joined battle with Nicanor. ²⁴ And by the help of the Almighty they slew above nine thousand of their enemies, and wounded and maimed the most part of Nicanor's host, and so put all to flight; ²⁵ and took their money that came to buy them, and pursued them far: but lacking time they returned: ²⁶ For it was the day before the sabbath, and therefore they would no longer pursue them. ²⁷ So when they had gathered their armour together, and spoiled their enemies, they occupied themselves about the sabbath, yielding exceeding praise and thanks to the Lord, who had preserved them unto that day, which was the beginning of mercy distilling upon them. ²⁸ And after the sabbath, when they had given part of the spoils to the maimed, and the widows, and orphans, the residue they divided among themselves and their servants. ²⁹ When this was done, and they had made a common supplication, they besought the merciful Lord to be reconciled with his servants for ever. ³⁰ Moreover of those that were with Timotheus and Bacchides, who fought against them, they slew above twenty thousand, and very easily got high and strong holds, and divided among themselves many spoils more, and made the maimed, orphans, widows, yea, and the aged also, equal in spoils with themselves. ³¹ And when they had gathered their armour together, they laid them up all carefully in convenient places, and the remnant of the spoils they brought to Jerusalem. ³² They slew also Philarches, that wicked person, who was with Timotheus, and had annoyed the Jews many ways. ³³ Furthermore, at such time as they kept the feast for the victory in their country, they burnt Callisthenes, that had set fire upon the holy gates, who had fled into a little house; and so he received a reward meet for his wickedness. [34] As for that most ungracious Nicanor, who had brought a thousand merchants to buy the Jews, [35] he was, through the help of the Lord, brought down by them of whom he made least account; and putting off his glorious apparel, and discharging his company, he came like a fugitive servant through the midland unto Antioch having very great dishonour, for that his host was destroyed. [36] Thus he, that took upon him to make good to the Romans their tribute by means of captives in Jerusalem, told abroad, that the Jews had God to fight for them, and therefore they could not be hurt, because they followed the laws that he gave them.

9 [1] About that time came Antiochus with dishonour out of the country of Persia. [2] For he had entered the city called Persepolis, and went about to rob the temple, and to hold the city; whereupon the multitude, running to defend themselves with their weapons, put them to flight; and so it happened, that Antiochus, being put to flight of the inhabitants returned with shame. [3] Now when he came to Ecbatane, news was brought him what had happened unto Nicanor and Timotheus. [4] Then swelling with anger, he thought to avenge upon the Jews the disgrace done unto him by those that made him flee. Therefore commanded he his chariotman to drive without ceasing, and to dispatch the journey, the judgment of God now following him. For he had spoken proudly in this sort, That he would come to Jerusalem and make it a common burying place of the Jews. [5] But the Lord Almighty, the God of Isreal, smote him with an incurable and invisible

plague: for as soon as he had spoken these words, a pain of the bowels that was remediless came upon him, and sore torments of the inner parts; [6] and that most justly: for he had tormented other men's bowels with many and strange torments. [7] Howbeit he nothing at all ceased from his bragging, but still was filled with pride, breathing out fire in his rage against the Jews, and commanding to haste the journey: but it came to pass that he fell down from his chariot, carried violently; so that having a sore fall, all the members of his body were much pained. [8] And thus he that a little afore thought he might command the waves of the sea, (so proud was he beyond the condition of man) and weigh the high mountains in a balance, was now cast on the ground, and carried in an horselitter, shewing forth unto all the manifest power of God. [9] So that the worms rose up out of the body of this wicked man, and while he lived in sorrow and pain, his flesh fell away, and the filthiness of his smell was noisome to all his army. [10] And the man, that thought a little afore he could reach to the stars of heaven, no man could endure to carry for his intolerable stink. [11] Here therefore, being plagued, he began to leave off his great pride, and to come to the knowledge of himself by the scourge of God, his pain increasing every moment. [12] And when he himself could not abide his own smell, he said these words, It is meet to be subject unto God, and that a man that is mortal should not proudly think of himself as if he were God. [13] This wicked person vowed also unto the Lord, who now no more would have mercy upon him, saying thus, [14] That the holy city (to the which he was going in haste to lay it even with the ground, and to make it a common buryingplace,) he would set at liberty: [15] And as touching the Jews, whom he had judged not worthy so much as to be buried, but to be cast out with their children to be devoured of the fowls and wild beasts, he would make them all equals to the citizens of Athens: [16] And the holy temple, which before he had spoiled, he would garnish with goodly gifts, and restore all the holy vessels with many more, and out of his own revenue defray the charges belonging to the sacrifices: [17] Yea, and that also he would become a Jew himself, and go through all the world that was inhabited, and declare the power of God. [18] But for all this his pains would not cease: for the just judgment of God was come upon him: therefore despairing of his health, he wrote unto the Jews the letter underwritten, containing the form of a supplication, after this manner: [19] Antiochus, king and governor, to the good Jews his citizens wisheth much joy, health, and prosperity: [20] If ye and your children fare well, and your affairs be to your contentment, I give very great thanks to God, having my hope in heaven. [21] As for me, I was weak, or else I would have remembered kindly your honour and good will. Returning out of Persia, and being taken with a grievous disease, I thought it necessary to care for the common safety of all: [22] Not distrusting mine health, but having great hope to escape this sickness. [23] But considering that even my father, at what time he led an army into the high countries, appointed a successor, [24] to the end that, if any thing fell out contrary to expectation, or if any tidings were brought that were grievous, they of the land, knowing to whom the state was left, might not be troubled: [25] Again, considering how that the princes that are borderers and neighbours unto my kingdom wait for opportunities, and expect what shall be the event, I have appointed my son Antiochus king, whom I often committed and commended unto many of you, when I went up into the high provinces; to whom I have written as followeth: ²⁶ Therefore I pray and request you to remember the benefits that I have done unto you generally, and in special, and that every man will be still faithful to me and my son. ²⁷ For I am persuaded that he, understanding my mind, will favourably and graciously yield to your desires. ²⁸ Thus the murderer and blasphemer having suffered most grievously, as he entreated other men, so died he a miserable death in a strange country in the mountains. ²⁹ And Philip, that was brought up with him, carried away his body, who also fearing the son of Antiochus, went into Egypt to Ptolemeus Philometor.

10

¹ Now Maccabeus and his company, the Lord guiding them, recovered the temple and the city: ² But the altars which the heathen had built in the open street, and also the chapels, they pulled down. ³ And having cleansed the temple they made another altar, and striking stones they took fire out of them, and offered a sacrifice after two years, and set forth incense, and lights, and shewbread. ⁴ When that was done, they fell flat down, and besought the Lord that they might come no more into such troubles; but if they sinned any more against him, that he himself would chasten them with mercy, and that they might not be delivered unto the blasphemous and barbarous nations. ⁵ Now upon the same day that the strangers profaned the temple, on the very same day it was cleansed again, even the five and twentieth day of the same month, which is Casleu. ⁶ And they kept the eight days with gladness, as in the feast of the tabernacles, remembering that not long afore they had held the feast of the tabernacles, when as they wandered in the mountains and dens like

beasts. [7] Therefore they bare branches, and fair boughs, and palms also, and sang psalms unto him that had given them good success in cleansing his place. [8] They ordained also by a common statute and decree, That every year those days should be kept of the whole nation of the Jews. [9] And this was the end of Antiochus, called Epiphanes. [10] Now will we declare the acts of Antiochus Eupator, who was the son of this wicked man, gathering briefly the calamities of the wars. [11] So when he was come to the crown, he set one Lysias over the affairs of his realm, and appointed him his chief governor of Celosyria and Phenice. [12] For Ptolemeus, that was called Macron, choosing rather to do justice unto the Jews for the wrong that had been done unto them, endeavoured to continue peace with them. [13] Whereupon being accused of the king's friends before Eupator, and called traitor at every word because he had left Cyprus, that Philometor had committed unto him, and departed to Antiochus Epiphanes, and seeing that he was in no honourable place, he was so discouraged, that he poisoned himself and died. [14] But when Gorgias was governor of the holds, he hired soldiers, and nourished war continually with the Jews: [15] And therewithall the Idumeans, having gotten into their hands the most commodious holds, kept the Jews occupied, and receiving those that were banished from Jerusalem, they went about to nourish war. [16] Then they that were with Maccabeus made supplication, and besought God that he would be their helper; and so they ran with violence upon the strong holds of the Idumeans, [17] and assaulting them strongly, they won the holds, and kept off all that fought upon the wall, and slew all that fell into their hands, and killed no fewer than twenty thousand. [18] And because certain, who were no less than nine thousand, were fled together into two very strong castles, having all manner of things convenient to sustain the siege, [19] Maccabeus left Simon and Joseph, and Zaccheus also, and them that were with him, who were enough to besiege them, and departed himself unto those places which more needed his help. [20] Now they that were with Simon, being led with covetousness, were persuaded for money through certain of those that were in the castle, and took seventy thousand drachms, and let some of them escape. [21] But when it was told Maccabeus what was done, he called the governors of the people together, and accused those men that they had sold their brethren for money, and set their enemies free to fight against them. [22] So he slew those that were found traitors, and immediately took the two castles. [23] And having good success with his weapons in all things he took in hand, he slew in the two holds more than twenty thousand. [24] Now Timotheus, whom the Jews had overcome before, when he had gathered a great multitude of foreign forces, and horses out of Asia not a few, came as though he would take Jewry by force of arms. [25] But when he drew near, they that were with Maccabeus turned themselves to pray unto God, and sprinkled earth upon their heads, and girded their loins with sackcloth, [26] and fell down at the foot of the altar, and besought him to be merciful to them, and to be an enemy to their enemies, and an adversary to their adversaries, as the law declareth. [27] So after the prayer they took their weapons, and went on further from the city: and when they drew near to their enemies, they kept by themselves. [28] Now the sun being newly risen, they joined both together; the one part having together with their virtue their refuge also unto the Lord for a pledge of their success and victory: the other side making their rage leader of their battle. [29] But when the battle waxed strong, there appeared unto the enemies from heaven five comely men upon horses, with bridles of gold, and two of them led the Jews, [30] and took Maccabeus betwixt them, and covered him on every side with their weapons, and kept him safe, but shot arrows and lightnings against the enemies: so that being confounded with blindness, and full of trouble, they were killed. [31] And there were slain of footmen twenty thousand and five hundred, and six hundred horsemen. [32] As for Timotheus himself, he fled into a very strong hold, called Gazara, where Chereas was governor. [33] But they that were with Maccabeus laid siege against the fortress courageously four days. [34] And they that were within, trusting to the strength of the place, blasphemed exceedingly, and uttered wicked words. [35] Nevertheless upon the fifth day, early, twenty young men of Maccabeus' company, inflamed with anger because of the blasphemies, assaulted the wall manly, and with a fierce courage killed all that they met withal. [36] Others likewise ascending after them, while they were busied with them that were within, burnt the towers, and kindling fires burnt the blasphemers alive; and others broke open the gates, and, having received in the rest of the army, took the city, [37] and killed Timotheus, that was hid in a certain pit, and Chereas his brother, with Apollophanes. [38] When this was done, they praised the Lord with psalms and thanksgiving, who had done so great things for Israel, and given them the victory.

11

[1] Not long after this, Lysias the king's protector and cousin, who also managed the affairs, took sore displeasure for the things that were done. [2] And when he had

gathered about fourscore thousand with all the horse-men, he came against the Jews, thinking to make the city an habitation of the Gentiles, ³ and to make a gain of the temple, as of the other chapels of the heathen, and to set the high priesthood to sale every year; ⁴ not at all considering the power of God, but puffed up with his ten thousands of footmen, and his thousands of horsemen, and his fourscore elephants. ⁵ So he came to Judea, and drew near to Bethsura, which was a strong town, but distant from Jerusalem about five furlongs, and he laid sore siege unto it. ⁶ Now when they that were with Maccabeus heard that he besieged the holds, they and all the people with lamentation and tears besought the Lord that he would send a good angel to deliver Israel. ⁷ Then Maccabeus himself first of all took weapons, exhorting the other that they would jeopard themselves together with him to help their brethren: so they went forth together with a willing mind. ⁸ And as they were at Jerusalem, there appeared before them on horseback one in white clothing, shaking his armour of gold. ⁹ Then they praised the merciful God all together, and took heart, insomuch that they were ready not only to fight with men, but with most cruel beasts, and to pierce through walls of iron. ¹⁰ Thus they marched forward in their armour, having an helper from heaven: for the Lord was merciful unto them ¹¹ And giving a charge upon their enemies like lions, they slew eleven thousand footmen, and sixteen hundred horsemen, and put all the other to flight. ¹² Many of them also being wounded escaped naked; and Lysias himself fled away shamefully, and so escaped. ¹³ Who, as he was a man of understanding, casting with himself what loss he had had, and considering that the Hebrews could not be overcome, because the Almighty God helped them, he sent unto them, [14] and persuaded them to agree to all reasonable conditions, and promised that he would persuade the king that he must needs be a friend unto them. [15] Then Maccabeus consented to all that Lysias desired, being careful of the common good; and whatsoever Maccabeus wrote unto Lysias concerning the Jews, the king granted it. [16] For there were letters written unto the Jews from Lysias to this effect: Lysias unto the people of the Jews sendeth greeting: [17] John and Absolom, who were sent from you, delivered me the petition subscribed, and made request for the performance of the contents thereof. [18] Therefore what things soever were meet to be reported to the king, I have declared them, and he hath granted as much as might be. [19] And if then ye will keep yourselves loyal to the state, hereafter also will I endeavour to be a means of your good. [20] But of the particulars I have given order both to these and the other that came from me, to commune with you. [21] Fare ye well. The hundred and eight and fortieth year, the four and twentieth day of the month Dioscorinthius. [22] Now the king's letter contained these words: King Antiochus unto his brother Lysias sendeth greeting: [23] Since our father is translated unto the gods, our will is, that they that are in our realm live quietly, that every one may attend upon his own affairs. [24] We understand also that the Jews would not consent to our father, for to be brought unto the custom of the Gentiles, but had rather keep their own manner of living: for the which cause they require of us, that we should suffer them to live after their own laws. [25] Wherefore our mind is, that this nation shall be in rest, and we have determined to restore them their temple, that they may live according to the customs of their forefathers. [26] Thou shalt do well therefore to send unto them, and grant them peace, that when they are certified of our mind, they may be of good comfort, and ever go cheerfully about their own affairs. ²⁷ And the letter of the king unto the nation of the Jews was after this manner: King Antiochus sendeth greeting unto the council, and the rest of the Jews: ²⁸ If ye fare well, we have our desire; we are also in good health. ²⁹ Menelaus declared unto us, that your desire was to return home, and to follow your own business: ³⁰ Wherefore they that will depart shall have safe conduct till the thirtieth day of Xanthicus with security. ³¹ And the Jews shall use their own kind of meats and laws, as before; and none of them any manner of ways shall be molested for things ignorantly done. ³² I have sent also Menelaus, that he may comfort you. ³³ Fare ye well. In the hundred forty and eighth year, and the fifteenth day of the month Xanthicus. ³⁴ The Romans also sent unto them a letter containing these words: Quintus Memmius and Titus Manlius, ambassadors of the Romans, send greeting unto the people of the Jews. ³⁵ Whatsoever Lysias the king's cousin hath granted, therewith we also are well pleased. ³⁶ But touching such things as he judged to be referred to the king, after ye have advised thereof, send one forthwith, that we may declare as it is convenient for you: for we are now going to Antioch. ³⁷ Therefore send some with speed, that we may know what is your mind. ³⁸ Farewell. This hundred and eight and fortieth year, the fifteenth day of the month Xanthicus.

12 ¹ When these covenants were made, Lysias went unto the king, and the Jews were about their husbandry. ² But of the governours of several places, Timotheus, and Apollonius the son of Genneus, also Hieronymus,

and Demophon, and besides them Nicanor the governor of Cyprus, would not suffer them to be quiet and live in peace. ³ The men of Joppa also did such an ungodly deed: they prayed the Jews that dwelt among them to go with their wives and children into the boats which they had prepared, as though they had meant them no hurt. ⁴ Who accepted of it according to the common decree of the city, as being desirous to live in peace, and suspecting nothing: but when they were gone forth into the deep, they drowned no less than two hundred of them. ⁵ When Judas heard of this cruelty done unto his countrymen, he commanded those that were with him to make them ready. ⁶ And calling upon God the righteous Judge, he came against those murderers of his brethren, and burnt the haven by night, and set the boats on fire, and those that fled thither he slew. ⁷ And when the town was shut up, he went backward, as if he would return to root out all them of the city of Joppa. ⁸ But when he heard that the Jamnites were minded to do in like manner unto the Jews that dwelt among them, ⁹ he came upon the Jamnites also by night, and set fire on the haven and the navy, so that the light of the fire was seen at Jerusalem two hundred and forty furlongs off. ¹⁰ Now when they were gone from thence nine furlongs in their journey toward Timotheus, no fewer than five thousand men on foot and five hundred horsemen of the Arabians set upon him. ¹¹ Whereupon there was a very sore battle; but Judas' side, by the help of God, got the victory; so that the Nomades of Arabia, being overcome, besought Judas for peace, promising both to give him cattle, and to pleasure him otherwise. ¹² Then Judas, thinking indeed that they would be profitable in many things, granted them peace: whereupon they shook hands, and so they departed to their tents. [13] He went also about to make a bridge to a certain strong city, which was fenced about with walls, and inhabited by people of divers countries; and the name of it was Caspis. [14] But they that were within it put such trust in the strength of the walls and provision of victuals, that they behaved themselves rudely toward them that were with Judas, railing and blaspheming, and uttering such words as were not to be spoken. [15] Wherefore Judas with his company, calling upon the great Lord of the world, who without rams or engines of war did cast down Jericho in the time of Joshua, gave a fierce assault against the walls, [16] and took the city by the will of God, and made unspeakable slaughters, insomuch that a lake two furlongs broad near adjoining thereunto, being filled full, was seen running with blood. [17] Then departed they from thence seven hundred and fifty furlongs, and came to Characa unto the Jews that are called Tubieni. [18] But as for Timotheus, they found him not in the places: for before he had dispatched any thing, he departed from thence, having left a very strong garrison in a certain hold. [19] Howbeit Dositheus and Sosipater, who were of Maccabeus' captains, went forth, and slew those that Timotheus had left in the fortress, above ten thousand men. [20] And Maccabeus ranged his army by bands, and set them over the bands, and went against Timotheus, who had about him an hundred and twenty thousand men of foot, and two thousand and five hundred horsemen. [21] Now when Timotheus had knowledge of Judas' coming, he sent the women and children and the other baggage unto a fortress called Carnion: for the town was hard to besiege, and uneasy to come unto, by reason of the straitness of all the places. [22] But when Judas his first band came in sight, the enemies, being smitten with fear and terror through the appearing of him who seeth all things, fled amain, one running into this way, another that way, so as that they were often hurt of their own men, and wounded with the points of their own swords. [23] Judas also was very earnest in pursuing them, killing those wicked wretches, of whom he slew about thirty thousand men. [24] Moreover Timotheus himself fell into the hands of Dositheus and Sosipater, whom he besought with much craft to let him go with his life, because he had many of the Jews' parents, and the brethren of some of them, who, if they put him to death, should not be regarded. [25] So when he had assured them with many words that he would restore them without hurt, according to the agreement, they let him go for the saving of their brethren. [26] Then Maccabeus marched forth to Carnion, and to the temple of Atargatis, and there he slew five and twenty thousand persons. [27] And after he had put to flight and destroyed them, Judas removed the host toward Ephron, a strong city, wherein Lysias abode, and a great multitude of divers nations, and the strong young men kept the walls, and defended them mightily: wherein also was great provision of engines and darts. [28] But when Judas and his company had called upon Almighty God, who with his power breaketh the strength of his enemies, they won the city, and slew twenty and five thousand of them that were within. [29] From thence they departed to Scythopolis, which lieth six hundred furlongs from Jerusalem, [30] but when the Jews that dwelt there had testified that the Scythopolitans dealt lovingly with them, and entreated them kindly in the time of their adversity; [31] they gave them thanks, desiring them to be friendly still unto them: and so they came to Jerusalem, the feast of the weeks approaching. ³² And after the feast, called Pentecost, they went forth against Gorgias the governor of Idumea, ³³ who came out with three thousand men of foot and four hundred horsemen. ³⁴ And it happened that in their fighting together a few of the Jews were slain. ³⁵ At which time Dositheus, one of Bacenor's company, who was on horseback, and a strong man, was still upon Gorgias, and taking hold of his coat drew him by force; and when he would have taken that cursed man alive, a horseman of Thracia coming upon him smote off his shoulder, so that Gorgias fled unto Marisa. ³⁶ Now when they that were with Gorgias had fought long, and were weary, Judas called upon the Lord, that he would shew himself to be their helper and leader of the battle. ³⁷ And with that he began in his own language, and sung psalms with a loud voice, and rushing unawares upon Gorgias' men, he put them to flight. ³⁸ So Judas gathered his host, and came into the city of Odollam. And when the seventh day came, they purified themselves, as the custom was, and kept the sabbath in the same place. ³⁹ And upon the day following, as the use had been, Judas and his company came to take up the bodies of them that were slain, and to bury them with their kinsmen in their fathers' graves. ⁴⁰ Now under the coats of every one that was slain they found things consecrated to the idols of the Jamnites, which is forbidden the Jews by the law. Then every man saw that this was the cause wherefore they were slain. ⁴¹ All men therefore praising the Lord, the righteous Judge, who had opened the things that were hid, ⁴² betook themselves unto prayer, and besought him that the sin committed might wholly be put out of remembrance. Besides, that noble Judas exhorted the people to keep themselves from sin, forsomuch as they saw before their eyes the things that came to pass for the sins of those that were slain. [43] And when he had made a gathering throughout the company to the sum of two thousand drachms of silver, he sent it to Jerusalem to offer a sin offering, doing therein very well and honestly, in that he was mindful of the resurrection: [44] For if he had not hoped that they that were slain should have risen again, it had been superfluous and vain to pray for the dead. [45] And also in that he perceived that there was great favour laid up for those that died godly, it was an holy and good thought. Whereupon he made a reconciliation for the dead, that they might be delivered from sin.

13 [1] In the hundred forty and ninth year it was told Judas, that Antiochus Eupator was coming with a great power into Judea, [2] and with him Lysias his protector, and ruler of his affairs, having either of them a Grecian power of footmen, an hundred and ten thousand, and horsemen five thousand and three hundred, and elephants two and twenty, and three hundred chariots armed with hooks. [3] Menelaus also joined himself with them, and with great dissimulation encouraged Antiochus, not for the safeguard of the country, but because he thought to have been made governor. [4] But the King of kings moved Antiochus' mind against this wicked wretch, and Lysias informed the king that this man was the cause of all mischief, so that the king commanded to bring him unto Berea, and to put him to death, as the manner is in that place. [5] Now there was in that place a tower of fifty cubits high, full of ashes, and it had a round instrument which on every side hanged down into the ashes. [6] And whosoever was con-

demned of sacrilege, or had committed any other grievous crime, there did all men thrust him unto death.
⁷ Such a death it happened that wicked man to die, not
having so much as burial in the earth; and that most
justly: ⁸ For inasmuch as he had committed many sins
about the altar, whose fire and ashes were holy, he
received his death in ashes. ⁹ Now the king came with
a barbarous and haughty mind to do far worse to the
Jews, than had been done in his father's time. ¹⁰ Which
things when Judas perceived, he commanded the multitude to call upon the Lord night and day, that if ever
at any other time, he would now also help them, being
at the point to be put from their law, from their country, and from the holy temple: ¹¹ and that he would not
suffer the people, that had even now been but a little
refreshed, to be in subjection to the blasphemous
nations. ¹² So when they had all done this together,
and besought the merciful Lord with weeping and fasting, and lying flat upon the ground three days long,
Judas, having exhorted them, commanded they should
be in a readiness. ¹³ And Judas, being apart with the
elders, determined, before the king's host should enter
into Judea, and get the city, to go forth and try the matter in fight by the help of the Lord. ¹⁴ So when he had
committed all to the Creator of the world, and exhorted his soldiers to fight manfully, even unto death, for
the laws, the temple, the city, the country, and the
commonwealth, he camped by Modin: ¹⁵ And having
given the watchword to them that were about him,
Victory is of God; with the most valiant and choice
young men he went into the king's tent by night, and
slew in the camp about four thousand men, and the
chiefest of the elephants, with all that were upon him.
¹⁶ And at last they filled the camp with fear and tumult,

and departed with good success. [17] This was done in the break of the day, because the protection of the Lord did help him. [18] Now when the king had taken a taste of the manliness of the Jews, he went about to take the holds by policy, [19] and marched toward Bethsura, which was a strong hold of the Jews: but he was put to flight, failed, and lost of his men: [20] For Judas had conveyed unto them that were in it such things as were necessary. [21] But Rhodocus, who was in the Jews' host, disclosed the secrets to the enemies; therefore he was sought out, and when they had gotten him, they put him in prison. [22] The king treated with them in Bethsura the second time, gave his hand, took theirs, departed, fought with Judas, was overcome; [23] heard that Philip, who was left over the affairs in Antioch, was desperately bent, confounded, intreated the Jews, submitted himself, and sware to all equal conditions, agreed with them, and offered sacrifice, honoured the temple, and dealt kindly with the place, [24] and accepted well of Maccabeus, made him principal governor from Ptolemais unto the Gerrhenians; [25] came to Ptolemais: the people there were grieved for the covenants; for they stormed, because they would make their covenants void: [26] Lysias went up to the judgment seat, said as much as could be in defence of the cause, persuaded, pacified, made them well affected, returned to Antioch. Thus it went touching the king's coming and departing.

14 [1] After three years was Judas informed, that Demetrius the son of Seleucus, having entered by the haven of Tripolis with a great power and navy, [2] had taken the country, and killed Antiochus, and Lysias his protector. [3] Now one Alcimus, who had been high priest, and had defiled himself wilfully in the times of their mingling with the Gentiles, seeing that by no means he could save himself, nor have any more access to the holy altar, ⁴ came to king Demetrius in the hundred and one and fiftieth year, presenting unto him a crown of gold, and a palm, and also of the boughs which were used solemnly in the temple: and so that day he held his peace. ⁵ Howbeit having gotten opportunity to further his foolish enterprise, and being called into counsel by Demetrius, and asked how the Jews stood affected, and what they intended, he answered thereunto: ⁶ Those of the Jews that he called Assideans, whose captain is Judas Maccabeus, nourish war and are seditious, and will not let the rest be in peace. ⁷ Therefore I, being deprived of mine ancestors' honour, I mean the high priesthood, am now come hither: ⁸ First, verily for the unfeigned care I have of things pertaining to the king; and secondly, even for that I intend the good of mine own countrymen: for all our nation is in no small misery through the unadvised dealing of them aforesaid. ⁹ Wherefore, O king, seeing thou knowest all these things, be careful for the country, and our nation, which is pressed on every side, according to the clemency that thou readily shewest unto all. ¹⁰ For as long as Judas liveth, it is not possible that the state should be quiet. ¹¹ This was no sooner spoken of him, but others of the king's friends, being maliciously set against Judas, did more incense Demetrius. ¹² And forthwith calling Nicanor, who had been master of the elephants, and making him governor over Judea, he sent him forth, ¹³ commanding him to slay Judas, and to scatter them that were with him, and to make Alcimus high priest of the great temple. ¹⁴ Then the heathen, that had fled out of Judea from Judas, came to

481

Nicanor by flocks, thinking the harm and calamities of the Jews to be their welfare. [15] Now when the Jews heard of Nicanor's coming, and that the heathen were up against them, they cast earth upon their heads, and made supplication to him that had established his people for ever, and who always helpeth his portion with manifestation of his presence. [16] So at the commandment of the captain they removed straightways from thence, and came near unto them at the town of Dessau. [17] Now Simon, Judas' brother, had joined battle with Nicanor, but was somewhat discomfited through the sudden silence of his enemies. [18] Nevertheless Nicanor, hearing of the manliness of them that were with Judas, and the courageousness that they had to fight for their country, durst not try the matter by the sword. [19] Wherefore he sent Posidonius, and Theodotus, and Mattathias, to make peace. [20] So when they had taken long advisement thereupon, and the captain had made the multitude acquainted therewith, and it appeared that they were all of one mind, they consented to the covenants, [21] and appointed a day to meet in together by themselves: and when the day came, and stools were set for either of them, [22] Judas placed armed men ready in convenient places, lest some treachery should be suddenly practised by the enemies: so they made a peaceable conference. [23] Now Nicanor abode in Jerusalem, and did no hurt, but sent away the people that came flocking unto him. [24] And he would not willingly have Judas out of his sight: for he loved the man from his heart. [25] He prayed him also to take a wife, and to beget children: so he married, was quiet, and took part of this life. [26] But Alcimus, perceiving the love that was betwixt them, and considering the covenants that were made, came to Demetrius, and told him that

Nicanor was not well affected toward the state; for that he had ordained Judas, a traitor to his realm, to be the king's successor. [27] Then the king being in a rage, and provoked with the accusations of the most wicked man, wrote to Nicanor, signifying that he was much displeased with the covenants, and commanding him that he should send Maccabeus prisoner in all haste unto Antioch. [28] When this came to Nicanor's hearing, he was much confounded in himself, and took it grievously that he should make void the articles which were agreed upon, the man being in no fault. [29] But because there was no dealing against the king, he watched his time to accomplish this thing by policy. [30] Notwithstanding, when Maccabeus saw that Nicanor began to be churlish unto him, and that he entreated him more roughly than he was wont, perceiving that such sour behaviour came not of good, he gathered together not a few of his men, and withdrew himself from Nicanor. [31] But the other, knowing that he was notably prevented by Judas' policy, came into the great and holy temple, and commanded the priests, that were offering their usual sacrifices, to deliver him the man. [32] And when they sware that they could not tell where the man was whom he sought, [33] he stretched out his right hand toward the temple, and made an oath in this manner: If ye will not deliver me Judas as a prisoner, I will lay this temple of God even with the ground, and I will break down the altar, and erect a notable temple unto Bacchus. [34] After these words he departed. Then the priests lifted up their hands toward heaven, and besought him that was ever a defender of their nation, saying in this manner; [35] Thou, O Lord of all things, who hast need of nothing, wast pleased that the temple of thine habitation should be among us: [36] Therefore now, O holy Lord of all holiness, keep this house ever undefiled, which lately was cleansed, and stop every unrighteous mouth. [37] Now was there accused unto Nicanor one Razis, one of the elders of Jerusalem, a lover of his countrymen, and a man of very good report, who for his kindness was called a father of the Jews. [38] For in the former times, when they mingled not themselves with the Gentiles, he had been accused of Judaism, and did boldly jeopard his body and life with all vehemency for the religion of the Jews. [39] So Nicanor, willing to declare the hate that he bare unto the Jews, sent above five hundred men of war to take him: [40] For he thought by taking him to do the Jews much hurt. [41] Now when the multitude would have taken the tower, and violently broken into the outer door, and bade that fire should be brought to burn it, he being ready to be taken on every side fell upon his sword; [42] choosing rather to die manfully, than to come into the hands of the wicked, to be abused otherwise than beseemed his noble birth: [43] But missing his stroke through haste, the multitude also rushing within the doors, he ran boldly up to the wall, and cast himself down manfully among the thickest of them. [44] But they quickly giving back, and a space being made, he fell down into the midst of the void place. [45] Nevertheless, while there was yet breath within him, being inflamed with anger, he rose up; and though his blood gushed out like spouts of water, and his wounds were grievous, yet he ran through the midst of the throng; and standing upon a steep rock, [46] when as his blood was now quite gone, he plucked out his bowels, and taking them in both his hands, he cast them upon the throng, and calling upon the Lord of life and spirit to restore him those again, he thus died.

15 ¹ But Nicanor, hearing that Judas and his company were in the strong places about Samaria, resolved without any danger to set upon them on the sabbath day. ² Nevertheless the Jews that were compelled to go with him said, O destroy not so cruelly and barbarously, but give honour to that day, which he, that seeth all things, hath honoured with holiness above all other days. ³ Then the most ungracious wretch demanded if there were a Mighty one in heaven, that had commanded the sabbath day to be kept. ⁴ And when they said, There is in heaven a living Lord, and mighty, who commanded the seventh day to be kept: ⁵ Then said the other, And I also am mighty upon earth, and I command to take arms, and to do the king's business. Yet he obtained not to have his wicked will done. ⁶ So Nicanor in exceeding pride and haughtiness determined to set up a public monument of his victory over Judas and them that were with him. ⁷ But Maccabeus had ever sure confidence that the Lord would help him: ⁸ Wherefore he exhorted his people not to fear the coming of the heathen against them, but to remember the help which in former times they had received from heaven, and now to expect the victory and aid, which should come unto them from the Almighty. ⁹ And so comforting them out of the law and the prophets, and withal putting them in mind of the battles that they won afore, he made them more cheerful. ¹⁰ And when he had stirred up their minds, he gave them their charge, shewing them therewithall the falsehood of the heathen, and the breach of oaths. ¹¹ Thus he armed every one of them, not so much with defence of shields and spears, as with comfortable and good words: and besides that, he told them a dream worthy to be believed, as if it had been so indeed, which did not a little rejoice them.

[12] And this was his vision: That Onias, who had been high priest, a virtuous and a good man, reverend in conversation, gentle in condition, well spoken also, and exercised from a child in all points of virtue, holding up his hands prayed for the whole body of the Jews. [13] This done, in like manner there appeared a man with gray hairs, and exceeding glorious, who was of a wonderful and excellent majesty. [14] Then Onias answered, saying, This is a lover of the brethren, who prayeth much for the people, and for the holy city, to wit, Jeremias the prophet of God. [15] Whereupon Jeremias holding forth his right hand gave to Judas a sword of gold, and in giving it spake thus, [16] Take this holy sword, a gift from God, with the which thou shalt wound the adversaries. [17] Thus being well comforted by the words of Judas, which were very good, and able to stir them up to valour, and to encourage the hearts of the young men, they determined not to pitch camp, but courageously to set upon them, and manfully to try the matter by conflict, because the city and the sanctuary and the temple were in danger. [18] For the care that they took for their wives, and their children, their brethren, and kinsfolk, was in least account with them: but the greatest and principal fear was for the holy temple. [19] Also they that were in the city took not the least care, being troubled for the conflict abroad. [20] And now, when as all looked what should be the trial, and the enemies were already come near, and the army was set in array, and the beasts conveniently placed, and the horsemen set in wings, [21] Maccabeus seeing the coming of the multitude, and the divers preparations of armour, and the fierceness of the beasts, stretched out his hands toward heaven, and called upon the Lord that worketh wonders, knowing that victory cometh

not by arms, but even as it seemeth good to him, he giveth it to such as are worthy: ²² Therefore in his prayer he said after this manner; O Lord, thou didst send thine angel in the time of Ezekias king of Judea, and didst slay in the host of Sennacherib an hundred fourscore and five thousand: ²³ Wherefore now also, O Lord of heaven, send a good angel before us for a fear and dread unto them; ²⁴ and through the might of thine arm let those be stricken with terror, that come against thy holy people to blaspheme. And he ended thus. ²⁵ Then Nicanor and they that were with him came forward with trumpets and songs. ²⁶ But Judas and his company encountered the enemies with invocation and prayer. ²⁷ So that fighting with their hands, and praying unto God with their hearts, they slew no less than thirty and five thousand men: for through the appearance of God they were greatly cheered. ²⁸ Now when the battle was done, returning again with joy, they knew that Nicanor lay dead in his harness. ²⁹ Then they made a great shout and a noise, praising the Almighty in their own language. ³⁰ And Judas, who was ever the chief defender of the citizens both in body and mind, and who continued his love toward his countrymen all his life, commanded to strike off Nicanor's head, and his hand with his shoulder, and bring them to Jerusalem. ³¹ So when he was there, and called them of his nation together, and set the priests before the altar, he sent for them that were of the tower, ³² and shewed them vile Nicanor's head, and the hand of that blasphemer, which with proud brags he had stretched out against the holy temple of the Almighty. ³³ And when he had cut out the tongue of that ungodly Nicanor, he commanded that they should give it by pieces unto the fowls, and hang up the reward of his madness before the temple. [34] So every man praised toward the heaven the glorious Lord, saying, Blessed be he that hath kept his own place undefiled. [35] He hanged also Nicanor's head upon the tower, an evident and manifest sign unto all of the help of the Lord. [36] And they ordained all with a common decree in no case to let that day pass without solemnity, but to celebrate the thirtieth day of the twelfth month, which in the Syrian tongue is called Adar, the day before Mardocheus' day. [37] Thus went it with Nicanor: and from that time forth the Hebrews had the city in their power. And here will I make an end. [38] And if I have done well, and as is fitting the story, it is that which I desired: but if slenderly and meanly, it is that which I could attain unto. [39] For as it is hurtful to drink wine or water alone; and as wine mingled with water is pleasant, and delighteth the taste: even so speech finely framed delighteth the ears of them that read the story. And here shall be an end.